Measuring National Well-being 2019

In replacement of 'Social Trends'

The data displayed in th   oading 29/01/20

Source: Office of National Sta   nt Licence V3.0

Measuring National Well-being 2019

CD containing supplementary articles and reference tables relating to:

Measures of National Well-being Dashboard

It monitors and reports how the UK is doing by producing accepted and trusted measures for the different areas of life that matter most to the UK public.

23 October 2019

The dashboard provides a visual overview of the data and can be explored by the areas of life (domains) or by the direction of change. It supports the Measuring National Well-being programme which provides a more detailed look at life in the UK. We describe well-being as "how we are doing" as individuals, as communities and as a nation, and how sustainable this is for the future. The full set of headline measures of national well-being are organised into 10 areas, such as health, where we live, what we do and our relationships. The measures include both objective data and subjective data.

For more detailed information, the national well-being measures dataset contains the latest data, back series, demographics where applicable and quality information.

We assess change over the short-term (mainly 1 year) and the long-term (mainly 5 years). Change is assessed over a 5 year basis in the dashboard below, however trend information can be found below in the graphs for each indicator.

The latest update provides a broadly positive picture of life in the UK, with the majority of indicators either improving or staying the same over the long-term. Areas of life that are improving include: our personal well-being, for example our life satisfaction, things we do are worthwhile and happiness. While areas showing no change include our feelings of loneliness and our satisfaction with our accommodation. Areas of deterioration include our trust in government and engaging in cultural activities.

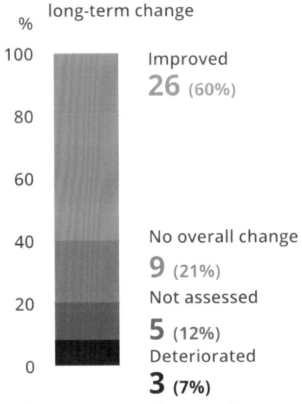

long-term change

%

Improved
26 (60%)

No overall change
9 (21%)

Not assessed
5 (12%)

Deteriorated
3 (7%)

*Figures may not sum due to rounding

View by indicator of change:

All indicators (43)   Positive Change (26)   Negative Change (3)   No Change (9)   Not assessed (5)

Personal Well-being

Includes individual's feelings of satisfaction with life, whether they feel the things they do in their life are worthwhile and their positive and negative emotions.

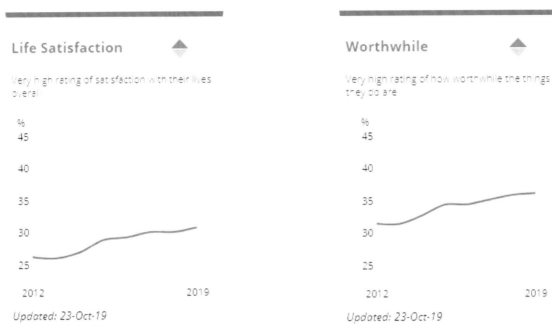

Life Satisfaction

Very high rating of satisfaction with their lives overall

Updated: 23-Oct-19

Worthwhile

Very high rating of how worthwhile the things they do are

Updated: 23-Oct-19

In the year ending March 2019, 30.7% of people aged 16 and over in the UK reported a very high rating of satisfaction with their lives overall (9 and 10 out of 10). An improvement over the short term (30.0% in the year ending March 2018) and the long-term (26.9% in the year ending March 2014).

In the year ending March 2019, 36.1% of people in the UK aged 16 and over reported a very high rating that the things they do were worthwhile (9 and 10 out of 10). No change over the short term (35.8% in the year ending March 2018) and an improvement over the long-term (32.7% in the year ending March 2014).

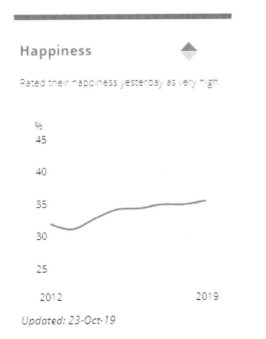

Happiness

Rated their happiness yesterday as very high

Updated: 23-Oct-19

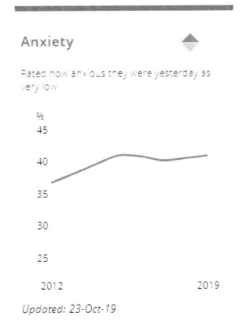

Anxiety

Rated how anxious they were yesterday as very low

Updated: 23-Oct-19

In the year ending March 2019, 35.4% of people aged 16 and over in the UK reported their happiness yesterday as very high (9 and 10 out of 10). No change over the short term (34.9% in the year ending March 2018) and an improvement over the long-term (32.7% in the year ending March 2014).

In the year ending March 2019, 40.9% of people aged 16 and over in the UK rated their anxiety as very low (0 to 1 out of 10). No overall change over the short term (40.5% in the year ending March 2018) and an improvement over the long-term (39.6% in the year ending March 2014).

Mental well-being ◆

Average rating of mental well-being

Score out of 35

30

25

20

2008   2015/16

Updated: 25-Apr-18

In 2015 to 2016, the average rating of positive mental well-being for people aged 16 and over in the UK was 25.2 out of 35. While there was an improvement over the short-term (24.6 out of 35 in 2012 to 2013), there was no overall change over the long-term (25.2 out of 35 in 2009 to 2010).

Our Relationships

Positive relationships have one of the biggest impacts on our quality of life and happiness. This domain includes satisfaction with personal relationships and feelings of loneliness.

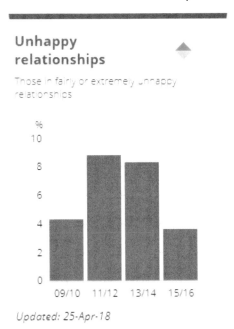

Unhappy relationships ◆

Those in fairly or extremely unhappy relationships

%
10

8

6

4

2

0
  09/10   11/12   13/14   15/16

Updated: 25-Apr-18

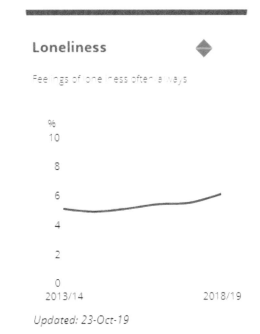

Loneliness ◆

Feelings of loneliness often / always

%
10

8

6

4

2

0
2013/14   2018/19

Updated: 23-Oct-19

The proportion of people in the UK aged 16 and over who reported that they were fairly or extremely unhappy with their relationship in 2015 to 2016 was 3.6%. This was an improvement for both the short-term (8.3% in 2013 to 2014) and the long-term (4.3% in 2009 to 2010).

The proportion of people aged 16 and over in England who reported feelings of loneliness often or always was 6.1% in the year ending March 2019. There was no overall change over the short-term (5.5% in the year ending March 2018), or over the long-term (5.1% in the year ending March 2014).

3

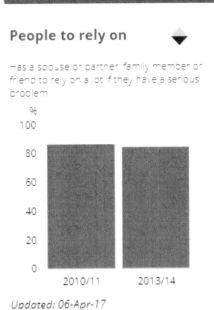

People to rely on

Has a spouse or partner, family member or friend to rely on a lot if they have a serious problem

Updated: 06-Apr-17

In 2013 to 2014, 84.0% of people in the UK aged 16 and over reported having someone to rely on if they had a serious problem. This has fallen over the long-term with 86.1% reporting they had someone to rely on in 2010 to 2011.

Health

An individual's health is recognised as an important component of their well-being. This domain contains both subjective and objective measures of physical and mental health.

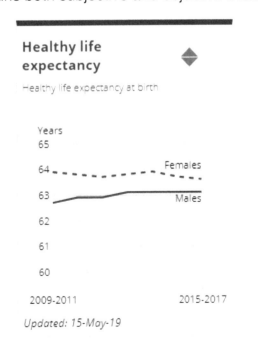

Healthy life expectancy

Healthy life expectancy at birth

Updated: 15-May-19

The healthy life expectancy at birth for males and females in the UK in 2015 to 2017 was 63.1 and 63.6 years respectively. This represented no overall change since 2012 to 2014 for both males (63.1) and females (63.8). There was also no overall change since 2010 to 2012 for males (62.9) and females (63.8).

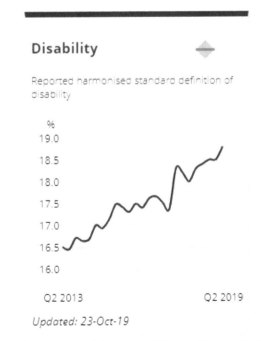

Disability

Reported harmonised standard definition of disability

Updated: 23-Oct-19

18.8% of people aged between 16 and 64 reported they had an illness or disability in April to June 2019, a similar proportion as the same period in the previous year. This change has not been assessed.

4

Health satisfaction ◆

Mostly or completely satisfied with their health

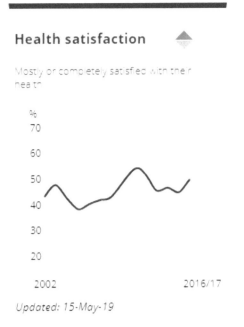

Updated: 15-May-19

Depression or Anxiety ◆

Some evidence indicating depression or anxiety

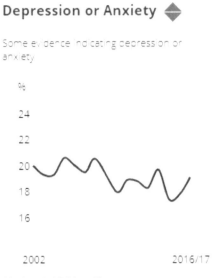

Updated: 15-May-19

In 2016 to 2017, around half (49.9%) of people aged 16 and over in the UK were mostly or completely satisfied with their health, no overall change over the short-term (51.0% in 2015 to 2016) and an improvement over the long-term (45.3% in 2011 to 2012).

In 2016 to 2017, 19.1% of people in the UK aged 16 and over showed some evidence of anxiety or depression. While over the short-term this measure had deteriorated (17.8% in 2015 to 2016), there was no overall change over the long-term (18.8% in 2011 to 2012).

What we do

Includes work and leisure activities and the balance between them.

Unemployment rate ◆

Unemployment rate (aged 16 and over seasonally adjusted)

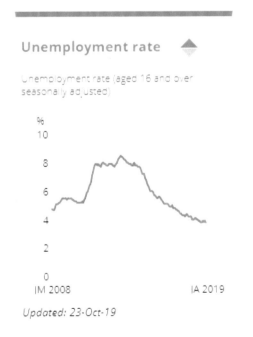

Updated: 23-Oct-19

Job satisfaction ◆

Satisfaction with their job

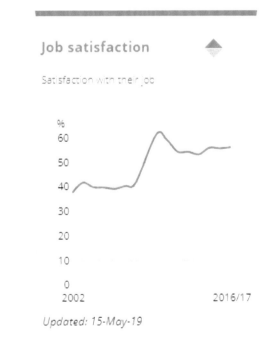

Updated: 15-May-19

There was an improvement in the unemployment rate in the UK over the long-term between the three months ending August 2019 (3.9%) and the three months ending August 2014 (6.0%). There was no change over the one year period (4.0% in the three months ending August 2018).

Over half of people aged 16 and over in the UK (56.0%) were mostly or completely satisfied with their job in 2016 to 2017. While over the short-term this measure showed no overall change (55.5% in 2015 to 2016), there was an improvement over the long-term (54.1% in 2011 to 2012).

Satisfaction with leisure time

Satisfaction with their amount of leisure time

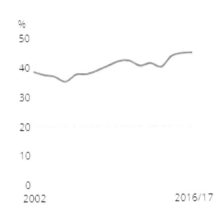

Updated: 15-May-19

The proportion of people aged 16 and over in the UK who were mostly or completely satisfied with their amount of leisure time was 44.8% in 2016 to 2017. While over the short-term this measure showed no overall change (44.6% in 2015 to 2016), there was an improvement over the long-term (40.4% in 2011 to 2012).

Volunteering

Volunteered more than once in the last 12 months

Updated: 15-May-19

17.1% of people in the UK aged 16 and over reported that they had participated in some kind of volunteering more than once in the last year in 2016 to 2017. This was a deterioration over the short-term (19.1% in 2014 to 2015) and no overall change over the long-term (16.5% in 2010 to 2011).

Art and culture participation

Engaged with/participated in arts or cultural activity at least 3 times a year

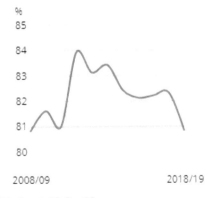

Updated: 23-Oct-19

In the year ending March 2019, just over 8 in 10 people in England (80.8%) had participated in an arts or cultural activity at least three times in the past year. This was unchanged over the short-term (82.3% in the year ending March 2018) but deteriorated over the long-term (83.4% in the year ending March 2014).

Sports participation

Adult participation in 30 mins of moderate intensity sport once per week

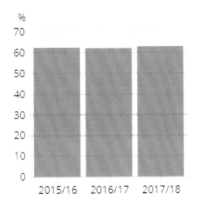

Updated: 15-May-19

Over 6 in 10 adults aged 16 and over in England took part in at least 150 minutes of sport and physical activities a week between November 2017 and November 2018 (62.6%). There was no overall change since the previous year (61.8%). Due to this measure originating from a new survey the long-term change cannot be assessed.

Where we live

Reflects an individual's dwelling, their local environment and the type of community in which they live. Measures include having a safe, clean and pleasant environment, access to facilities and being part of a cohesive community.

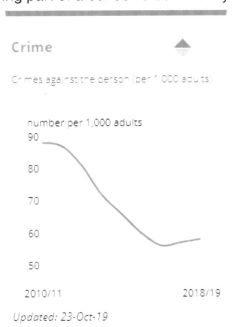

Updated: 23-Oct-19

In the year ending March 2019, there were an estimated 58 personal crimes per 1,000 adults (aged 16 and over) in England and Wales. There was no overall change over the short-term (57 crimes per 1,000 adults in the year ending March 2018) and an improvement over the long-term (72 crimes per 1,000 adults in the year ending March 2014).

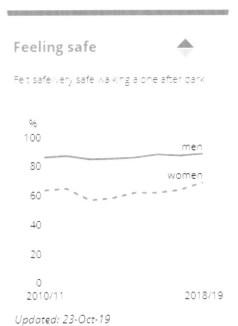

Updated: 23-Oct-19

In the year ending March 2019, 88.4% of men and 68.8% of women aged 16 and over in England and Wales reported that they felt fairly or very safe walking alone after dark. An improvement over the long term for men (84.7%) and women (56.7%) in the year ending March 2013. Over the short-term there was no change for men and an improvement for women (87.2% and 63.7% respectively in the year ending March 2018).

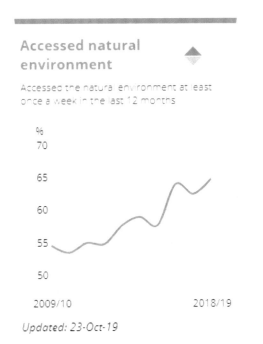

Updated: 23-Oct-19

Over 6 in 10 people in the UK (64.7%) visited the natural environment at least once a week in the 12 months prior to interview in the year ending March 2019. There was no overall change from the previous year (62.4%) and an improvement over the long-term (57.6% in the year ending March 2014).

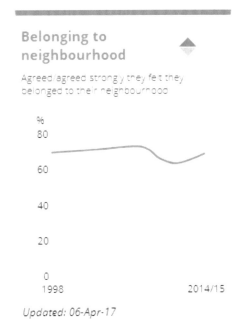

Updated: 06-Apr-17

The proportion of people in the UK aged 16 and over who agreed or agreed strongly they felt they belonged to their neighbourhood in 2014 to 2015 was 68.8%. While change was not assessed over the short-term period, there was an improvement over the long-term (66.0% in 2009 to 2010).

Access to key services ◆

Average minimum travel time to reach nearest services

minutes
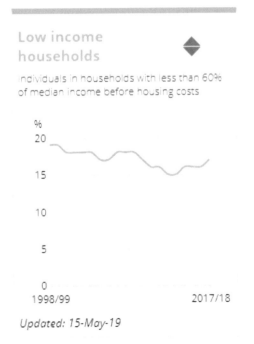

Updated: 26-Sep-18

The average minimum travel time by public transport or walking to an average of 8 main services was 17.7 minutes in England in 2016. As there is only three data points at present, the change has not been assessed.

Satisfaction with accommodation

Fairly/very satisfied with their accommodation

%
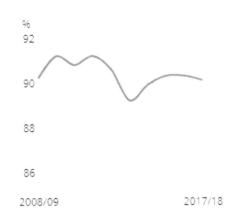

Updated: 23-Oct-19

Around 9 in 10 people aged 16 and over in England (90.1%) were satisfied with their accommodation in the year ending March 2018. This has remained unchanged over both the short-term and the long-term (90.3% in the year ending March 2017 and 90.6% in the year ending March 2013).

Personal Finance

Includes household income and wealth, its distribution and stability.

Low income households ◆

Individuals in households with less than 60% of median income before housing costs

%

1998/99   2017/18

Updated: 15-May-19

In the year ending March 2018 the proportion of individuals living in households in the UK with less than 60% of median income before housing costs was 17%. There was no overall change in both the short-term (16% in the year ending March 2017) and the long-term (15% in the year ending March 2013).

Household wealth ◆

Median wealth per household, including pension wealth

£

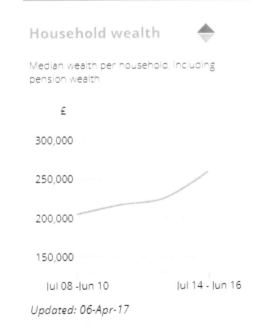

Jul 08 -Jun 10   Jul 14 - Jun 16

Updated: 06-Apr-17

In July 2014 to June 2016 the median wealth per household, including pension wealth was £259,400. While change was not assessed over the short-term there was an improvement over the long-term (£216,500 in July 2010 to June 2012).

Household income

Real median houshold income

£ per year (2015/16 prices)

30,000

25,000

20,000

15,000

10,000

1999/2000   2017/18

Updated: 15-May-19

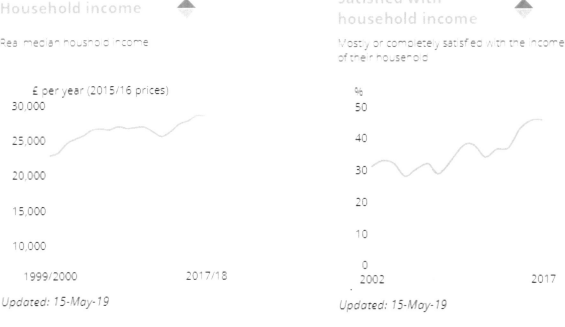

Satisfied with
household income

Mostly or completely satisfied with the income
of their household

%
50

40

30

20

10

0
2002   2017

Updated: 15-May-19

Real median household income was £28,418 in the UK in the year ending March 2018. There was no overall change over the short-term (£28,437 in the year ending March 2017) and and improvement over the long-term (£25,488 in the year ending March 2013).

In 2016 to 2017, 45.7% of people in the UK aged 16 and over were mostly or completely satisfied with the income of their household. There was no change over the short-term (45.6% in 2015 to 2016) and and improvement over the long-term (34.0% in 2011 to 2012).

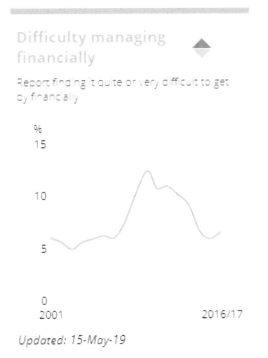

Difficulty managing
financially

Report finding it quite or very difficult to get
by financially

%
15

10

5

0
2001   2016/17

Updated: 15-May-19

In 2016 to 2017, 6.6% of people in the UK aged 16 and over reported finding it quite or very difficult to get by financially. While there was no overall change over the short-term (5.9% in 2015 to 2016), there was an improvement over the long-term (10.9% in 2011 to 2012).

9

Economy

Provides an important contextual domain for national well-being and includes measures of inflation and public sector debt.

Disposable income

UK Real net national disposable income per capita CVM SA

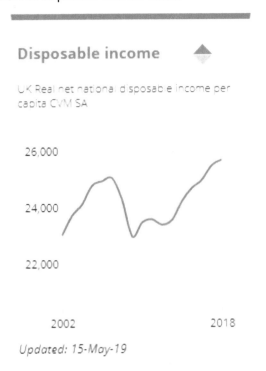

Updated: 15-May-19

The real net national disposable income per head in the UK was £26,065 in 2018, an improvement from the previous year (£25,979) and over the 5 year period (£23,765 in 2013).

Public sector debt

PS: Net Debt (excluding public sector banks) as a % of GDP: NSA

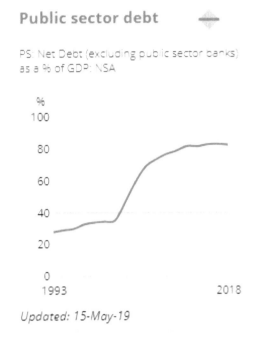

Updated: 15-May-19

In 2018, public sector net debt in the UK stood at 84.2% of GDP, compared with 84.5% in 2017. This change has not been assessed.

Inflation

CPIH ANNUAL RATE 00: ALL ITEMS 2015=100

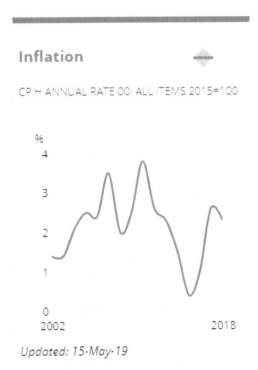

Updated: 15-May-19

In 2018 the rate of inflation in the UK was 2.3%, compared to 2.6% a year earlier. This change has not been assessed.

Education and Skills

Includes aspects of education and the stock of human capital in the labour market with some more information about levels of educational achievement and skills.

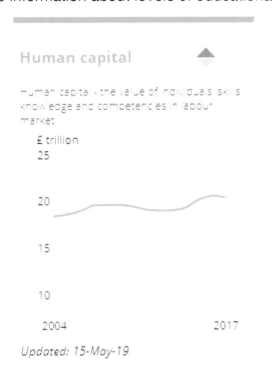

Human capital

Human capital - the value of individuals skills, knowledge and competences in labour market

£ trillion

Updated: 15-May-19

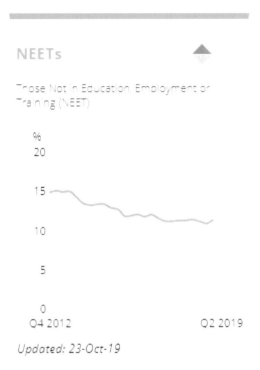

NEETs

Those Not In Education, Employment or Training (NEET)

%

Updated: 23-Oct-19

In 2017, the value of full human capital amounted to £20.4 trillion. This was an deterioration from the previous year's data (£20.6 trillion) and an improvement over the long-term (£19.0 trillion in 2012).

The percentage of all young people aged 16 to 24 in the UK who were NEET was 11.5% in April to June 2019. While there was no overall change since the previous year (11.1%) there was an improvement over the long-term (13.2% in April to June 2014).

No qualifications

UK residents aged 16 to 64 with no qualifications

%

Updated: 25-Apr-18

In 2018, 7.8% of UK residents had no qualifications, there was no change over the short-term (8.0% in 2017) and an improvement over the long-term (9.4% in 2013).

Governance

Includes democracy and trust in institutions

Voter turnout ▲

Voter turnout in UK General Elections

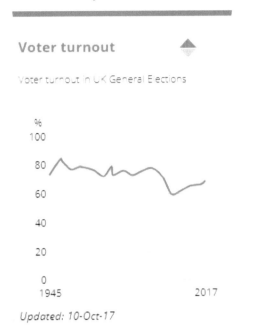

Updated: 10-Oct-17

Voter turnout at the UK general election in 2017 was 68.8%, an improvement on 2015 (66.2%) and 2010 (65.1%)

Trust in government ▼

Those who have trust in national government

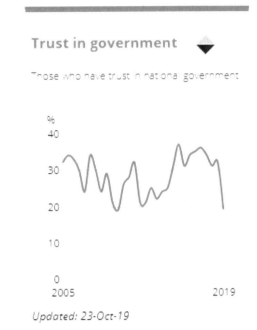

Updated: 23-Oct-19

In the spring of 2019, 19% of people aged 15 and over in the UK reported that they 'tended to trust' their national government. This was a deterioration over the short-term (31% in 2018) and over the long-term (25% in 2014).

Environment

Reflects areas such as climate change, the natural environment and the effects our activities have on the global environment.

Greenhouse gas emissions ▲

Total greenhouse gas emissions

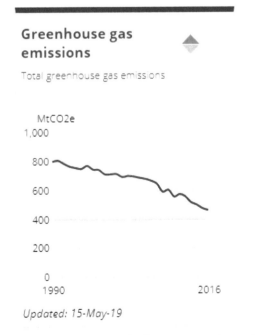

Updated: 15-May-19

The UK's greenhouse gas emissions were estimated at 460.2 million tonnes carbon dioxide equivalent (MtCO2e) in 2017. This decreased (improved) both for the short-term (473.1 MtCO2e in 2016) and the long-term (570.4 MtCO2e in 2012).

Protected areas ▲

Protected areas in the UK

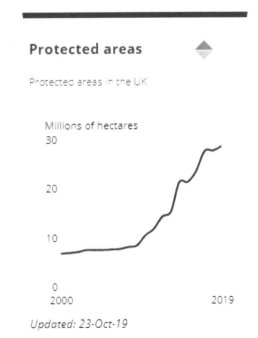

Updated: 23-Oct-19

In the UK in 2019, 28.6 million hectares of land and sea was designated as a nationally or internationally important protected area. This was an improvement on the previous year (27.7 million hectares) and over the long-term (21.2 million hectares in 2014).

Renewable energy

Energy consumed within the UK from renewable sources

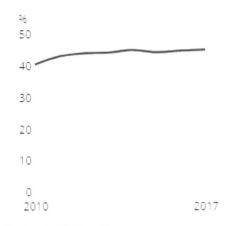

%

12

10

8

6

4

2

0

2004   2018

Updated: 23-Oct-19

Household recycling

Waste from households that's recycled

%

50

40

30

20

10

0

2010   2017

Updated: 15-May-19

11.0% of energy consumption came from renewable sources in 2018. This has improved over both the short term (9.9% in 2017) and the long term (5.7% in 2013).

The household recycling rate for the UK in 2017 was 45.0%. An assessment of change is made by measuring progress towards the EU target of recycling 50% of waste from households by 2020. Change is only assessed as improved if growth is sufficient to meet this target, therefore there was no overall change over the short-term (44.7% in 2016) and the long-term (43.9% in 2012).

Related

Personal well-being in the UK

Statistical bulletin | Released on 23 October 2019

Estimates of life satisfaction, feeling that the things done in life are worthwhile, happiness and anxiety at the UK, country, regional, county and local authority level.

Measuring National Well-being

Article | Released on 25 April 2018

This article, forming part of the Measuring National Well-being programme which today publishes the latest assessments of change, focuses on the main differences between age groups.

Contact

qualityoflife@ons.gov.uk

Compendium

National Measurement of Loneliness: 2018

This compendium provides comprehensive information on the loneliness measurement landscape, the recommended national indicators of loneliness and the question testing underpinning our recommendations.

Contact:
Dawn Snape or Silvia Manclossi
qualityoflife@ons.gov.uk
+44 (0)1633 582486

Release date:
5 December 2018

Next release:
To be announced

Chapters in this compendium

Compendium

Introduction: Developing national indicators of loneliness

Why loneliness should be investigated, the rationale for national indicators across all ages and how we define loneliness.

Contact:
Dawn Snape or Silvia Manclossi
qualityoflife@ons.gov.uk
+44 (0)1633 582486

Release date:
5 December 2018

Next release:
To be announced

Table of contents

1 . Why does "loneliness" matter?

Loneliness is a feeling that most people will experience at some point in their lives. However, prolonged and extreme exposure to loneliness can seriously impact an individual's well-being, and their ability to function in society. As loneliness has been shown to be linked to poor physical and mental health, and poor personal well-being with potentially adverse effects on communities, it is an issue of increasing interest to policy-makers at local and national levels as well as internationally.

In January 2018, the Prime Minister tasked Office for National Statistics (ONS) with developing national indicators of loneliness suitable for use on major studies to inform future policy in England, including people across society and of all ages. We have worked with the cross-government Tackling Loneliness Team and a Loneliness Technical Advisory Group (TAG) comprising experts in loneliness measurement and analysis to agree a working definition of loneliness, and ideal criteria for the indicators and for the collection of data.

The Jo Cox Commission on Loneliness published its manifesto in 2017, setting out a series of recommendations to central government as well as local authorities and wider civil society. In response to their recommendations, the Prime Minister set out the government's plans in January 2018, which included appointing a Minister for Loneliness and committing the government (as well as other commitments) to:

- develop the evidence-base around the impact of different initiatives in tackling loneliness, across all ages and within all communities

- establish appropriate indicators of loneliness across all ages with ONS so these figures can be included in major research studies

Agreeing a definition for loneliness is crucial for proceeding with the government's work programme, but it has specific implications when considering and establishing measurement. There are many definitions for loneliness that are currently in use and the lack of harmonisation could lead to users being unable to compare measures of loneliness between different datasets and outputs. A consistent definition of loneliness will be useful to those in central or local government who are considering how best to measure loneliness in accordance with the government's Loneliness Strategy announced in October 2018. It will also be helpful to those working in academia or the private sector who would like to measure loneliness as part of their work and make a positive contribution to the evidence base on loneliness.

2 . Why do we need national indicators?

As part of their call to action (PDF, 2.6MB), the Jo Cox Commission highlighted the need for a "national indicator of loneliness" to enable better measurement of progress towards preventing and alleviating loneliness. This is based on their observation that:

"Over the years, studies on loneliness have reached different conclusions about the levels and overall distribution of loneliness across the UK and among different groups. Studies have found relatively consistent levels of chronic loneliness among older people – with between five and 15 per cent reporting that they are often or always lonely. However, we have much less robust data on loneliness among children, young people and adults of working age."

One of the reasons why studies may have reached different conclusions is that various approaches have been used to measure loneliness, potentially leading to quite different results. Additionally, terms such as "loneliness" and "social isolation" are often used interchangeably, though they are separate concepts requiring different approaches to measurement. This can confuse the picture further.

The rationale for recommending national measures of loneliness is to address these deficits in the evidence base by:

- encouraging more consistent use of standard measures of loneliness, enabling more robust comparisons between studies

- adapting measures for use among children and young people, to enable consistent measurement of loneliness among those aged from 10 to 15 years

- addressing the lack of conceptual clarity by recommending measures focused on the subjective experience of loneliness (rather than social isolation or other related concepts)

3 . Defining "loneliness" and the criteria required in national indicators

There are a range of ways in which national measures of loneliness may be used; these include:

- improving our understanding of loneliness across all ages

- monitoring loneliness across the population and for specific sub-groups

- capturing changes in prevalence or groups most affected over time

- enabling comparisons of local estimations of loneliness with national estimates or between estimates of local service providers with estimates for the wider population in the area

- bringing greater measurement consistency and build the evidence on loneliness in a more coherent way

- enabling decision-makers in government, private sector and the third sector to take action on the basis of the findings

- enabling resources to be effectively prioritised and targetted at those most in need

- enabling service providers to measure and demonstrate the impact of their work

This range of uses meant looking at various criteria we might seek in our national indicators of loneliness. Therefore, first of all, it was crucial to define:

- what we meant by the term "loneliness" and how it could be defined

- what the ideal standard(s) associated with indicators of loneliness were

The definition of loneliness adopted for our purposes is aligned to the definition used by the Jo Cox Commission and in the Loneliness Strategy, which is based on a definition first suggested by Perlman and Peplau in 1981:

"A subjective, unwelcome feeling of lack or loss of companionship. It happens when we have a mismatch between the quantity and quality of social relationships that we have, and those that we want."

Although it was unlikely that any single measure could fulfill all our ideal criteria, the following served as a useful checklist for comparing how well different measures performed:

- appropriate for relevant age groups (from age 10 years and over)

- suitable for use with diverse ethnic groups (ideally including those with limited English)

- captures self-perceived loneliness (whether respondents consider themselves to be lonely)

- captures severity of loneliness – including frequency, intensity and duration

- does no harm to respondents

- does not stigmatise loneliness

- reliable, but sensitive to change over time

- able to be used easily on national surveys as well as local resident surveys, local programme evaluations and so on (without adding too much time, expense, respondent burden)

- tested for administration via different modes with clear guidance available

- produces internationally-comparable findings

- validated for use with "clinical" populations (to meet the needs of people with chronic health problems, including mental health challenges)

4 . Identifying where and how to collect loneliness data

As well as considering what we wanted in the indicators, we also took into account the types of surveys where the measures could most helpfully be used. Working with the Loneliness Technical Advisory Group (TAG), we identified a range of criteria regarding the design, sample and geographical coverage of the surveys on which we would ideally like the measures to be placed, including:

- longitudinal surveys to measure durations of loneliness and transitions in and out of loneliness

- cross-sectional surveys to enable regular monitoring of prevalence across the population using representative samples

- large samples to enable greater granularity (smaller geographical areas, further breakdowns by sociodemographic characteristics, further information about specific groups).

- ethnic boosts for understanding differences between ethnic groups, including immigrants

- surveys of children and young people as well as adults to capture the full age range

- surveys incorporating well-being measures and measures of mental and physical health or illness, and other relevant impacts and risk factors

- surveys linked to activities associated with loneliness or increased social connectedness such as sport, volunteering, culture or arts

- geographical coverage of England at a minimum

The way the survey is administered is also an important consideration, but the "ideal" form of administration is likely to vary depending on the needs of the group in question. For example, older people may find face-to-face surveys preferable to those administered online, while younger people may prefer the latter.

Feedback from the TAG members also suggested that there may be "good enough" approaches that could be adopted if the "ideal" is not feasible. For example, it may be possible to measure durations of loneliness by asking questions about this on cross-sectional surveys like the BBC Loneliness Experiment, as well as seeking to include the indicators on longitudinal surveys.

To contribute to the wider roll-out of the Loneliness Strategy, we considered possible surveys that could include the loneliness measures and made suggestions to colleagues from the Loneliness Strategy Team at the Department for Digital, Culture, Media and Sport (DCMS) who liaised with survey managers about their possible inclusion. The list of surveys which will include our recommended indicators for loneliness can be found in Measuring loneliness: guidance for use of the national indicators on surveys.

5 . Addressing the need for indicators across all ages

Loneliness can occur at any point in life and is an experience likely to affect most of us at some point. It becomes a more serious issue, associated with poor health outcomes, when it is a frequent experience. The Loneliness Strategy summarised some of the most important known effects of loneliness in the following way:

"Feeling lonely frequently is linked to early deaths. Its health impact is thought to be on a par with other public health priorities like obesity or smoking. Research shows that loneliness is associated with a greater risk of inactivity, smoking and risk-taking behaviour; increased risk of coronary heart disease and stroke; an increased risk of depression, low self-esteem, reported sleep problems and increased stress response; and with cognitive decline and an increased risk of Alzheimer's. What's more, feeling lonely can make a person more likely to perceive, expect and remember others' behaviour to be unfriendly. This can increase social anxiety and cause them to withdraw further, creating a vicious cycle."

"… Feeling lonely frequently has a direct impact on individuals and can also have wider effects for society. For example, lonely people are more likely to be readmitted to hospital or have a longer stay. There is also evidence that lonely people are more likely to visit a GP or A&E and more likely to enter local authority funded residential care. At work, higher loneliness among employees is associated with poorer performance on tasks and in a team, while social interaction at work has been linked to increased productivity. A study by the Co-op and New Economics Foundation attempted to calculate the cost of this, estimating that loneliness could be costing private sector employers up to £2.5 billion a year due to absence and productivity losses".

The evidence on loneliness is currently quite patchy. We have much more robust and extensive data on loneliness in older people, but much less for other age groups including children and young people. The same quality and quantity of data does not exist for younger people's experiences of loneliness. We know much less about why younger people become lonely and how this compares with factors associated with loneliness in older people.

Questions about loneliness are sometimes included on major studies of children and young people (for example, the Millennium Cohort Study; the Environmental Risk Longitudinal Twin Study). However, there are currently no national studies regularly collecting data on loneliness in children and young people below the age of 16 years, while studies like the English Longitudinal Study of Ageing have been consistently collecting data on loneliness in older people for many years. We also need to understand more about the factors most associated with loneliness, what the effects of loneliness are for different people and how we can prevent or alleviate it. If more people measure loneliness in the same way, we will build a much better evidence base more quickly. This is why the Prime Minister asked Office for National Statistics (ONS) to develop national indicators of loneliness for people of all ages, suitable for use on major studies.

Compendium

Mapping the loneliness measurement landscape

Review of existing loneliness measures and shortlisting of existing measures for testing.

Contact:
Dawn Snape or Ed Pyle
qualityoflife@ons.gov.uk
+44 (0)1329 447141

Release date:
5 December 2018

Next release:
To be announced

Table of contents

1 . Review of existing loneliness measures

Many different approaches have been used to measure loneliness. These include both loneliness multi-item scales and single item measures. Some measures ask about loneliness directly, while others ask about emotions associated with loneliness from which loneliness is then inferred. There are advantages and disadvantages associated with each.

Office for National Statistics (ONS) undertook a programme of scoping work and consultation with experts on existing approaches to measuring loneliness. We developed a list of current measures of loneliness, which are either in use or have been used in the past. Members of the Loneliness Technical Advisory Group (TAG) provided invaluable support through meetings and correspondence to collate this information. Specifically, we gathered information on:

- findings from studies including loneliness measures (for example, surveys and evaluations)

- any cognitive question testing already carried out

- any results of pilot work

- types of surveys on which loneliness measures have been used (for example, longitudinal or cross-sectional)

- any adaptations made to the questions or response scales and the reasons why this was done

- any comparative data on findings using different single item measures, different scales for loneliness measurement and combinations of these

- any longitudinal data of loneliness using these measures

- mode effects (how the method of administering the survey may affect responses)

1.1 Direct measures of loneliness

As loneliness is a subjective emotional state, which we may each experience differently and which may vary over the life course, asking people directly is an important way of allowing them to express their own emotions and to capture self-perceived loneliness. Some existing surveys use a single item question on its own, while others include a single item question along with a loneliness scale comprising several questions exploring aspects of loneliness. There are several versions of single item questions currently in use, focusing on specific issues such as intensity or frequency of loneliness. Typically, respondents are required to define "loneliness" for themselves rather than being offered a definition. Table 1 provides examples of some direct measures of loneliness used in the UK.

Table 1: Examples of direct measures of loneliness

Survey	Question or item wording	Response categories
Community Life Survey (CLS)	How often do you feel lonely?	1.Often/Always 2.Some of the time 3.Occasionally 4.Hardly ever 5.Never
English Longitudinal Study of Ageing (ELSA) / Understanding Society	How often do you feel lonely?	1. Hardly ever or never 2. Some of the time 3. Often
British Household Panel Survey	How often do you feel lonely?	1. Very often 2. Quite often 3. Occasionally 4. Hardly ever
Health behaviours in school aged children – England	Thinking about the last week, have you felt lonely?	1. Never 2. Rarely 3. Quite often 4. Very often 5. Always
Mental Health of Children and Adolescents in Geat Britain	In the past two weeks, I felt lonely.	1. Mostly true 2. Sometimes true 3. Not true

Community Life Survey (CLS) and English Longitudinal Study of Ageing (ELSA) are both major surveys covering England and both include the question, "How often do you feel lonely?". These are some of the largest surveys that currently collect data on loneliness in England and, as a result, there is more evidence for this specific wording than other versions of the single item questions.

Despite using the same question wording, they have different response categories, as shown in Table 1. Fewer response categories tend to be more beneficial for telephone data collection and for certain age groups as they are easier to remember. However, in terms of measuring the impact of interventions and changes over time, more response categories may be more useful in detecting changes over time.

Although a single-item measure might be beneficial in encouraging wider adoption and roll-out, posing minimal extra burden on respondents and survey costs, there are also some possible disadvantages. These include:

- the potential for under-reporting due to a perceived stigma attached to loneliness; this seems to be more evident for males, introducing a possible gender bias (Borys and Perlman, 1985)

- that respondents must define "loneliness" for themselves, which may lead to people describing different types of feelings and experiences as "loneliness", some of which may not align with the definition of loneliness used for policy or analytical purposes

- the difficulty of capturing the severity of loneliness in a single item measure (as "severity" is defined as a combination of the frequency, intensity and duration of self-perceived loneliness)

1.2 Indirect measures of loneliness

Non-direct measurement of loneliness relies on researchers designing measures to capture specific aspects of the concept of loneliness and defining someone as more or less lonely depending on their answers to these questions. This means we are more likely to identify people who feel similar, but it is ultimately the designer of the measurement scale who decides whether what they are feeling is loneliness.

The review highlighted three indirect measures, which are either currently in use on an existing national survey in the UK, or which were assessed as meeting aspects of our ideal criteria well. These have been summarised in Table 2.

Table 2: Examples of indirect measures of loneliness

Scales	Items	Response categories
The three-item UCLA Loneliness scale on ELSA	1. How often do you feel that you lack companionship? 2. How often do you feel left out? 3. How often do you feel isolated from others?	1. Hardly ever or never 2. Some of the time 3. Often
The six-item De Jong Gierveld Loneliness scale	1. I experience a general sense of emptiness 2. I miss having people around me 3. I often feel rejected 4. There are plenty of people I can rely on when I have problems 5. There are many people I can trust completely 6. There are enough people I feel close to	1. Yes 2. More or less 3. No
The Campaign to End Loneliness scale	1. I am content with my friendships and relationships 2. I have enough people I feel comfortable asking for help at any time 3. My relationships are as satisfying as I would want them to be	1. Strongly Disagree 2. Disagree 3. Neutral 4. Agree 5. Strongly Agree 6. Don't Know

Loneliness scales are often used either in addition to or instead of single-item questions on loneliness. The loneliness scales vary in length, with longer and shorter versions available for some, for example, the UCLA scale and the De Jong Gierveld scale. The number of items in the scale is an important issue in this context, as the intention is for the loneliness measure to be used on national surveys. An important consideration has been to avoid over-burdening respondents, which could compromise response rates, and to keep costs and survey space within feasible limits.

2 . Shortlisting of existing measures for testing

After the initial scoping review of measures and further discussion with the Technical Advisory Group (TAG), the decision was taken to base our preliminary recommendations on existing measures rather than developing new ones. This was based on the following main reasons:

- the desire to see them widely and consistently used, which would be more likely if we could encourage more researchers to choose measures already established and in use

- the existence of measures that have produced helpful insights, are well-tested and have a track record in relation to how well they perform for different population groups and using different approaches to data collection

- the advantages associated with building on the existing evidence base to bring further comparable insights into loneliness quicker than would be the case if new measures were used

Based on these considerations, we decided to focus on the following measures for further testing:

- the direct question of loneliness currently in use on the Community Life Survey (CLS)

- the short form (three-item) of the UCLA loneliness scale currently in use on the English Longitudinal Study of Ageing (ELSA) and the Understanding Society study

The UCLA loneliness scale was designed to measure relational connectedness, social connectedness and self-perceived isolation. There are several versions including a 20-item and a three-item scale. Due to our requirement to use the measure on national surveys, only the three-item scale was considered. Although the UCLA scale uses negative wording (for example, focusing on a perceived lack of social connection), it is well-established internationally, aiding wider comparisons and suggesting translations are readily available if required. It has also been found to perform well both in self-completion questionnaires and in telephone interviews.

The use of both a direct question and a scale measure is the approach currently taken by ELSA and Understanding Society. This enables measurement of loneliness via a scale that has been assessed as valid and reliable, as well as allowing the respondent to report for themselves whether they feel lonely, providing further insight into the subjective feeling of loneliness for different people. Also, there is variation in how people understand the term "loneliness" and some people might be reluctant to admit to loneliness, and this might be particularly true of certain groups such as men. Those who are most lonely may find it upsetting to discuss their feelings and experiences of loneliness. A multi-item measure that does not mention loneliness directly can be helpful to address these issues.

We undertook a programme of work to test our preliminary recommended measures involving question testing on surveys across all age groups (from the age of 10 years) and cognitive question testing (see the Cognitive testing of loneliness questions and response options and Testing of loneliness questions in surveys chapters). All of the existing and new evidence was brought together to inform the recommended measures for loneliness, which have now been proposed as interim harmonised principles for use across the Government Statistical Service (GSS).

We will work with colleagues at the Department for Digital, Culture, Media and Sport (DCMS) and the GSS Harmonisation Team to encourage the roll-out of these indicators and suggest taking stock and making any refinements necessary within two years, after surveys using these measures have data available for analysis. After this, we will consider any further refinements needed to the indicators or guidance for their use before proposing the final Harmonised Principle (see the Recommended national indicators of loneliness chapter). To accompany the loneliness measurement recommendations, we have also developed a guidance report with suggestions for how to incorporate the measures in relevant surveys and interpret the results.

Compendium

Cognitive testing of loneliness questions and response options

Findings from our cognitive testing of loneliness questions with children and young people.

Contact:
Ian Sidney or Ed Pyle
qualityoflife@ons.gov.uk
+44 (0) 1633 455542

Release date:
5 December 2018

Next release:
To be announced

Table of contents

29

1 . Introduction

Many different approaches have been used to measure loneliness. These include both loneliness multi-item and single-item measures. Some measures ask about loneliness directly while others ask about emotions associated with loneliness, from which loneliness is then inferred. There are advantages and disadvantages associated with each. We undertook a programme of scoping work and consultation with experts on existing approaches to loneliness measurement. From this, two preliminary measures (both a direct and an indirect measure of loneliness) were selected as meeting many criteria we required for the loneliness indicators.

However, before making a final recommendation on the measures, cognitive and survey testing of our preliminary recommended measures of loneliness was conducted. This was intended to provide further information on how they would work for people of different ages and backgrounds and how well they would perform on different types of surveys. The main findings from the survey testing have been reported in the Testing of loneliness questions in surveys chapter, while this chapter focuses on our cognitive testing work. Our cognitive testing involved qualitative interviews in which respondents were first asked to answer the proposed loneliness questions, followed by discussion of their interpretations of the questions and use of the response scales. As the questions were already in use among adults, the cognitive testing focused on how well the questions would work with children and young people.

In particular, this chapter outlines:

- the questions and response options that were tested

- the methodological approach for the cognitive testing

- the findings from the cognitive testing for children (aged 10 to 15 years)

- the findings from the cognitive testing for young adults (aged 16 to 24 years)

- children's and young adults' preferences for response categories

- children's and young adults' preferences on where they would complete these questions

- children's and young adults' opinions on the impact these questions would have on survey respondents

The findings and recommendations in this chapter were used to inform our recommended national indicators and the guidance for measuring loneliness in national surveys.

2 . Questions and response options tested

Following an initial scoping review and short-listing of loneliness measures with experts, we cognitively tested four questions to capture different aspects of loneliness. The first three questions were from the UCLA three-item loneliness scale, which is currently used in the English Longitudinal Study of Ageing and the last is a direct question about how often the respondent feels lonely, currently used on the Community Life Survey.

2.1 Young adults

These questions were tested with young adults aged 16 to 24 years:

1. How often do you feel that you lack companionship?

2. How often do you feel left out?

3. How often do you feel isolated from others?

4. How often do you feel lonely?

Response categories: Hardly ever or never / Some of the time / Often

2.2 Children and young people

An adapted version of the measures was tested for use with children and young people aged 10 to 15 years. The wording for the children's measure was changed to a more "plain English" version, reflecting concerns that the words "companionship" and "isolation" are difficult for children to read and may be interpreted in a range of different ways. We revised the questions and tested them qualitatively (to understand children's ease of use and interpretations) and on a survey of children conducted by The Children's Society.

The following questions were tested with children and young people aged between 10 and 15 years:

1. How often do you feel that you have no one you can talk to?

2. How often do you feel left out?

3. How often do you feel alone?

4. How often do you feel lonely?

Response categories: Hardly ever or never / Some of the time / Often

3 . Methodology

Children's and young adults' understanding of the questions, the meanings of the words and concepts, and the suitability of the response options were cognitively tested. The cognitive testing was the first part of a semi-structured interview, which focused on respondents' understanding and experiences of loneliness. The interviews lasted approximately 60 minutes for young adults (aged 16 to 24 years old) and around 30 minutes for children and young people (aged 10 to 15 years old). The cognitive part of the interview asking about understanding of the questions lasted for approximately half of the interview.

3.1 Approach to sampling and recruitment

Recruitment of respondents took place during July 2018. The main sampling criteria were agreed and monitored throughout recruitment of study respondents to try to achieve a balanced sample.

Several methods were used to recruit respondents including asking Office for National Statistics (ONS) to circulate information about the research to people with children and young people aged 10 to 24 years (see Annex 1). Recruitment was also carried out in collaboration with children's charities, namely The Children's Society and Whizz-Kidz. The latter acted as an intermediary, passing on information about the research to potential respondents on our behalf, while researchers from The Children's Society collaborated with ONS throughout and were actively involved in the design of study materials, respondent recruitment and interviews.

The sample design sought an even balance between males and females, age groups, region, and rural and urban areas. Other characteristics such as ethnicity and disability were to be monitored to help ensure a mixture of views and experiences among respondents. The achieved sample had slightly more females than males and more respondents living in urban than rural areas. The age breakdown of respondents included an even mix of children and young people in two age groups (sixteen children aged 10 to 11 years and fifteen young people aged 12 to 15 years) and young adults, also in two age groups (sixteen young adults aged 16 to 18 years and sixteen aged 19 to 24 years).

All respondents were given a token of appreciation to thank them for taking part. These were in the form of a £15 high street store voucher for those aged 10 to 15 years and £30 in cash for those aged 16 to 24 years.

3.2 Achieved sample

In total 63 interviews were completed. Table 1 provides a breakdown of the characteristics of the respondents.

Table 1 : Breakdown of children and young people respondents' characteristics: by age, sex, and location

England

Children and young people (10- to 15-year-olds)

	South West / Midlands	South East / London	North	Total	Rural	Urban
Females	4	10	4	18	5	13
Males	4	2	8	14	5	9

Young Adults (16 to 24-year olds)

	South West / Midlands	South East / London	North	Total	Rural	Urban
Females	6	5	6	17	4	13
Males	3	6	5	14	2	12

Source: Office of National Statistics

Most interviews were conducted during August 2018 in the participant's own home, with six conducted in a youth centre and four at ONS premises. The interviews were predominantly completed face-to-face with no one else present although several younger children were interviewed with a parent or guardian present.

3.3 Topic guides, recording and transcription

The interviews were based on a topic guide used as an aide memoir that also allowed flexibility for responding to topics raised by respondents. Small changes were made to the topic guide as the research progressed in order to make the interview flow more smoothly and to enable questions emerging from previous interviews to be addressed. A copy of the final topic guides can be found in Annex 2 and Annex 3.

In keeping with best practice, all interviews were recorded with permission of the respondents (and their parents where appropriate) and transcribed word for word. Prior to turning on the recorder, respondents were reminded of the reason for the interview and what would happen with their information and that the findings from the study would be reported anonymously with their data held confidentially. They were also informed that they could stop the interview at any time and that they did not have to answer any questions that made them feel uncomfortable.

Children and young people along with a parent or guardian were asked to read and if in agreement sign a consent form (Annex 4). Parents and guardians in conjunction with their children were then asked if they would like to be present during the interview. A similar process was conducted with young adults and they were asked to sign a consent form, though their parents or guardian were not present (Annex 5). A copy of the signed consent form was left with the respondents so that they could contact the interviewer at a later date if required.

Our analysis, as described in Section 3.4, is based on the transcribed data.

3.4 Approach to analysis

The qualitative data from the cognitive interviews were analysed in a multi-stage process:

- immediately after the interviews the interviewers wrote up the main themes based on the original topic guide; slight revisions were then made to the topic guide to incorporate any emerging themes to be explored in subsequent interviews

- regular meetings were held between interviewers and other members of the research team to share and explore emerging initial themes

- the transcribed interview data were used for the full thematic analysis, with the thematic framework developed collaboratively by the research team

- to generate early themes, the same transcript was analysed by several members of the team to ensure a consistent approach

- finally, all transcripts were analysed using the agreed thematic framework

This report presents the findings from part of the interview data involving cognitive testing of respondents' interpretations of the loneliness questions and possible alternatives. Substantive findings about children and young people's experiences and perspectives on loneliness have been published separately.

4 . Findings from cognitive testing with children and young people

This section presents the findings from cognitive testing of children and young people (aged 10 to 15 years), focusing on their understanding and interpretations of each of the four loneliness questions.

4.1 "How often do you feel that you have no one to talk to?"

4.1.1 Understanding of the question

Children interviewed generally showed good understanding of the question, "How often do you feel that you have no one to talk to?".

A common interpretation was that the question was asking if they had someone to talk to about their feelings and issues important to them in particular:

"So basically, how often is there no one around which you can trust to say stuff to. […] Yeah because you won't tell someone everything who you've just met. Like you won't go I live at blah, blah to a complete stranger who you've never met before." (Male, 12)

Similarly:

"How often do you feel like you can go to someone and express how you feel and your emotions and what you're thinking about?" (Female, 15)

The "double negative" aspect of the question could be challenging to interpret, as highlighted by the need for a respondent to re-phrase it aloud before answering:

"I always have someone to talk to, so that's hardly ever." (Male, 15)

The lack of a specified timeframe for the question could also be problematic:

"[…]trying to remember because it's really hard to remember back all the way to first school, like year 1 and Reception." (Male, 12)

4.1.2 Alternative interpretations

We found some variation in children's understanding of what it means to have someone to talk to. For some, the question simply asked if they had anyone to talk to at all:

Interviewer: "How often do you feel that you have no one to talk to, can you tell me what you think that question is asking you?"

Child: "How often is there people around to talk to?" (Male, 14)

4.1.3 Understanding of "companionship"

We tested the "How often do you feel that you have no one to talk to?" question in place of the UCLA original item "How often do you feel that you lack companionship?" due to concerns that younger children may have difficulty understanding the concept of "companionship" or reading the word. Our testing supported this view, as there was variation in whether children aged 10 and 11 years had ever heard the word, or knew what it meant. Among those who understood the concept of companionship, there was little consensus on its interpretation. A companion could be synonymous with a friend or family member:

"Like your friends like they're your companion, I guess." (Female, 14)

"Is it like a companion where you're together or something, like your friends or family?" (Male, 12)

Alternatively, companionship could imply a closer relationship than just someone to talk to. For example, a companion was considered to be someone they could rely on to be there for them and who they felt comfortable with. This view was more common among older children:

"Companionship sounds more like a closer relationship than just someone there, because you can really, if you feel comfortable with them, talk to them. But I'm not best friends with my form tutor or my parents, so companionship's maybe more of like a closer bond." (Female, 14)

Another interpretation was that it referred to relationships with pets. It is possible that is interpretation has its roots in children's stories that often include animal "companions" and may be where many children first encounter the concept of companionship.

"Like a friend, someone that you do a lot of things with[…] or like a pet, a dog." (Female, 11)

4.1.4 Preferred question wording

Respondents who preferred the revised version ("How often do you feel that you have no one to talk to?") felt it was easier to understand:

"[I would prefer the no one to talk to question] because if they're like my age but slightly older, sometimes people aren't quite sure, like they think they know what it means slightly but not fully. So, I'd probably keep [how often do you feel you have no one to talk to]." (Female, 11)

Similarly:

"Well I think the first one [about no one to talk to] because I think the second one's [companionship] a bit too vague. Because lacking companionship, like some people might not exactly understand what that means, like lacking companionship does that mean that you don't have friends or that you don't spend time with your friends or that you don't feel that you like your friends or like being around your friends." (Male, 14)

They also believed that other children would have no difficulties understanding and responding to the question, "How often do you feel that you have no one to talk to?".

4.2 How often do you feel left out?

4.2.1 Understanding of the question

Children commonly had a good understanding of the question, "How often do you feel left out?" and had no difficulty responding. They understood being "left out" as meaning excluded or marginalised in relation to group activities or relationships. For example:

"It's where they don't want to play with you, you're not allowed to play and you're sitting in a corner and then ten people are just playing over there, football, and they won't let you play." (Male, 12)

"Left out in my opinion would be that you're with a group of people and they've sort of gravitated towards each other but away from you. So, you're sort of left on your own, on your little island, the figurative island and away from them. And I guess you're sort of isolated because people, they probably won't to talk to you because they're talking to each other. And yeah, I think that's a good explanation of it." (Male, 14)

4.2.2 Alternative interpretations

Being left out could also be interpreted as social exclusion in a wider sense:

"How often do you feel like you have no place, or like serve no purpose or feel isolated within society?" (Female, 15)

Considering why people are left out, it could be either be something imposed by others or it could be self-imposed:

"So like when you're with your friends, how often do they leave you out the group, how often do they not let you join in with what they're doing or talking about?" (Female, 11)

"[…]If you tell yourself oh they don't want me there or they don't want me to do that, then you can get yourself in that mindset and be like I'm not going to go because I know they don't want me. But also, people can also shut you out and not let you do stuff with them and deliberately leave you out." (Female, 14)

When discussing what being left out feels like, it was very much about being alone with no social support:

"Well when you've got no one, you've got no friends or you've got no one there to talk to, and you're just always by yourself." (Female, 11)

4.3 "How often do you feel alone?"

4.3.1 Understanding of the question

Children also showed a good understanding of the question, "How often do you feel alone?", and had little difficulty answering the question. Again, understandings varied. The question could imply how often you feel by yourself:

"When you have no-one really or, yeah, you just feel alone[…] You could be in a group, but they don't include you. You could feel lonely, but you wouldn't be alone." (Female, 14)

It could also mean being around people who aren't engaging with you:

"Alone means there's people around you but they aren't talking." (Male, 11)

4.3.2 Alternative interpretations

Although all children were asked about "feeling" alone, some misunderstood or interpreted this as "being" alone:

"I'd probably think of alone as being by yourself." (Female, 11)

"Like how do you feel when you're by yourself, not a lot of people around you, socialising." (Female, 10)

Being alone was not always seen as a negative thing, and there was some indication that time away from other people provided a way to get desired privacy or a way to calm down:

"Yeah because you want a moment to yourself, some privacy, yes." (Male, 12)

"You can be alone by yourself if you have got into an argument and you want to calm down, you can be alone." (Female, 10)

Choice was an influential factor when deciding if being alone was a positive or negative thing. Young people felt that being alone by choice could be a positive experience, but that being alone without choosing was negative:

"I think that sometimes it's good to be alone. You don't want to constantly be surrounded by people. But I think it should be a choice. You don't want to be alone without wanting to be. It's not a very nice feeling." (Female, 13)

A distinction was also drawn between being left out and being alone, with being left out leading to being alone if you had no one else to go to:

"Being left out is just being left out of one thing, but then you can find something else to do; whereas being alone is like you've got no one else to go to if you've been left out of something." (Female, 11)

4.3.3 Understanding of "isolated"

Again, we tested the "How often do you feel alone?" question in place of the UCLA original item "How often do you feel isolated?" due to concerns that younger children may have difficulty understanding the concept of "isolated". This concern was shared by respondents who felt that some children would not understand the word "isolated":

"Some people might not fully understand what isolation is. They might feel like it's something different than it is. But most people will know what alone means and lonely, so again it's more straightforward." (Female, 13)

"Because isolated is quite a more dramatic word than alone. So, they might not understand it or they might just like, I don't know how to explain it, but they might just like feel more sad." (Female, 10)

"Isolation" appeared to have a wider range of interpretations than "alone". For example, isolation was seen as more extreme or severe than being alone:

"If you're isolated it's like you're on your own and no one else can get to you. It's a bit different to alone I think. Because sometimes you can feel alone even though there's other people around you or people like there, you just maybe make yourself feel more alone because you want to be by yourself instead of forced to be by yourself, maybe isolated is more[…]" (Female, 14)

Similarly:

"[…] isolated I feel it's a much harsh term. Like isolated could imply that you feel that there's no one around you, that no one wants to talk to you, there's no way you'll talk to anyone. And yeah I think that alone and isolated probably on the same spectrum but I think isolated is more extreme than alone." (Male, 14)

Isolation was also associated with punishment in schools such as when a child is separated from their classmates and sent to do their work alone somewhere else:

"It means when you're alone. Because we have isolation at school where you're put on a table by yourself outside the office, so you don't distract other people. […] Alone, by yourself, no one." (Male, 11)

This connection to punishment could contribute to the perceived severity of the word "isolated" among children.

Another interpretation of isolation was that of self-isolation and withdrawing oneself from others:

"I think alone because there are very few people cut themselves off from your world because people generally do have friends and family to talk to. So being alone I think is more common than being isolated." (Female, 14)

"To me, if you're isolated, it means that you're not only being like left out you've also got to the point where you're pushing people away or isolating yourself." (Female, 13)

4.3.4 Preferred question wording

When asked whether young people felt it better to ask "How often do you feel alone?" or "How often do you feel isolated?", "alone" was preferred over "isolated" due to concern that other children would not understand the question and the belief that "isolation" was a far more severe experience.

4.4 How often do you feel lonely?

4.4.1 Understanding of the question

Children understood the question well, but felt that it was similar to or the same as, "How often do you feel alone?".

"When you have no-one really or, yeah, you just feel alone[…]You could be in a group, but they don't include you. You could feel lonely, but you wouldn't be alone." (Female, 14)

This also highlights a clear understanding of the difference between feeling alone and being alone, the former being a state of mind, regardless of the physical presence of others:

"Like how often do you feel like by yourself at home, at school, anywhere round where you are by yourself, no one talking to you, just by yourself, no one but there's a lot of people around you." (Male, 13)

Respondents also noted that a defining aspect of loneliness was a negative feeling:

"Lonely is just like you're by yourself but you're sad. But alone is just you're by yourself" (Male, 13).

4.4.2 Alternative interpretations

Another aspect of "feeling lonely" is that it could be seen as a more prolonged and potentially damaging emotional state than "feeling alone":

"How often, I feel like alone is like a short period of time you can feel alone, but then lonely is like a long period of time. So, you can feel lonely for a long time but alone is more like you feel alone for a day and then you can kind of snap out of it or you can kind of go get better again and, you know, do something." (Female, 14)

"I'd say being alone would be a much more present feeling, something you feel right now; being lonely would be something a lot more prolonged. I think lonely would be where you've spent so much time alone that it's started to have a negative effect on your mental wellbeing […] where it starts to feel negative, where you start to think, I don't like this" (Male, 14)

5 . Findings from cognitive testing with young adults (aged 16 to 24 years)

A total of 31 young adults between the ages of 16 and 24 years took part in similar cognitive interviews as those reported in Section 4 with children and young people. The questions and response options tested with this group were the same questions used on the English Longitudinal Study of Ageing (ELSA) and Community Life Survey (CLS), although the latter survey uses a five-item response scale. The CLS also includes this age group as part of its adult general population sample but only has the direct question on loneliness. This testing enabled further insights into how young adults in the UK respond to the UCLA questions, first developed among university students in the United States.

In general, the four questions were answered by the 16- to 24-year-old respondents without any difficulty. In the following sections we focus on interpretations of each question.

5.1 How often do you feel you lack companionship?

5.1.1 Understanding of the question

Respondents of this age generally understood the question about lacking companionship in terms of lacking friends or friendship, but a range of interpretations were offered as to the depth and nature of the relationship implied by the word "companionship".

Respondents thought that companionship meant having someone they could talk to, who would understand them and offer support when required:

"It's sort of like if I was having a bad day or if I was, you know, if I needed someone to talk to I would have access to someone to talk to, like a friend or a close family member who I could look at and look for help from." (Female, 23)

"Well I suppose it's probably asking if you, no matter where you are if you feel like you don't have any company or someone to talk to. You're just, doesn't really matter who they are it's just if you have someone who you're with or you can speak to, or like a friend or family. And I suppose yeah, makes sense yeah." (Male, 19)

They also noted that this was not a word they would normally use, which may help to explain why there were varying interpretations as to the type of relationship implied by it:

"I laughed because we would never say that. Why would you? You wouldn't say it." (Female, 18)

"It depends. Everybody's got a different definition of companionship. What one person would consider companionship is going to be different from what somebody else considers it to be." (Female, 23)

"Companionship to me is like a relationship between two people in a way, or multiple people. Like, there's a bond there between them. It could be friend. It could be romantic. It can be anything." (Male, 16)

5.1.2 Alternative interpretations

Companionship could be interpreted as a more superficial friendship, potentially lacking depth or closeness:

"So I see it in terms of being close to someone. You can have companions but still like kind of be[…] it's a bit like glass between the friendship and it doesn't actually feel like you know them well. Then you'll have people you know who you feel very warm around – more intimate – relationships where you feel like very comfortable. You know you can be companions with someone and still feel like you lack companionship if that makes sense." (Female, 23)

"Companionship is probably more open, because at least if you have a companion you can at least try and build on that relationship[…] you just meet someone. You wouldn't say you were friends with someone immediately after you meet them. But then you might go to have a drink at Costa or something. That's a companion." (Male, 18)

It could also imply a more romantic or intimate relationship. This was mentioned by respondents of both sexes from across the age range:

"I would say it's more like probably like dating life and stuff like that really especially with my sort of age." (Male, 23)

"I guess you could look at it in terms of general friendship maybe also in the sense of a relationship like a more intimate kind of companionship. That's sort of how I see it." (Female, 23)

This theme also carried through into a sense of discomfort that the word could be interpreted as a romantic relationship and should be avoided for that reason:

"Maybe change the word companionship, because some people can take that as an affectionate, so you've got a companion in your life could be like wife, girlfriend, boyfriend, stuff like that." (Male, 16)

"I suppose I feel like perhaps especially, more men would feel a bit, maybe the word companion would feel a bit flowery or[...] I feel like I know that a lot of my male friends probably wouldn't say they would have a companion because while you have a great relationship, you can have a really great relationship with another guy, it's kind of, I think calling them your companion wouldn't feel right." (Male, 17)

The term "companion" was also interpreted in quite different ways by disabled respondents. A companion could be someone who provides care or support with daily activities (as in companion care) or alternatively, a companion may be a friend, but not a paid carer:

"A lot of people think of, especially in the disability sector, companionship is relying on someone else[...] in the disability sector companion is quite often a negative connotation because it's kind of like a carer. So for me companion makes it feel like I rely on someone, whereas actually rather than being supported by someone." (Female, 21)

"Well do you lack a person there that's not helping, not designed to help you. Basically somebody who's not there as a helper, but more as a friend I suppose[...] Somebody who isn't a carer. Because carers, as nice as they are, are paid to be there, they're there to support you, and they shouldn't really be used as a substitute." (Male, 22)

5.1.3 Understanding of "no one to talk to"

We also compared interpretations of the companionship question with the "plain English" adaptation of the question used with children and young people ("Having no one to talk to"). Respondents commonly felt that this was more straightforward and easier to understand:

Respondent: They're the same[...]

Interviewer: Which one is better?

Respondent: Having someone to talk to[...] not many people know the meaning of companionship (Female, 18)

"I prefer 'having someone to talk to' [than companionship]. Companionship just it doesn't really explain what it is. And having someone to talk to is just having someone to talk to. It explains it without, I don't know, it's just better, clearer." (Female, 18)

When asked to explain what they thought companionship meant, one interpretation is that it's about "having someone to talk to". However, there was also a belief that you can have someone to talk to without having the depth of relationship that might be implied by companionship:

"It is a massive thing because I suppose it is kind of separate from parents, I wouldn't think of a parent as a companion. Having a companion is, it's someone who you can talk to about anything. With parents there will always be certain topics that you just can't talk about because it's not the kind of thing that you talk about. And it's having someone around your age, perhaps who go through similar situations, who perhaps also doesn't really know the answer. Sometimes you don't need an answer you just want to talk through something and say how you're feeling and get it out and having that mutual trust with someone or even multiple people is a huge thing just to get things off your chest. I think if I didn't have that I wouldn't talk to anyone really. I wouldn't talk to my parents about it." (Male, 17)

Similarly, a distinction was also drawn between having someone to talk in a professional capacity versus having a companion one could talk to:

"Well it may be because having someone to talk and a companion in my opinion, I would go to like probably my boyfriend or something like that, and maybe sometimes my dad. But someone to talk to can be like a counsellor or something like that. I've been through that and they've been my 'someone' to talk to. But I wouldn't ever describe them as a companion. I'd call a companion someone to talk to and a companion like. The companion and someone to talk to can be used together but I don't think, like in that sense of the way, but not in the other side of it. Does that make sense? It makes sense in my brain but." (Female, 20)

5.2 "How often do you feel left out?"

5.2.1 Understanding of the question

Respondents were able to answer this question using the response options offered without a problem. Similarly to the findings for children aged 10 to 15 years, feeling "left out" was understood by the majority of respondents as not being included in social situations, activities or discussions:

"You're asking how often am I feeling like I'm left out of situations with my friends, with my family, people maybe not telling me things or inviting me somewhere, those kinds of situations." (Female, 18)

5.2.2 Alternative interpretations

Respondents were asked if they could suggest an alternative to "How often do you feel left out?". This helped to clarify that feeling left out could be experienced in a number of ways including:

- others not giving you an opportunity to join in activities, reflecting an externally imposed sense of exclusion:

"How often do you feel that you are not given an opportunity to engage in a pastime, or how often do you feel you're not involved in an activity." (Male, 16)

- feeling unable to approach or talk to people or on a different level with those around you, reflecting a sense of emotional exclusion from others:

"Do you feel isolated, do you feel you can't approach people? Do you feel you can't talk to people, communicate and all of that." (Male, 17)

"I think it's about, you've got like communication, if you're not on the same level, if everyone's talking or everyone's got a dynamic which you're not part of, even when you're with them you feel left out. It's like, in essence, third-wheeling really." (Male, 18)

It was also suggested that there are many ways that people can be left out, making this open to a range of interpretations:

"I think it's like anything if you're going to interview people about loneliness, you're going to have to ask them have you felt left out. But isn't it left out in what sense? Kind of left out of what? So, you can see a way it can be an open-ended question". (Female, 23)

There are a range of situations in which young adults said they felt left out:

"Like sort of, of a conversation or something like that. If you're sat around a table or even if people make plans. Or, you know, if you feel like, I feel like things go on around me that I'm unaware of but I feel like I should be aware of. Like family, like group chats and stuff, there's a lot of things that go on. And then they'll, like my family will chat but they'll chat separately. And then they'll be like oh you knew this. No, I didn't, you didn't tell me. There's a lot of, you know, that sort of thing. Or you're sort of sat there at the table and you're just like I don't really feel like I have any contribution or no one's bringing my opinion into it or. I would say if you went out with friends and had plans, but that doesn't really, I don't really go out or anything so." (Female, 20)

With such a wide range of ways that individuals could feel left out, this may have implications as to how often it occurs and hence how frequently respondents report it in surveys. However, this specific question was generally answered quickly by respondents and only on reflection did they think more deeply about its full meaning.

There were also comments from disabled people suggesting that isolation can be closely related to social inclusion and accessibility, and a sense of exclusion may be a very common experience:

"Do you feel included in your community? Do you feel included in your friendship groups? Do you feel like you're not involved in those[…] it's quite personal in terms of access and disabled access there is a lot of social inclusion issues. So feeling left out is something I feel every single day." (Female, 21)

5.3 "How often do you feel isolated from others?"

5.3.1 Understanding of the question

As with the previous two questions, respondents were able to answer the question on how often they feel isolated from others with ease. Their interpretations focused different aspects of isolation:

- socially or emotional isolation, implying little or no meaningful communication with others even though others may be physically close

- physical isolation through distance from others though contact may still be possible remotely (for example, by phone, text or social media)

These different dimensions of isolation may mean people take different things into account when responding:

"How often do I feel like I'm kept separated from other people. I can't maybe contact people or talk to them. Yeah, I'd say that was a little bit more of a challenging question for me to think about[…]. Yeah, I'd say because is it like a physical isolation from them or is it, yeah, I wasn't too sure where to take that question[…] Do we mean that I can't contact somebody on my phone? Do I mean that they don't want to talk to me? Do you mean I can't physically see them? Like, that is what I mean like I didn't know quite where to take that question." (Female, 18)

5.3.2 How often do you feel alone?

Respondents were also asked what they thought the difference was between "How often do you feel isolated" and "How often do you feel alone"? The questions were thought to ask very similar things, though some distinctions between them were noted. For example, being alone can be a positive choice, whereas isolation is unlikely to be. Similar findings emerged as for children and young people, in which "isolation" was seen as a more extreme state than "feeling alone":

"It depends on the value of the question because if you ask people how often do you want to be alone, I want to be alone most days. I don't want to talk to people. But if you'd ask somebody how often do they want to be isolated, they'd say they wouldn't want to be isolated because it sounds a bit more negative and dire in a sense than how often do you want to be alone. Because you can be in a busy place where it's noisy and people are talking – I want to be alone. I can't be doing with this right now. I just want a cup of coffee. And you could have a grumpy day, like I don't like mornings; I just want to be alone until 10:00am. But you wouldn't say I want to be isolated till 10:00am." (Female, 23)

"How often you feel alone is not really a big thing. It's like because everyone feels alone at some point. Literally everybody will feel alone at some point in their life. I feel like with isolated not as many people will feel that, […] and people will feel like they won't really have much support." (Male, 16)

Isolation was also thought to reflect a more prolonged and negative mental state than feeling alone, which could be a transient experience:

"For me kind of isolation is more kind of impacting than being left out. If you're left out you can kind of renew it. You can try again, go to a different place with your friends or do something else. You can fight to change being left out. Whereas feeling isolated is something very internal and it's an emotional symptom of being left out for so long that you kind of internalise. So for me kind of feeling isolated is now a mental barrier where I can't let people in emotionally or I feel like I can't do certain things or I won't do certain things because of my previous experiences." (Female, 21)

These feelings were echoed by other respondents who also felt that being alone could be a first stage towards being isolated. This point was reflected in an example from a young person who described a transition from "feeling alone" to "feeling isolated", which happened after increasingly withdrawing from situations in which they might feel left out. Self-imposed isolation was also something noted by respondents as potentially associated with mental health issues.

5.3.3 Preferred wording

Respondents preferred "feeling alone" to "isolation" because it was clearer wording, but they understood the meaning of isolation and applied it appropriately in the examples they gave. It was not associated with punishment as it was with those aged 10 to 15 years.

5.4 "How often do you feel lonely?"

5.4.1 Understanding of the question

Respondents were also asked the direct question, "How often do you feel lonely?". They did not find this difficult to answer, but noted it felt similar to the other questions:

"I'd say it was quite similar to the isolated one. I'd look at it and feel like how often do I feel like I'm by myself, alone, don't have, like I said, people to talk to, people to kind of offload any of my issues onto. And yeah just feeling very like you can't talk to people, trust people, yeah, in those situations." (Female, 18)

"Well it's just a combination of all three above together. It's like for me it just feels like a summary." (Male, 23)

5.4.2 Alternative interpretations

In keeping with the findings from younger respondents, "being lonely" was differentiated from being alone:

"You can feel lonely in a room full of people[…] it's not a physical thing. Lonely is a state of mind." (Female, 17).

Respondents clearly associated alone with a physical attribution, using the term "being alone", and lonely with an emotional one using the term "feeling lonely":

"Loneliness which is where you don't have anyone to fall back on, where you have that kind of emotional impact of having to go at it on your own, whether that be physical or emotional[…] I think being alone is a very physical thing if you don't see anyone. Being lonely is the emotional thing of not feeling understood, not feeling valued, not feeling like you have anyone to lean on, like you have no one who respects you and respects your dignity." (Female, 21)

6 . Response scales

During the cognitive interviews, respondents were asked how they felt about the response options for the questions and whether they would prefer specific alternatives.

6.1 Children and young people's use of the response scales

6.1.1 Alternative response scales considered

A specific suggestion put to children and young people was whether they would prefer to answer the questions on a 0 to 10 scale with 0 being "Never" and 10 being "Always" or using labelled response categories such as: "Hardly ever or never", "Some of the time" or "Often". The labelled response categories were used as part of the question testing so they had experience of this.

Labelled response scales

Those who preferred labelled response categories felt that words were easier to understand and more meaningful in terms of loneliness than numerical categories:

"I think words are better[…] it lets me draw more on my thoughts because it's prompting me more than a number I guess." (Male, 14)

"[…] it's easier to understand if you say words. People might not understand if you use a scale." (Female, 14)

Numerical response scales

Among those who reported that they would prefer the 0 to 10 scale, this was primarily because this approach enabled more response options:

"I think I'd prefer a 0 to 10 scale just because it's got more of range that you could like go into a bit more detail." (Female, 13)

"[…]You've got more of a range instead of just three answers[…] I think maybe numbers it'll have a wider range of choice." (Male, 13)

A possible trade-off was also noted between more choice in a 0 to 10 scale versus ease of understanding in response options with labels:

"Because there's more choice. It's easier to give a better answer[…] [but] it's easier to understand if you say words. People might not understand if you use a scale." (Female, 14)

A final observation is that children who answered "hardly ever or never" tended to treat this as two distinct response options and pick one:

Interviewer: "How often do you feel that you have no one to talk to: hardly ever or never, some of the time or often?"

Respondent: "Never."

6.2 Young adults' use of response scales

6.2.1 Alternative response scales considered

As with children and young people, young adults (aged 16 to 24 years) were also asked their views on whether they preferred the three-item labelled response categories used when they answered the questions ("Hardly ever or never", "Some of the time" and "Often") or a 0 to 10 scale with 0 being never and 10 being always.

There were advocates for both the labelled response scale and the numerical scale with spontaneous suggestions for other possible approaches including: a 0 to 5 numerical scale; a labelled five-item scale; and an open text box to enable people to give more details regarding how they feel.

Fans of the three-item labelled scale felt it offered sufficient response options. Similar to the findings for children and young people, there was a view it was easier to answer in words than numbers:

"Words is more straightforward[…][and] lets you be a little bit more specific[…] probably easier." (Male, 19)

Those who preferred labelled responses thought it was difficult to quantify an emotion:

"I think that because it's sort of like a subjective thing and a sort of emotional topic I don't think you can like quantify it and say 6 out of 10 because like your feelings can be different about different matters[…] I think the other answers are probably better for like description purposes because even if you said like, say if I felt left out eight of ten but because being left out can be different circumstances so I think it's more difficult, I don't think it's like appropriate to quantify it." (Female, 24)

The use of words in the response scale could also help to anchor the question in people's own experiences:

"I quite like the hardly ever, sometimes answer for this[…] because it helps you to think of specific situations and it helps you to clarify how often you feel that emotion and how often it kind of comes up[…] because I think it is one where you have to think about literal events or times that you felt like that." (Female, 24)

By contrast, the main advantage cited with the numerical scale was the wider breadth of response options:

I thought they were quite good categories. I mean I could choose. I'm trying to think. Maybe it would be nice to have a larger scale made like a 1 to 10 kind of thing, rather than limiting that. If you said one is never, and I suppose it's giving you quite a range then, but maybe that would be nicer to do it that way." (Female, 18)

"With three categories, it was three that you gave us before? I just think there's not much like what's the word, I can't think of the word – leeway. Whereas if it's like one to 10 you can proper put a finger on it". (Female, 17)

Young adults were clearly very used to taking part in surveys and this was also reflected in their responses:

"I think if you had a scale like you do like online ones, you can have all the time, some of the time, occasionally, hardly ever and then never, like a scale of five or so, and you give a little bit more differentiation there's more places people can fall[…] But it might be easier for people to relate to certain things: you might get more accurate or direct answers[…] I wanted to say a mix between all of the time and some of the time for some of those questions and occasionally and never, but if there wasn't an in-between option." (Male, 16)

Those who preferred more response options felt this would allow a more specific response, better reflecting individual experiences:

"I think that kind of gives it a bit more of a sliding scale because sometimes it's, you sit sometimes you think hardly never and sometimes it's finding that spot to explain your answer." (Female, 24)

"More of a scale might have been better[…] I just think it's easier to gauge because you can sort of giving something out of ten is I think more specific. Because sometimes you might have put yourself between a category or someone might find it hard to think between sometimes and often or something like that." (Male, 16)

7 . Views about where and how to ask the questions

Respondents were also asked about the environment in which they would prefer to answer these questions. We were particularly interested in exploring issues of where respondents would be most comfortable answering the question, confidentiality and the importance of support being available, if required.

7.1 Children's and young people's preferred environment for completing the questions

We asked children and young people whether they would prefer to answer the loneliness questions at home or at school.

7.1.1 At home

Among those who preferred to answer the questions at home, reasons given related to concerns about confidentiality and risk of embarrassment if peers or friends found out their responses:

"[At home] there's nobody to, there's nobody watching you really because you can trust your mum and not [others] at school[…] because usually they would go around telling everyone. That wouldn't really be that comfortable." (Male, 12)

"Probably at home, because I don't really want to be putting the same answers down as my friends or talking about it with them afterwards." (Female, 14)

"[…] what happened with us after the height and weight checks everyone was going 'oh what's your height?' 'oh yes, I'm taller than you'. Like not yes like ha ha, I'm better, like yes, I've grown. Like that. So, people might feel under pressure to tell other people. So, it would be better if you do it at home and then no one knows when you've done it and they can't ask." (Male, 11)

Creating a "safe" environment in which children and young people can answer the questions is important to enable them to answer honestly and to be clear there won't be negative repercussions from doing so.

Completing the survey on a computer at school was viewed as problematic in this regard if others could see their screen:

"It might be better at home because at school lots of people look at each other's screens. And go oh why are you looking at that. If you give me something I won't tell that you were looking at that. Or they can find out information you don't want them to know." (Male, 11)

The importance of not having to answer in front of others who aren't trusted completely was also highlighted by respondents:

"Because at school there's teachers there and you could feel like your answer could just like, if they didn't expect you to answer that you could just feel like weird or judged." (Female, 14)

"[…]So, with me, if I had to answer in front of my parent, I don't think my answers would change because I trust my parents. But maybe if someone didn't trust their parents as much, or if it was in front of a teacher or someone like that, they might be inclined to lie." (Female, 13)

7.1.2 Preference to answer loneliness-related questions alone

Concerns about confidentiality and fear for potential embarrassment or stigma, were also noted as reasons for preferring to be alone when answering loneliness-related questions:

"If family or friends are there they probably feel like they want to put the same answer as their friends, or if something was on their minds, they wouldn't want their family to know[…]" (Female, 14)

Although there were concerns expressed about being able to see others' screens at school, a self-administered survey, by computer, was suggested as preferable to an interviewer-led approach:

"I think they'd prefer to do it on a computer because I feel like some people, if someone's an introvert or something like that, they'd feel more comfortable doing it [by] themselves […]. They might feel inclined to be less honest if they're in front of people. […] It might make them inclined to lie." (Female, 13)

7.1.3 At school

Among those saying they would prefer to answer the questions at school rather than at home, they were still keen to suggest steps that should be implemented to ensure confidentiality or privacy and avoid others knowing their answers. These suggestions largely related to answering the questions alone:

"A private room at school with a laptop where you can just submit your answer and it's gone. And you can choose whether people know your name or they don't." (Male, 11)

"Probably by just letting me get on by myself probably because it would be a lot easier I'll find." (Male, 12)

7.2 Young adults' preferred environment for completing the questions

Similarly, to children and young people, young adults (aged 16 to 24 years) were also asked where and how they would prefer to answer the questions, focusing particularly on home or school or college.

As with the younger respondents, a consistent theme was that it was important to have privacy when answering the questions. Without this, people may not be inclined to answer openly:

"When you're with your group you act up in front of them don't you? Act like the big one. So they'll not answer honestly." (Female, 18)

"Not comfortable. I don't think I'd give a true, especially if I was around my parents, I wouldn't want, if it was people I didn't know that wouldn't bother me, but people I'm close to I wouldn't want them to know." (Female, 20).

7.2.1 The right conditions for answering the questions

Another similar idea to the findings for children and young people is that it is important to provide a safe and private space for answering the questions, where they feel at ease and can answer at their own pace:

"[...]it would be at home because you'd have the time, you'd have the facilities. You wouldn't have to rush. You'd make yourself a cup of tea and yeah, I've got to do this now. And it'd be just out of convenience really." (Female, 23)

"And a lot of times in college, I know when we got surveyed and stuff you never really finish. You just want to get it done as quickly as possible and get rid of it. That's usually what it was like at school because that's just the way it is. But at home, I think you'd answer it a bit more in-depth and stuff, yeah." (Male, 20)

"Home's probably better[...] first year of uni, it's a little bit more, you don't quite have your own space, but at home you definitely do." (Male, 18)

Place was also an important consideration for people with additional needs, with home noted as potentially being an easier and more comfortable option:

"Personally, I'd prefer to do it in my own space because it's a lot less clinical. And I know a lot of people, especially with additional needs know that there's a lot of anxiety around going to a different place already with oh is it going to be accessible, are the people's attitudes going to be accessible? Whereas when you're in your own environment it's a lot kind of easier to relax into the questions rather than having to go somewhere." (Female, 21)

7.2.2. Influence of people around you

Many respondents thought that it could be problematic if they had to answer these questions in front of others including friends, family and carers. There are clear implications for ethics and data quality if respondents are asked to complete surveys in front of other people where the confidentiality of their answers cannot be guaranteed:

"You probably wouldn't answer it clearly because they wouldn't want to tell their family and friends that that might be a problem. If I had my mum and dad behind me, if I did have a lack of companionship, I wouldn't answer that in front of my family. Probably the reason being that you wouldn't want to admit it, maybe, if you were a young adult or a young child or whatever." (Male, 20)

"Some people try and impress people and they want to try and impress their friends and say oh no I'm never left out. People just wouldn't answer that." (Male, 20)

These issues should also be considered carefully and sensitively in circumstances where people may need support from a carer to participate:

"I have only got capacity to go somewhere else when there's a person with me. And quite frankly going somewhere else I'd have to watch who I then said it to." (Male, 16)

7.2.3 Potential to get support

A further view was that answering these questions around others might promote more open discussion and greater support:

"Probably school[…] if you had friends around you and you answered the question in front of them, they might realise." (Male, 19)

In terms of accessing support, young adults differed in their view as to where this might be more easily available at home or school and depended on the type of support required:

"Probably on a computer at home, or at school. Having it at school[…] because you've got the teachers and your schools friends around there. So they help you understand the meaning of it. I don't understand things or read well[…] Having your family to talk to about it. And probably being too scared to if they don't want to talk about it." (Female, 17)

"I think it would be better to do it at home because you can just talk about more. I don't know, if you're at school you're like around other people and you wouldn't feel like you could talk about it as much[…] I just think you could just tell the truth at home." (Female, 17)

7.2.4 Mode of response

Respondents discussed the advantages and disadvantages of a range of modes of completion, including face-to-face interviews, telephone and online. A computer-based interview was appealing for a number of reasons including: ease, speed of completion and could be completed at home in private:

"[…]it'd probably be a bit easier to click an option rather than just actually admit it over the phone probably, yeah […] on your own, probably at home. If you were say on your phone or on your laptop or something it would probably be the best way to answer it, yeah." (Male, 20)

Some concern was expressed about telephone interviews, which could be less comfortable for respondents:

"I definitely wouldn't do the phone one[…] I get very nervous. I don't mind face-to-face because you can get your message across to someone properly[…] I don't mind the internet because it's quick and easy. I'd probably pick the internet because I can easily slot that into my time." (Female, 17)

There was also concern about including the questions on a household survey, both because of a possible lack of privacy and the potential for raising difficult issues within the family:

"Yeah. If there was a way that it could be, you sit somewhere, do it and it's gone that's it. Done, dusted, they won't see it. Whereas if it's sent out to a household they could, I know what my mother's like." (Female, 20)

Finally, despite the privacy potentially afforded by completing the questions online, there were also concerns raised about the security of internet-based modes of completion:

"With online, because a lot of big things nowadays is big scares like something's going to be hacked or there's been a leak on iCloud or whatever, and I know that obviously won't affect a lot of things, but it would be quite scary in a way [...]I'd probably say paper or, if the option's there, in person is quite nice. Because it's just like quite genuine and you can see someone's expression and see how they're reacting to this. But then with paper as well you write it down, it gets sent off[...]" (Male, 16)

7.3 Perceived impacts of the questions

7.3.1 Children and young people's views and experiences

Children were asked how they felt when answering the questions and whether they thought the questions could be upsetting for others. Although they acknowledged that all the questions had the potential to be upsetting to those affected by the issues, they did not relate this to themselves – even those who said they had experienced aspects of loneliness or had no one to talk to:

"It could be upsetting for some people. If someone is going through a time where they are lonely and they've got no one, it could upset them [...] I think they could feel quite embarrassed, because some people might find it embarrassing because they're not as popular as anyone else." (Female, 11)

They emphasised that the questions might be upsetting depending on the experiences of the person answering them:

"It depends what they've been through, because if maybe they were a really lonely person it might be quite upsetting for them, but maybe if, a person who's had a lot of friends or maybe been a bit lonely it might be hard to answer it but you would know what to say in the end like I did. Or if you're just a person who's had friends from the beginning you probably would find it quite easy to talk about." (Male, 13)

Respondents also noted that if people had experienced loneliness, this may discourage them from answering the questions honestly:

"Some people who do feel lonely might not want to admit it because it might not be like a thing they want to admit, because like they might feel like it makes them sound weak or whatever or like they don't have friends or whatever." (Female, 14)

"It could be unnerving for the people who are lonely because they might not want to say and they could be like yeah I'm never alone when you can see in their eyes that they are." (Male, 11)

Although they felt the questions could be upsetting, respondents also recognised the value of asking about loneliness and encouraging people to talk about it:

"I think it's quite important to keep asking them because most children wouldn't reach out and say I feel left out of this. Whereas, if you're asking them, it's giving them an opportunity to share how they feel. [...] Because I think that would be one of the main reasons that people could start to become isolated and start pushing people away if they think if I'm constantly being left out, why should I make efforts with people, why should I go and speak to someone. And I think that could be the root cause of leading to like things becoming worse." (Female, 13)

7.3.2 Young adults' views and experiences of answering loneliness questions

Among the young adult group (aged 16 to 24 years), as with the younger group, respondents felt the questions could be upsetting for those who were lonely or had little social support:

"Yeah, I know there would be [people who would be upset]. Like a couple of my friends, like people at my school, people I know, people I care about, I know they'd find it quite hard to answer that question due to upbringing or the situations they're in at the moment. And yeah, I think that's just it. Like they would find it quite difficult to answer due to circumstances." (Male, 16)

"Quite upsetting if that's how they felt. Like if they were alone and they got asked on it, it would be a bit awkward […] they might just reflect on themselves that they've got no one to talk to." (Female, 17)

Asking the questions and moving on quickly to other topics was suggested as a way to make it easier for people to answer and to minimise potential upset:

"Not as much, because it's just one little question. If you're having a conversation about it you've got to talk about it." (Female, 17)

"My feeling is just answer it, move on." (Male, 16)

However, those who said that they did feel aspects of loneliness also said that the questions were not particularly upsetting to them:

"I felt OK. I'm relatively open about talking. I talk quite a bit. But yeah, I feel if I don't talk about it then what's the point in having the ability to speak. Like I've got to talk about something and if a question's asked, I might as well answer it. And I don't really feel uncomfortable. I was all right with it, to be honest, pretty good." (Male, 16)

As noted previously, due to the sensitivity of the topic, providing a safe space where people can give honest answers in privacy is particularly important to avoiding adverse impacts:

"Maybe they wouldn't want to admit it, I think. It's quite a sensitive topic, really, to admit that you're lonely. It's quite a tough thing to do but I feel like if you were with someone, one-to-one you would answer that quite honestly." (Male, 20)

"I can see how it could be [upsetting] if it was asked to a certain type of person. And I mean, obviously there's people in school, you see it going on, they can be bullied. They'd be laughed at. There were a few people in my school that ended up moving schools. You can see how it probably would upset some of them. […] I don't know. Only people that are probably lonely." (Female, 23)

8 . Overall recommendations

8.1 Findings and recommendations on question wording for children and young adults

Children and young people aged under 16 years understood the questions well and were confident about how to respond to the adapted, plain English versions tested.

There were a range of interpretations given to the word "companionship" among children and young people as well as for those aged 16 to 24 years. This was not an easy term for people aged under 25 years and there was a lack of clarity about the nature and depth of relationship implied by it. Apart from varying interpretations from platonic to romantic relationships and with different degrees of closeness, a companion might also include a pet, and for those requiring assistance with independent living, the term is also connected to professional carers (for example, companion care).

Much of the ambiguity was removed for children aged 10 to 15 years by adapting the question from "lacking companionship" to "having no one you can talk to".

Despite the varying interpretations of the question among those aged 16 to 24 years, we do not recommend alternative wording of the "companionship" question for adults. This is because it is part of a well-tested and validated scale currently in use on major surveys of adults in the UK and internationally, and it is important to retain the question wording to maintain comparability. For those undertaking surveys where these different interpretations of the question may be particularly relevant (for example, surveys of those with long-term health conditions or disabilities), it may be helpful to offer further clarification of what is meant by "companionship".

For children and young people under 16 years, the word "isolated" could be viewed as an externally-imposed separation from others, associated with punishment for bad behaviour at school. For both those under 16 years and those aged 16 to 24 years, the term was thought to imply a prolonged, severe and deeply-felt separation from others. For those aged 16 years and over, there was more recognition that isolation may be externally imposed or self-imposed and may involve a sense of emotional separation from others, physical separation or both.

For those under 16 years, we adapted the question about feeling "isolated" from others to ask, "How often do you feel alone?". Our testing of this showed this was well understood by children and was not associated with the idea of punishment. Different interpretations were noted in relation to "being alone", which could be a positive experience (for example, taking time out for oneself) and "feeling alone", which implied a more negatively experienced sense of aloneness not of one's choosing.

The question, "How often do you feel left out?" was well-understood by children and young people aged 10 to 15 years and those in the older age group aged 16 to 24 years. For children and young people, this was interpreted as being excluded from activities or friendship groups and might be temporary or more enduring. Some in their mid-teens and beyond also noted that this could relate to wider exclusion from full participation in society, such as social exclusion that may be experienced by minority groups. This was specifically noted by respondents both in relation to ethnicity and disability.

The direct question on loneliness, "How often do you feel lonely?" was well understood by respondents of all ages and was viewed similarly to the question on frequency of "feeling alone" for children and young people and to the question on frequency of "feeling isolated" for young adults. For both children and young adults, the term "lonely" was clearly associated with a state of mind and it was widely acknowledged that one could feel lonely even in the company of others.

8.2 Findings and recommendations on response scales

All the questions were tested qualitatively using a three-item response scale. This is consistent with how the questions are currently asked on the English Longitudinal Study of Ageing (ELSA) and Understanding Society.

When asked about ease of using the response scales and other possible options, a preference for more response options was expressed as the three-item scale didn't allow much distinction for expressing how frequently people feel a particular way. Coupled with this, there was a concern that the three-item response scale may not allow sufficient sensitivity for monitoring changes in the prevalence of loneliness over time.

To address these issues, we have recommended that the three-item response scale be retained for the first three questions based on the UCLA loneliness scale while a five-item response scale is used for the final, direct question on loneliness. This has the advantage of maintaining consistency with ELSA and Understanding Society on the first three questions from the UCLA scale, while ensuring that the final question is consistent with the loneliness question on the Community Life Survey (CLS).

One disadvantage of this solution is that the response scale used for CLS includes the word "occasionally", which experts from our Technical Advisory Group suggested may be difficult for some children to read and understand. This was not included in the main cognitive testing, as it only arose in relation to the perceived limitations of the three-item scale highlighted during the testing itself.

As part of scoping work on previously used loneliness measures, we have found that a similar question on loneliness with a five-item response scale was used for several years among 10- to 15-year-olds on the British Household Panel Survey (predecessor to the Understanding Society study). That scale included the word "occasionally" and we have not found any evidence to suggest it was problematic for respondents. To understand any possible issues with this more fully, we are working with The Children's Society to test this response scale among an additional group of children and we will update our guidance with any further suggestions that may be advised to maximise children's comprehension of the response options.

Although more plain English versions of the scale exist, which could be used instead, it would be very helpful to have a single question on loneliness asked in the same way to everyone from the age of 10 years upwards and comparable with the existing prevalence measure of loneliness from the CLS. Our recommendations reflect this goal.

8.3 Preferences and recommendations on how and where to ask the questions

On the advice of The Children's Society, we also asked children and young people where and how they would prefer to answer these questions. This arises from a concern to ensure that support is available if they are in any way upset by the questions or would like to discuss them further.

Our conversations with children and young people reflected an awareness of the possible need for further support among those particularly affected by the issues raised, but along with this was a strongly-felt suggestion that ensuring privacy and confidentiality to respondents should be an important priority. This was viewed as important regardless of the interview setting, but young people particularly worried about peer pressure at school to share responses. They also worried about their responses being seen by others, resulting in teasing or bullying at school or difficult conversations with family members if completed at home. Fear and embarrassment associated with others knowing their responses could result in a lack of honesty in how young people respond to the questions. This, along with possible embarrassment about answering the questions face-to-face or over the phone, was also associated with a preference for self-completion formats, either online or on paper, and administered in a way that guarantees confidentiality.

This is possibly reinforced by our experience with the cognitive testing, which involved asking these questions early in a face-to-face interview that usually took place in the respondent's home. Their responses to the initial questions often suggested that they were not often lonely. Later in the interviews when they were possibly more at ease, they sometimes gave clear examples of feeling lonely, being left out or having no one to talk to. They also gave examples of other people whom they thought were lonely.

It is also important to remember that these questions will not normally be asked in the context of a survey focused entirely on loneliness. Generally, surveys cover many topics, with loneliness only expected to comprise between one and four questions and taking no more than two minutes of total survey time. In this context, confidentiality is still important, but loneliness may not be the main issue young people want to discuss (or want to avoid discussing) afterwards. As part of a longer and wider-ranging survey, young people may be more comfortable answering the questions.

Compendium

Testing of loneliness questions in surveys

Overview of our loneliness question testing, methodology and findings.

Contact:
Ellie Osborn, Charlotte Hassell,
Georgina Martin or Abbie
Cochrane
qualityoflife@ons.gov.uk
+44 (0)1633 651830

Release date:
5 December 2018

Next release:
To be announced

Table of contents

1 . Introduction

Many different approaches have been used to measure loneliness. These include both loneliness multi-item and single-item measures. Some measures ask about loneliness directly while others ask about emotions associated with loneliness, from which loneliness is inferred. There are advantages and disadvantages associated with each.

We undertook a programme of scoping work and consultation with experts on existing approaches to loneliness measurement. From this, two preliminary measures (both a direct and an indirect measure of loneliness) were selected as meeting many criteria we required for the loneliness indicators. However, before a final recommendation on the tools to be used to measure loneliness could be made, cognitive and survey testing of our preliminary recommended measures of loneliness was conducted. This was carried out to understand how they work for people of different ages and backgrounds and how well they perform on different types of surveys. The main findings from the cognitive testing have been reported in Cognitive testing of loneliness questions and response options. The main aim of the survey testing covered here was to fill knowledge gaps, particularly in relation to:

- how well our preliminary recommended measures worked for people of different ages

- whether they gave us useful information about different aspects of loneliness and therefore merit being used together on the same survey

- whether responses may be affected by the order in which the questions are being asked, for example, using the indirect measure of loneliness before or after the direct measure

- how long the questions took to ask and answer

This chapter outlines:

- the questions and surveys that were used for testing

- the specific aims of the testing for each survey

- the statistical analysis used

- the main findings from testing

- our conclusions and recommendations

The findings in this chapter were used to inform our recommended national indicators and the guidance for measuring loneliness in national surveys.

2 . Overview of the surveys used for testing

We undertook question testing on two surveys, the Opinions and Lifestyle Survey and the Good Childhood Index Survey.

The Opinions and Lifestyle Survey (OPN) is an omnibus survey conducted by Office for National Statistics (ONS). Data are collected over the phone for UK residents aged 16 years and over. The survey is conducted over eight months of the year, and data are available two months later. The survey achieves a sample size of approximately 1,100 respondents each month. Alongside a variety of demographic variables, such as age, employment status and living situation, the survey frequently includes questions commissioned by outside parties. This flexibility, combined with the rapid fieldwork and data delivery, means that the survey is commonly used for question testing.

The UCLA scale and a direct question on loneliness were included on the OPN in July and August 2018. Both had a three-item response scale.

Two different orders (direct measure asked before the indirect measure and direct question asked after the indirect measure) were tested in both months, by randomly splitting the sample and creating two independent groups.

The Good Childhood Index Survey is run ad hoc (usually every few months) by The Children's Society, and was first conducted in 2010. The survey typically achieves a sample of approximately 2,000 households, and collects data on children aged 10 to 17 years. Questions are answered at home, through an online survey. The survey collects information on children's well-being, which is used to build The Children's Society's Good Childhood Index, and includes questions targeted towards the theme of the annual Good Childhood Reports.

The Children's Society agreed to test the recommended children's loneliness questions on Wave 17 of the survey. The wording of the recommended loneliness questions was modified to be simpler for children to understand. Data were collected during May and June of 2018.

The loneliness questions selected for testing have also been included on the English Longitudinal Study for Ageing (ELSA) for several years and the direct measure of loneliness has been used on the Community Life Survey (CLS) since 2014.

The ELSA is a longitudinal survey carried out every two years in England on residents aged 50 years and over. The achieved sample size is typically between 7,000 and 9,000 respondents. The first wave of data was collected in 2002 to 2003, and eight waves of data have been collected to date. Wave 8 data was collected in 2016 to 2017 and published in 2018. ELSA collects information on a variety of topics, including demographic variables such as age and retirement status, aspects of physical and mental health, household structure and relationships with family and friends.

As part of their assessment, ELSA includes questions on people's loneliness. Respondents are asked both the direct question of loneliness and the UCLA three-item scale, both with three response options (Hardly ever or never, Some of the time, Often). The loneliness questions are answered via a self-completion questionnaire.

The Community Life Survey (CLS) is a major survey of adults aged 16 years and over in England, held annually and designed to track measures that are important to understanding society and local communities. It asks questions that cover volunteering, views about the local area, community cohesion and participation, and subjective well-being.

The questions are asked either face-to face or are completed online. Respondents are asked the direct question of loneliness with five response options (Often/Always, Some of the time, Occasionally, Hardly ever or Never).

These two established surveys were used for comparability as well as the plausibility of using the combined (direct and indirect) measure of loneliness. This analysis focuses on establishing the reliability of the UCLA scale in relation to the direct measure of loneliness, for both adults and children, as well as analysing order effects and the effect of important demographic variables on loneliness.

3 . Questions and response options tested

Table 1 presents the measures and response categories tested for each survey.

Measures	Items	Response categories	Survey
The 3-item UCLA Loneliness scale	1. How often do you feel that you lack companionship? 2. How often do you feel left out? 3. How often do you feel isolated from others?	1. Hardly ever or never, Some of the time, Often 2. Hardly ever or never, Some of the time, Often 3. Hardly ever or never, Some of the time, Often	ELSA OPN
The 3-item UCLA Loneliness scale for children	1. How often do you feel that you have no one to talk to? 2. How often do you feel left out? 3. How often do you feel alone?	1. Hardly ever or never, Some of the time, Often 2. Hardly ever or never, Some of the time, Often 3. Hardly ever or never, Some of the time, Often	Good Childhood Index
The direct measure of loneliness	How often do you feel lonely?	Hardly ever or never, Some of the time, Often	ELSA OPN Good Childhood Index
		Often/ Always, Some of the time, Occasionally, Hardly ever, Never	CLS

4 . Aims of the survey testing

Overall, testing on the survey responses was aimed to check the reliability and validity of using the preliminary recommended loneliness measures on national surveys. Simply put, high reliability means that the questions are measuring the same concepts consistently, and high validity means that the question are measuring what we expect them to be measuring. The reliability and validity should yield similar estimates across all surveys. Each individual survey was used to answer specific research questions as described in this section.

English Longitudinal Study of Ageing

- To assess the relatedness of the University of California, Los Angeles (UCLA) scale and the direct measure of loneliness over a time series.

- To assess how consistent the reliability and validity is over time for the direct measure and the UCLA scale.

- To assess any effects of long-term limiting illness and sex on responses to the direct measure of loneliness and the UCLA scale.

Community Life Survey

- To assess the effect of important demographics on responses to the direct measure of loneliness.

- To compare the effect of important demographics on the direct measure of loneliness with the findings from the Opinions and Lifestyle Survey (OPN) and the English Longitudinal Study for Ageing (ELSA).

Opinions and Lifestyle Survey

- To assess the relatedness of the UCLA scale and the single-item question and to compare the findings with the established ELSA.

- To assess the effect of key demographics on responses to the direct measure of loneliness and the UCLA scale, and to compare the findings with the established CLS.

- To assess the effect of question ordering on responses to the direct measure of loneliness and the UCLA scale.

Good Childhood Index Survey

- To assess the relatedness of the children's UCLA scale and the direct measure of loneliness.

- To assess the reliability of the adapted wording of the children's UCLA scale.

- To explore any differences in responses to the questions in children when compared with adults' responses on other surveys.

- To assess effect of age and sex on responses to the children's UCLA scale and the direct measure of loneliness.

5 . Methodology

Missing data and weighting

"Missing data" refers to incidences when respondents have either refused to answer the questions on loneliness or have answered "don't know". When missing data was found, listwise deletion was used, which means the entire response was excluded from analysis if any single value from the University of California, Los Angeles (UCLA) scale or direct measure of loneliness was unanswered. This is because if, for example, a respondent had not answered the direct measure of loneliness but had answered the UCLA, the case could not be used in the analysis comparing the two.

Weights were included in the descriptive analysis to compensate for unequal selection probabilities and differential non-response. Weights were not used when statistical tests were run as the software used could not account for them correctly (for example, in the calculation of the degrees of freedom in a chi-Square test).

Presentation of the UCLA scores

In reporting the findings from the analysis, we used the UCLA questions for adults and children as intended by the developers of the scale – that is, by assigning a score to each response and creating a total score by summing the individual scores.

For example:

- "Hardly ever or never" equals 1

- "Some of the time" equals 2

- "Often" equals 3

The lowest possible combined score on the loneliness scale is 3 (indicating less frequent loneliness) and the highest is 9 (indicating more frequent loneliness). There is no standard accepted score above which a person would be considered lonely, so no threshold for loneliness was used in interpreting the analyses.

Statistical tests

To check the reliability and validity of the proposed loneliness measures, we used a number of different statistical tests, which are detailed in this section.

A p-value of less than 0.05 was taken as significant, as is reported in the statistics in the following section. This means that the test is showing a statistically significant result, and association between two variables is greater than would be expected by chance.

Pearson's chi square of association was used to see whether there was any association among selected variables. A chi-square test compares the observed frequencies with those you would expect to get by chance if there were no association. This test is used on categorical or ordinal data. Cramer's V was used as a follow-up test, as it tells us the strength of the association and therefore which factors have the greatest influence and the strongest relationships. The X^2 value is reported, as is standard when reporting the chi-square test, as well as the degrees of freedom, number of cases analysed (N) and the p value. For Cramer's V, a coefficient is reported, which can be interpreted similarly to a correlation coefficient. The closer the coefficient is to 1.00, the stronger the relationship between the variables is. Direction or causality cannot be expressed using a chi square.

A Goodman-Kruskal correlation was used to check how well the UCLA scores were associated with the direct measure of loneliness. This particular correlation test was used because the data are ordinal, that is, the data represent categories that make sense in a certain order, as opposed to numbers on a scale. The correlation coefficient (G) has been reported in the findings; if the number is closer to 1.00 then the correlation is high and the variables are closely related, whereas if it is closer to 0.00 then there is little to no correlation.

Cronbach's alpha was used to assess the internal reliability of the children's UCLA scale. Internal reliability is the degree to which questions in a scale can be said to measure the same concept; in this case it was used to check whether each UCLA question is measuring the same concept. This test is commonly used, and it measures how closely related a set of responses are as a group. The alpha coefficient is reported, which once again can be interpreted similarly to a correlation coefficient: high internal reliability is denoted with an alpha much closer to 1.00.

6 . Main findings from the survey testing

English Longitudinal Study for Ageing

The analysis used waves 4 to 8 of the English Longitudinal Study for Ageing (ELSA) data, unless otherwise stated. When using the Opinions and Lifestyle Survey (OPN), a sub-sample of those aged 50 years and over was analysed to ensure it was comparable to ELSA. Descriptive statistics, such as the percentage of people who responded in a particular way, were run on wave 8 and cross-sectional weights were used. The latest methodology on the waves and weights (PDF, 382.8KB) is available. For details of the full OPN sample, please see Table 3.

Frequency of loneliness

Around two-thirds of respondents reported "Hardly ever or never" feeling lonely, that is, 69.0% of respondents on ELSA and 65.0% on OPN. The difference in those reporting often feeling lonely was even smaller when comparing the ELSA and OPN, at 6.8% and 6.3%, respectively (Figure 1). Respondents also reported similar scores in response to the UCLA scale (Figure 2).

The similarity between frequencies when comparing the OPN to the ELSA suggest that the OPN has measured the same concept of loneliness. The differences might be due to mode effects (the mode in which the survey is administered such as telephone or face-to-face interview). However, without more rigorous testing and analysis of the different modes used, it is difficult to say whether this definitively accounts for the differences in proportions reporting frequent and less frequent loneliness.

Figure 1: Reported frequency of loneliness for the direct measure

ELSA and OPN

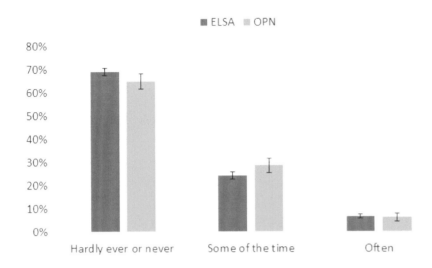

Source: Office for National Statistics: English Longitudinal Study of Ageing (ELSA); Opinions and Lifestyle Survey (OPN)

Notes:

1. ELSA data is from wave 8 (2016 to 2017).

2. OPN data is July to August 2018.

3. 95% confidence intervals are displayed on the chart.

Figure 2: Reported frequency of loneliness on the UCLA scale for wave 8 of the English Longitudinal Study for Ageing and the Opinions and Lifestyle Survey

ELSA and OPN

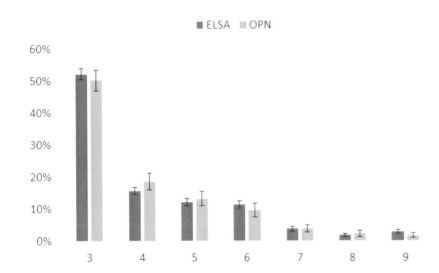

Source: English Longitudinal Study of Ageing (2016-2017) and Opinions and Lifestyle Survey (2018)

Notes:

1. ELSA data is from wave 8 (2016 to 2017).

3. 95% confidence intervals are displayed on the chart.

UCLA compared with direct measure of loneliness

For each wave of the ELSA data, both the UCLA and the responses to the direct measure of loneliness showed strongly significant positive correlations (G = 0.875-0.888, p<.000). This indicates that if a person scored highly in one measure, they also tended to score highly in the other (that is, if a person rated themselves as lonely on the UCLA items they would also rate themselves as lonely on the direct measure of loneliness).

Using ELSA data from wave 8, a Cronbach's alpha test on the three questions comprising the UCLA scale showed high internal validity, with an alpha coefficient of 0.824.

These coefficients from the correlations and validity tests can be used as a "benchmark" for testing the OPN data. As the correlation scores for the ELSA ranged from 0.875 to 0.888, we would expect the OPN to have correlations in a similar region, and also for the internal consistency of the UCLA to have a similar alpha coefficient.

Demographics and loneliness

A chi-square test was used to see if sex and long-term illness or disability (independently) affected responses to the direct measure of loneliness and the UCLA scale, as has been found in previous testing. Sex was significantly associated with both items; females were more likely than males to say they often felt lonely compared with hardly ever or never feeling lonely (direct measure: X^2 (2, N = 3117) = 48.388, p<.000, compared with UCLA: X^2 (6, N = 3065) = 23.784, p<.005).

Reporting having a disability or long-term limiting illness was also significantly associated with different answers on the direct measure of loneliness and UCLA (direct measure: X^2 (2, N = 3116) = 53.230, p<.000, compared with UCLA: X^2 (6, N = 3064) = 73.195, p<.000); odds ratios suggest respondents are more likely to respond "Often" on the direct measure of loneliness if they report having a disability or long-term illness than if they do not.

Community Life Survey

In April 2018, we reported the factors most associated with loneliness in the article, Loneliness – What characteristics and circumstances are associated with feeling lonely?. The analysis was carried out using data from the 2016 to 2017 Community Life Survey (CLS) and identified a number of demographics associated with loneliness, such as sex, employment, marital status and age. These factors were also analysed here as part of the testing programme using OPN data to see if findings would be consistent. The analysis previously published on the CLS was carried out using a five-item response scale for the direct measure of loneliness (see Table 1). No analysis was possible for the UCLA scale as it was not used on the CLS survey. The statistical test used with the OPN data (a chi-square) was run using the CLS data to compare the results.

Demographics and loneliness

The variables tested were all found to have a significant relationship with the direct measure of loneliness, and are presented in Table 2. Some of the demographic variables presented on the CLS were not categorised in a similar way to the OPN or the questions were asked differently and therefore were not comparable. For example, employment had different categories on the CLS compared with OPN, in that the OPN did not have those defined as economically inactive.

The findings suggest that responses to the direct measure of loneliness are significantly associated with individual characteristics such as sex and age and show the same patterns of association across the two surveys. Although the effects sizes are small, tenure has the strongest relationship.

Table 2: Factors significantly associated with direct measures of loneliness on the Community Life Survey, 2016 to 2017

Variable	Categories	Chi-square statistic	Effect size1
Tenure	Owner Renter	$X2 (4, N = 8997) = 338.527$, $p < 0.000$	0.194
Marital status	Single Married/civil partnership Divorced/separated Widowed	$X2 (12, N = 9781) = 813.782$, $p < 0.000$	0.167
Health (self-reported)	Very good Good Fair Bad Very bad	$X2 (16, N = 7336) = 545.705$, $p < 0.000$	0.136
Sex	Male Female	$X2 (4, N = 9969) = 173.457$, $p < 0.000$	0.132
Age group	16 to 24 25 to 34 35 to 44 45 to 54 55 to 64 65 to 74 75 and over	$X2 (24, N = 9695) = 241.587$, $p < 0.000$	0.079

Source: Community Life Survey

Notes

1. Using Cramer's V coefficient. The closer the value is to 1.00 the bigger the effect size.

Opinions and Lifestyle Survey

Over the two months during which the questions were tested, the OPN combined sample size was 2,208 persons. The weighted demographic composition of the total sample is shown in Table 3.

Table 3: Weighted counts and proportions by age and sex of the Opinions and Lifestyle Survey testing, July and August 2018

	16 to 24	25 to 44	45 to 54	55 to 64	65 to 74	75 and over	Total
Male	14.2%	32.6%	17.1%	14.9%	12.2%	8.9%	48.9%
Female	13.6%	31.0%	17.0%	14.9%	12.6%	11.0%	51.1%
Total	13.9%	31.8%	17.1%	14.9%	12.4%	9.9%	100.0%

Source: Office for National Statistics

Frequency of loneliness

As shown in Figure 3, nearly two-thirds (65.0%) of respondents to the OPN survey reported that they hardly ever or never felt lonely in response to the direct question on loneliness.

This compares with half of respondents who had the lowest score on the UCLA scale (50.3%), meaning that they answered hardly ever or never to all three UCLA questions (Figure 4). This suggests that OPN respondents were more likely to report that they were never or hardly ever lonely when asked directly than when asked indirectly using the UCLA scale. This is also consistent with findings from other studies, such as ELSA.

Figure 3: Reported frequency of loneliness for the direct measure

OPN

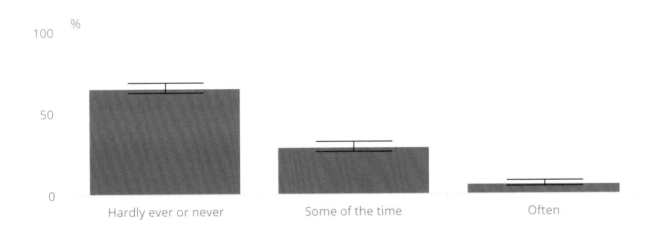

Figure 3: Reported frequency of loneliness for the direct measure

OPN

Source: Office for National Statistics, Opinions and Lifestyle Survey (OPN)

Notes:

1. July to August 2018.

2. 95% confidence intervals are displayed on the chart.

Figure 4: Reported frequency of loneliness for each score of the UCLA

OPN

Figure 4: Reported frequency of loneliness for each score of the UCLA

OPN

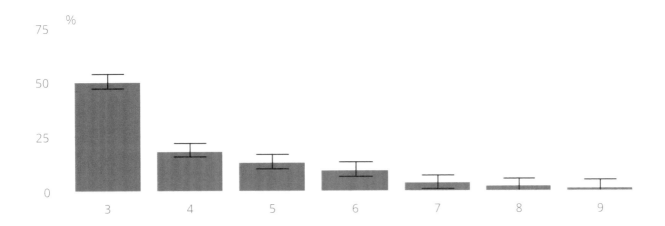

Source: Office for National Statistics, Opinions and Lifestyle Survey (OPN)

Notes:

1. July to August 2018.

2. 95% confidence intervals are displayed on the chart.

3. UCLA refers to the University of California, Los Angeles measure of loneliness.

As would be expected, people who scored hardly ever or never on the direct measure of loneliness also scored lower on the UCLA scale, and the other way around, with those answering some of the time on the direct measure most frequently scoring 6 on the UCLA (Figure 5).

Figure 5: Reported frequency of loneliness for each score of the UCLA

OPN

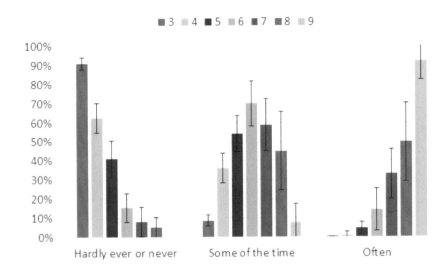

Source: Office for National Statistics

Notes:

1. July to August 2018.

2. 95% confidence intervals are displayed on the chart.

3. UCLA refers to the University of California, Los Angeles measure of loneliness.

Direct question of loneliness compared with UCLA scale

There was a significant strong positive correlation between UCLA scores and the responses to the direct measure of loneliness (G=.844, p<.000). That is, if a person scored highly in one measure, they were likely to score highly in the other measure. This suggests that the measures are related and both are capturing aspects of loneliness. This result is similar to the correlation coefficients produced for each wave of the ELSA data. Although the measures are related and move in similar directions, people appear to under-report loneliness on the direct measure compared with the indirect measure (UCLA). This is shown by the fact that people more frequently reported that they were "Hardly ever or never" lonely to the direct question than reported having the lowest loneliness to the indirect question.

The UCLA scale items also had fairly high internal consistency, with a Cronbach's alpha of 0.76, although this is lower than the alpha coefficient found using the ELSA data. Further investigation is needed to determine why the internal consistency of the UCLA scale is lower on the OPN than ELSA. Possible reasons are a difference in understanding of the UCLA by people of different ages, with the OPN sample having a wider age range than ELSA, or the fact that the ELSA is self-completed and the OPN is carried out via phone interview.

Demographics and loneliness

Chi-square tests were conducted on the OPN data to explore whether there were similar associations between loneliness and demographics, such as sex and age, as those found in the CLS analysis. A significant association was found between the direct measure of loneliness and sex, X^2 (2, N = 2203) = 28.6, p<.000, and the association between UCLA and sex was also found to be significant, X^2 (6, N = 2189) = 17.3, p<.05.

This indicates that there is a significant difference in males and females, on both the direct measure of loneliness and the UCLA scale. Women report higher levels of loneliness, which appears to be most sensitive on the middle categories (that is, "Some of the time" on the direct measure of loneliness and around score 6 on the UCLA scale), which is shown in Figures 6 and 7.

Figure 6: Reported frequency of loneliness for the direct measure, by sex

OPN

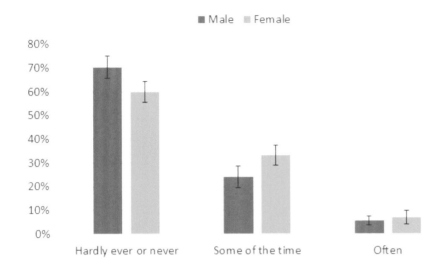

Source: Office for National Statistics, Opinions and Lifestyle Survey (OPN)

Notes:

1. July to August 2018.

2. 95% confidence intervals are displayed on the chart.

Figure 7: Reported frequency of loneliness on the UCLA scale, by sex

OPN

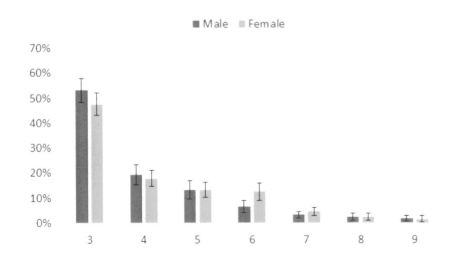

Source: Office for National Statistics, Opinions and Lifestyle Survey (OPN)

Notes:

1. When using the UCLA scale, men and women reported no significant difference in levels of loneliness.

2. UCLA refers to the University of California, Los Angeles measure of loneliness.

OPN data were also analysed to see if we would find the same significant associations with loneliness as identified using the CLS data (Table 4). It was not possible to replicate all the analysis reported for the CLS data due to differences in the questions asked on the surveys (see OPN section).

Table 4: Factors significantly associated with the direct measure of loneliness, Opinions and Lifestyle Survey

Variable	Categories	Chi-square statistic	Effect size1
Marital status	Single Married/civil partnership Divorced/separated Widowed	X2 (6, N = 2203) = 196.11, p<.000	0.211
Health (self-reported)	Very good Good Fair Bad Very bad	X2 (8, N = 2196) = 125.37, p<.000	0.169
Tenure	Owner Renter	X2 (2, N = 2159) = 49.95, p <.000	0.152
Sex	Male Female	X2 (2, N = 2203) = 28.55, p<.000	0.114
Age group	16 to 24 25 to 34 35 to 44 45 to 54 55 to 64 65 to 74 75 and over	X2 (12, N = 2203) = 38.77, p<.005	0.089

Source: Opinions and Lifestyle Survey

Notes

1.Using Cramer's V coefficient. The closer the value is to 1.00 the bigger the effect size.

Table 5: Factors significantly associated with the UCLA scale, Opinions and Lifestyle Survey

Variable	Categories	Chi-square statistic	Effect size1
Marital status	Single Married/civil partnership Divorced/separated Widowed	X2 (18, N = 2189) = 180.79, p<.000	0.166
Health (self-reported)	Very good Good Fair Bad Very bad	X2 (24, N = 2185) = 186.73, p<.000	0.146
Tenure	Owner Renter	X2 (6, N = 2146) = 97.66, p<.000	0.213
Sex	Male Female	X2 (6, N = 2189) = 17.28, p<.01	0.089
Age group	16 to 24 25 to 34 35 to 44 45 to 54 55 to 64 65 to 74 75 and over	X2 (36, N = 2189) = 52.94, p<.05	0.063

Source: Office for National Statistics

Notes

1. Using Cramer's V coefficient. The closer the value is to 1.00 the bigger the effect size.

Order effects

Chi-square tests of association were conducted to explore whether people responded differently to the questions depending the order in which they were presented. A significant association was found between UCLA and order (X^2 (2, N = 2189) = 17.1, p<.01), however, no significant association was found between the direct measure of loneliness and question order (X^2 (2, N = 2203) = 1.78, p=0.41). This suggests that the order in which the questions are presented to respondents affects their responses to the indirect questions on loneliness (the UCLA scale) but does not affect their responses to the direct question on loneliness.

Figure 8: Reported frequency of loneliness for each score of the UCLA, by order of questioning

OPN

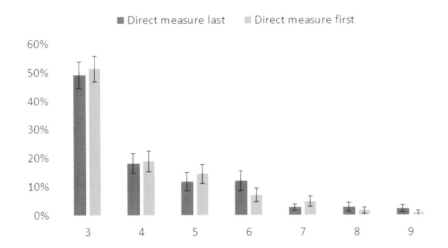

Source: Office for National Statistics, Opinions and Lifestyle Survey (OPN)

Notes:

1. July to August 2018.

2. 95% confidence intervals are displayed on the chart.

3. UCLA refers to the University of California, Los Angeles measure of loneliness.

Although the association between order and UCLA score was found to be significant, Figure 8 shows that order did not affect the UCLA uniformly. The difference in UCLA score was only seen in certain score ranges. In this case, respondents who scored 6 were most affected by order change. This indicates that those who experience very high or very low levels of loneliness are not affected by the difference between direct and indirect language, however, those who may experience more moderate degrees of loneliness will be impacted by order. In other words, the direct language of the single item appears to impact those who experience moderate degrees of loneliness, making them more likely to change their responses. Because of this, it is recommended that the direct measure of loneliness follows the UCLA, unless it is used alone; this is consistent with established surveys such as the ELSA.

Question debriefing with OPN interviewers

The OPN telephone interviewers were de-briefed about their experiences of asking the questions in a telephone interview. The following are main points raised by the interviewers:

- many interviewers described a little apprehension about asking these questions before the testing had begun but were surprised at how easily and well they were received

- the questions did not seem to cause upset among respondents

- no one refused to answer the questions or stopped answering part way through

- the questions did not take long to ask and answer (they estimated about two minutes in total including the preamble)

- interviewers believed the questions were answered honestly, that respondents thought about their answer before answering, and they attributed this in part to the use of a word rather than numerical response scale

- they thought a broadly worded introduction (not mentioning loneliness) should be recommended with the questions as this helps to inform respondents about what is coming and helps make the questions flow

- they felt it was helpful that the loneliness questions followed the personal well-being questions on this survey, as it created a useful flow and suggested that putting the loneliness questions with health-related questions would also work well

Good Childhood Index Survey

The analysis carried out on the OPN was also run on the data available for children aged 10 to 15 years. As there has been comparatively less research into children's loneliness using the direct measure of loneliness and the UCLA scale, we conducted more descriptive analysis on these data to establish a fuller picture of how children respond to these measures. The Children's Society survey asks respondents their gender, while the other surveys analysed here have included the respondent's sex. To aid comparisons, and because of small sample sizes for children identifying as transgender, the analysis here only includes those who identified as the same sex assigned at birth.

Frequency of loneliness

When asked how frequently they felt lonely using the direct question, 11.3% of children reported that they felt lonely often, while 54.6% of children reported that they hardly ever or never felt lonely (Figure 9). While adults seem to most frequently score 3 on the UCLA scale with a consistent decline in the proportion of respondents receiving each higher score, the pattern is a bit different for children. While they also most frequently score 3, there is another peak in the proportion of respondents scoring in the middle of the scale, as shown in Figure 10.

Figure 9: Reported frequency of loneliness for the direct measure

Good Childhood Index, ages 10 to 15

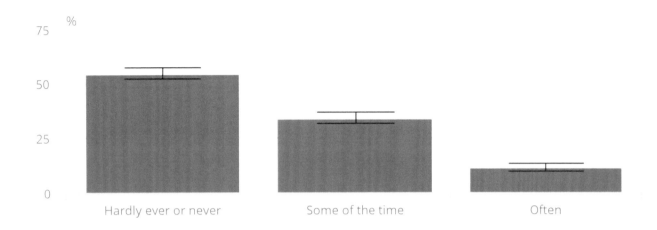

Figure 9: Reported frequency of loneliness for the direct measure

Good Childhood Index, ages 10 to 15

Source: The Children's Society, Good Childhood Index Survey

Notes:

1. May to June 2018.

2. 95% confidence intervals are displayed on the chart.

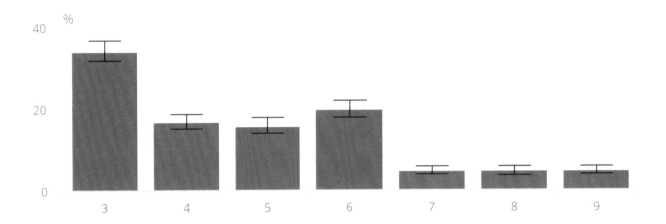

Figure 10: Reported frequency of loneliness for each score of the UCLA

Good Childhood Index, ages 10 to 15

Source: The Children's Society, Good Childhood Index Survey

Notes:

1. May to June 2018.

2. 95% confidence intervals are displayed on the chart.

3. UCLA refers to the University of California, Los Angeles measure of loneliness.

UCLA compared with direct question of loneliness

As found for the other surveys, there was a strong, positive relationship between answers to the direct measure of loneliness and the UCLA scores (G = 0.877, p < 0.00). It can therefore be concluded that the direct measure and the UCLA scale are strongly related in children as well as in adults. Finally, the Cronbach's alpha test produced an alpha statistic of 0.846, indicating a high level of internal consistency within the adapted version on the UCLA scale for children.

Demographics and loneliness

The relationship between the direct measure of loneliness and sex was assessed using a chi-square test of association. This found a significant association between sex and responses to the single-item question (= x^2 (2, N=1538) = 7.2356, p<.05). The relationship between sex and the UCLA scale was assessed in the same manner, and again found a significant association (=x^2 (6, N=1537) = 27.256, p <.000). Despite these significant results, further testing found that Cramer's V was 0.069 for the direct measure of loneliness and 0.133 for the UCLA scale, indicating a very weak association between sex and responses.

Figures 11 and 12 show the responses to the direct question of loneliness and the UCLA scale by sex. Both the direct measure and the UCLA scale showed that girls were less likely to report extreme values than boys, with girls' answers more likely to cluster around the middle scores of the direct question of loneliness and the UCLA scale.

Figure 11: Reported frequency of loneliness for the direct measure, by sex

Good Childhood Index, ages 10 to 15

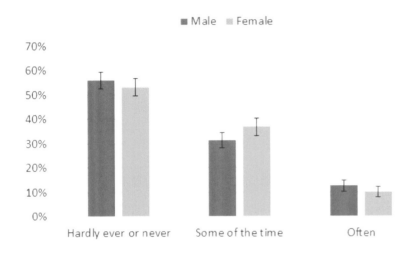

Notes:

1. May to June 2018.

2. 95% confidence intervals are displayed on the chart.

Figure 12: Reported frequency of loneliness for each score of the UCLA, by sex

Good Childhood Index, ages 10 to 15

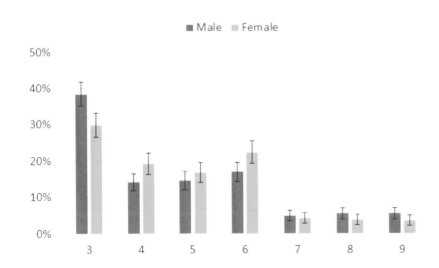

Notes:

1. May to June 2018.

2. 95% confidence intervals are displayed on the chart.

3. UCLA refers to the University of California, Los Angeles measure of loneliness.

Further chi-square tests were conducted to assess the relationship between age and both the direct question of loneliness and the UCLA scale. The test was conducted using age groups of 10 to 12 and 13 to 15 years. Testing found that age was significantly related to responses to the direct question of loneliness (= x^2 (2, N=1538) = 12.964, p <.000). Cramer's V was 0.092, indicating a very weak effect between age and responses to the direct question. A significant relationship was also identified between age and responses to the UCLA scale (= x^2 (6, N=1537) = 38.988, p <.000, with a Cramer's V coefficient of 0.159, indicating a weak association between age and the UCLA scale.

Figures 13 and 14 show the responses to the direct measure question and the UCLA scale by age group. Younger children (aged 10 to 12 years) were more likely than older children (aged 13 to 15 years) to report that they often felt lonely on the direct measure of loneliness, or to report a high UCLA score.

Figure 13: Reported frequency of loneliness for the direct measure, by age groups

Good Childhood Index

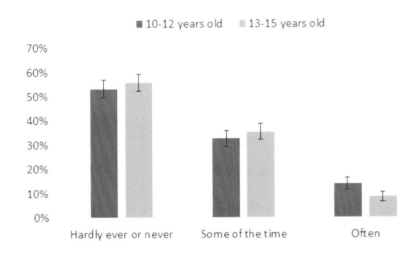

Source: The Children's Society, Good Childhood Index Survey

Figure 14: Reported frequency of loneliness for each score of the UCLA, by age groups

Good Childhood Index

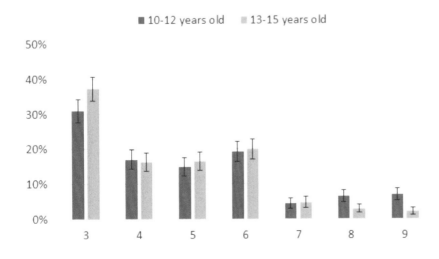

Source: The Children's Society, Good Childhood Index Survey

1. May to June 2018.

2. 95% confidence intervals are displayed on the chart.

3. UCLA refers to the University of California, Los Angeles measure of loneliness.

7 . Conclusions

Many different approaches have been used to measure loneliness, including both multi-item scales and direct measures. There is also a variety of different approaches to survey administration are in use among the surveys that currently include the questions. Through our survey testing, we aimed to understand how our preliminary recommended measures of loneliness worked for people of different ages and backgrounds and how well they performed on different types of surveys.

Overall, when comparing responses to loneliness questions on surveys like ELSA, the Community Life Survey, and the Opinions Survey, the findings are consistent and relationships identified between loneliness and other factors are also similar. It is encouraging that the UCLA scale used on ELSA produces comparable findings when used on surveys covering a wider age range and performed well in tests of reliability and validity. The adapted version of the UCLA scale for use with children also performed well in similar testing. We suggest that this combination of indirect and direct measures of loneliness is therefore suitable for use on major studies.

There is a strong positive association between the UCLA scale and the direct measure of loneliness, with those who report feeling lonely on one often reporting feeling lonely on the other as well.

Assessment of the UCLA scale's internal consistency shows that it is high across all surveys tested. This indicates that the questions within the UCLA scale are measuring the concept of loneliness and that it is a reliable measure of loneliness when used on young people and adults, as well as in its adapted version for children.

The importance of question order comes into play in cases where both measures are included. A significant order effect was found, with responses to the UCLA scale affected if preceded by the direct question of loneliness. The direct question is not sensitive to order effects with the UCLA scale.

Opinions and Lifestyle Survey (OPN) interviewers described a little apprehension about asking the loneliness questions before the testing had begun but were surprised at how easily and well the questions were received. The questions did not seem to cause upset among respondents. Also, the questions did not take long to ask and answer.

Recommendations based on the findings

We suggest the use of both direct and indirect measures of loneliness as the "gold standard" where possible. This enables us to measure responses on a scale that has been assessed as valid and reliable, as well as allowing the respondent to say for themselves whether they feel lonely, providing further insight into the subjective feeling of loneliness for different people. Also, there is variation in how people understand the term "loneliness" and some people might be reluctant to admit to loneliness, and this might be particularly true of certain groups. A multi-item measure that does not mention loneliness directly can be helpful to address these issues. The recommended measures are well-tested, and have a positive track record for performing well in general population surveys using different approaches to data collection.

Although the combination of a direct and an indirect measure provides a more holistic picture of loneliness, where it is not possible to use all four questions as survey space is a major constraint, we would recommend at a minimum the use of the direct question to measure prevalence of loneliness.

Question order is important for comparability between surveys, as findings seem to indicate that asking the direct question of loneliness first impacts responses to the UCLA, within mid-level categories. For this reason, it is recommended that the direct question of loneliness follows the UCLA questions. The three UCLA questions should be kept together and in the order in which they are presented in Table 1 to ensure comparability of the findings with other surveys.

An adapted version of the UCLA questions should be used for children. The findings in this section show that this version is as reliable and valid as the general version for adults, and measures feelings of loneliness in those aged 10 to 15 years well. More substantive findings on the understanding of the UCLA questions among children can be found in Cognitive testing of loneliness questions and response options.

Interviewers noted that specifically mentioning "loneliness" rather than "relationships" in the introduction could have an effect on respondents' answers. Overall, it is recommended that the introduction or preamble should not mention loneliness and should introduce the topic as focusing on the participant's relationships with others.

Compendium

Recommended national indicators of loneliness

Overview of our recommendations for national measures of loneliness.

Contact:
Dawn Snape or Silvia Manclossi
qualityoflife@ons.gov.uk
+44 (0)1633 582486

Release date:
5 December 2018

Next release:
To be announced

Table of contents

1 . Recommended measures for adults and children

Based on our review of existing measures and the results of our cognitive testing and survey testing programme, we recommend four questions to capture different aspects of loneliness. The first three questions are from the University of California, Los Angeles (UCLA) three-item loneliness scale and the last is a direct question about how often the respondent feels lonely, currently used on the Community Life Survey. The questions recommended for use with adults aged 16 years and over are detailed in this section.

Proposed indicators of loneliness for adults aged 16 years and over

Three-item version of UCLA scale

The three-item version of the UCLA scale asks indirectly about loneliness using the following questions:

- How often do you feel that you lack companionship?

- How often do you feel left out?

- How often do you feel isolated from others?

Response categories: "Hardly ever or never", "Some of the time" or "Often".

Responses to each question can be scored to provide a single loneliness score.

Direct measure

A single-item measure currently used on the Community Life Survey, which asks people directly about their experience of loneliness:

"How often do you feel lonely?"

Response categories: "Often or always", "Some of the time", "Occasionally", "Hardly ever" or "Never".

For clarity, we are not recommending that the direct measure of loneliness be combined with the UCLA scale into a composite score, but rather that the indirect (UCLA) measure and direct (single-item) measure should ideally be used together as a loneliness question module. The two approaches to measurement provide a more holistic picture of loneliness (as shown by findings from the English Longitudinal Study of Ageing).

Where it is not possible to use all four questions, as survey space is a major constraint, we would recommend at a minimum the use of a direct question on loneliness: "How often do you feel lonely?". This will provide an estimate of the prevalence of loneliness based on respondents' own perspectives and will give the greatest comparability with other surveys.

An adapted version of the measures is recommended for use with children and young people aged 10 to 15 years. The wording for the children's measure was changed to a more "plain English" version, reflecting concerns that the words "companionship" and "isolation" are difficult for children to read and may be interpreted in a range of different ways. We revised the questions and tested them cognitively (to understand children's ease of use and interpretations) and on a survey conducted among children by The Children's Society. The findings showed that the revised questions were appropriate for use with children.

Proposed indicators of loneliness for children aged 10 to 15 years

Modified version of UCLA scale

For children (aged 10 to 15 years), we suggest a slightly modified version of the UCLA scale using the following questions:

- How often do you feel you have no one to talk to?

- How often do you feel left out?

- How often do you feel alone?

Response categories: "Hardly ever or never", "Some of the time" or "Often".

Direct measure

The Direct measure currently used on the Community Life Survey, which asks children directly about their experience of loneliness:

"How often do you feel lonely?"

Response categories: "Often or always", "Some of the time", "Occasionally", "Hardly ever" or "Never".

To accompany the loneliness recommendations, we have also developed a guidance report for incorporating the measures in relevant surveys and interpreting the results.

2 . Harmonisation of national indicators of loneliness

Harmonisation is about ensuring consistency in the use of definitions, survey questions, administrative data and in the presentation of outputs across the Government Statistical Service (GSS). Harmonisation is important in maximising the usefulness of data collected and statistics produced. Ensuring comparability across the GSS is important as it maximises the power of data and analyses without compromising quality.

The Interim Harmonised Principle for loneliness has been agreed by the cross-government National Statistics Harmonisation Group (NSHG) and approved by the National Statistics Harmonisation Steering Group (NSH SG). From today (5 December 2018), the loneliness indicators outlined in this section will form part of a new GSS Interim Harmonised Principle for loneliness that can be accessed through the GSS web pages.

We will encourage the roll-out of the Interim Harmonised Principles for loneliness across the GSS and more widely, and suggest taking stock and making any refinements necessary within two years, after survey data have been analysed, before proposing the final GSS Harmonised Principle. The GSS Harmonisation Team will monitor implementation of the loneliness principle to ensure harmonisation is adhered to.

We would welcome your feedback on how well the loneliness indicators work and any improvements you would suggest, before submitting them for final approval as GSS Harmonised Principles in 2020. Please get in touch with us by contacting:

- QualityofLife@ons.gov.uk

- Harmonisation@Statistics.gov.uk

Compendium

Acknowledgments

A list of acknowledgements for the loneliness compendium.

Contact:
Dawn Snape or Silvia Manclossi
qualityoflife@ons.gov.uk
+44 (0)1633 582486

Release date:
5 December 2018

Next release:
5 December 2018

Table of contents

1 . Acknowledgements

This publication represents the outcome of a collaborative effort. The Office for National Statistics (ONS) Quality of Life and Social Analysis Team is grateful for the expert advice, contributions and assistance provided by many people throughout this project. Most notably, this includes the cross-government Tackling Loneliness Team based in the Department for Digital, Culture, Media and Sport, the academics and other experts who comprised the Loneliness Technical Advisory Group (TAG), and our collaborators at The Children's Society who helped with survey testing and qualitative interviews with children. We are also grateful to colleagues from across ONS who have helped with data collection, analysis and interpretation.

We would specifically like to acknowledge the help provided at important stages of the project by the following people and organisations:

- Andrea Wigfield and Sarah Alden (University of Sheffield)

- Andrew Steptoe and Camille Lassole (University College London)

- Andy Staniford (Department for Business, Energy & Industrial Strategy)

- Cam Lugton (Public Health England)

- Cherish Watton, Sarah Lamb and Tim Leech (WaveLength)

- Christina Victor (Brunel University)

- Darren Stillwell (Department for Transport)

- David Marjoribanks (Money Advice Service)

- David McDaid and Nava Ashraf (London School of Economics)

- Ellie Baggott, Maria Willoughby, Ramona Herdman and Rosanna White (Department for Digital, Culture, Media and Sport)

- Farhana Mann (University College London)

- Gwyther Rees (University of York)

- Huw Thomas (relate)

- Ingrid Abreu-Scherer, Nancy Hey and Silvia Brunetti (What Works Centre for Wellbeing)

- Julianne Holt-Lunstad (Brigham Young University)

- Julie Barnett (University of Bath)

- Kate Jopling (Jopling Consulting)

- Kellie Payne and Laura Alcock-Ferguson (Campaign to End Loneliness)

- Larissa Pople (The Children's Society)

- Laura Venning, Richard Dowsett and Tamsin Shuker (Big Lottery Fund)

- Lauren Bowes (Home Office)

- Leila Tavakoli (Department of Health and Social Care)

- Louise Arseneault (King's College London)

- Matt Baumann (Ageing Better)

- Nicole Pitcher (Cochrane France)

- Olivia Christophersen (Department for International Development)

- Pamela Qualter (University of Manchester)

- Raj Patel (University of Essex)

- Sophie Pryce, Philip Talbot and Vinal Karania (Age UK)

- Stephen Hall (Department for Environment, Food and Rural Affairs)

- Susan Cooke (British Red Cross)

- Tim Matthews (King's College London)

- Ula Tymoszuk (Royal College of Music)

Compendium

Annexes: Cognitive testing of loneliness questions with children and young people and young adults

A series of annexes relating to the loneliness compendium, which provides comprehensive information on loneliness measurement, national indicators of loneliness and the question testing underpinning our recommendations.

Contact:
Ian Sidney or Ed Pyle
qualityoflife@ons.gov.uk
+44 (0)1633 455542

Release date:
5 December 2018

Next release:
To be announced

Table of contents

1 . Annex 1: ONS calls for volunteer interviewees to help produce better statistics on loneliness

The Well-being, Inequalities, Sustainability and Environment (WISE) Division, alongside the Department for Digital, Culture, Media and Sport (DCMS), have been asked by the Prime Minister to undertake a programme of work to improve our understanding of, and in turn alleviate, loneliness.

To help provide better statistics on the subject and help policymakers make better decisions on how to support people, we're looking for volunteers in England between the ages of 10 and 24 years to be interviewed during July about their attitudes, ideas and experiences of loneliness. All the information will be kept confidential and respondents will receive an incentive as a thank you for taking part.

Jo Cox Loneliness Commission

The late Jo Cox MP campaigned to raise the profile of loneliness stating, "young or old loneliness does not discriminate", and the Jo Cox Loneliness Commission presented a number of recommendations to government to help tackle the problem.

In her response, the Prime Minister Theresa May committed government to improving the evidence base and establishing indicators to measure loneliness across all ages. Specifically, in her announcement in January 2018, the Prime Minister indicated that government would be "establishing appropriate indicators of loneliness across all ages with the Office for National Statistics so these figures can be included in major research studies."

The current evidence base on loneliness is patchy – while it is richer and more comprehensive for adult age groups, we know less about experiences of loneliness for younger age ranges. We know loneliness can be an issue across all age groups but need to better understand how certain factors interact to increase the risk of loneliness, and what could reduce or even protect from future feelings of loneliness.

If you know anyone living in England who may be willing to take part to help us improve our evidence base to inform better decisions on what help and support is provided, please contact either Name or Name for more information.

2 . Annex 2: Loneliness topic guide for children and young people (aged 10 to 15 years)

Interviewing tips

Use open questions – who, how, what, why, when? Closed questions are not as effective so try to turn closed into open wherever possible.

Do not be afraid to use silence – give respondents enough time to think and say what they want to. Some people need more time than others so be aware of that. Encouragement – reassure with "umm", "yes" or head nodding, for example. This shows you are listening and interested but do not lead respondents by over-using them. Hanging probes – you can leave a question or statement hanging for respondents to finish such as, "So you think…?".

Summaries – you can recap what respondents have said then ask if you have it right or not to check you've understood. You can also ask them to summarise their thoughts; this can often provide great quotes for reports too!

Paraphrasing – paraphrasing a lot of information is a further way to check you have understood their point.

Do not assume – never think you know what respondents mean. Try your hardest to take nothing at face value. Use probes, paraphrases and summaries to check you have understood what respondents say. As a general rule of thumb, it's good to remember that if the respondent did not say it on the recording, it does not count.

Tone – the interview should be conversational and you should try to sound relaxed so respondents are put at ease. One of the best ways to achieve this is to know the topic guide inside out so you do not sound script-bound. Remember that the probes are not set in stone; a good interviewer finds their own way to ask the probes without changing the meaning of the research objective.

Interview checklist

Topic guide, respondent's contact and address details, two copies of the consent form, a show card with the Loneliness measure questions, the useful contacts list, a dictaphone, voucher incentive, pens, notepad, and batteries.

Tips for getting them to talk

You can use an activity that often helps children to open up and focus. You give them a pen and a sheet of paper with concentric circles on it (these can be drawn by hand but we'll try to get a printed one). Ask them to write their name or "Me" in the centre then ask them to think about people in their lives and add them in the circles with the closest people near him or her and the people less close to him or her further out. This can be used to generate conversation, such as "Have any of these people been lonely?", or "Why do you think they are not lonely?".

Section 1 Introduction

Loneliness is something we're hearing a lot about lately in the news. It's a normal part of life, but we do not understand enough about it and what we can do to help people in our lives who may feel lonely. That's what we'd like to talk about today. We're speaking to children and young people as well as to adults to understand more about loneliness and what we can do about it. What you have to say will help us advise the Prime Minister on how we can tackle loneliness in the UK.

Loneliness questions

a. How often do you feel you have no one to talk to?

b. How often do you feel left out?

c. How often do you feel alone?

d. How often do you feel lonely?

Answers:

Hardly ever or never

Some of the time

Often

There are no right or wrong answers. We just want to find out what you think. Your answers will be kept private, and we will not tell anybody what you've said. Just so you are aware, if you tell me something that makes me concerned about your safety or the safety of someone else, then we'll need to talk about it, and I might have to share that with the Project Leader. We may also need to talk to your parent, guardian or teacher. You do not have to answer any question if you do not want to, and we can stop at any time. We usually record the interviews so that we can listen back to it later and make notes. Does that sound OK to you? Do you have any questions you want to ask before we start?

You also get a shopping voucher as a thank you for taking part. (Give them the voucher and ask the respondent and the adult to both sign two consent forms, keeping one copy for yourself.)

Section 2: Cognitive question testing

To get this right, we are thinking very hard about the type of questions we should be asking people about loneliness. So, I want to start by asking you four questions and I will ask you to answer these using three response options. Once we have completed this we can discuss your thoughts about the questions.

Interviewer – Read out each question one at a time and give the respondent the three answer options. Wait for a response before delivering the next question. (Try not to engage or answer any questions from the respondent at this time.)

Loneliness measure questions

How often do you feel that you have no one you can talk to?

1. In your own words, can you tell me what this question is asking you?

2. Can you think of another way of asking this question?

3. Can you give me some examples of who you might have that you can talk to? Who do you think other people might have to talk to?

4. How important do you think it is to have someone to talk to? Why?

5. How did you feel after answering this question? Do you think most children would feel that way? Do you think this question could be upsetting for children aged 10 to 15 years to answer?

6. How well do you think children between 10 to 15 years old would understand this question?

7. Children could be asked to answer this question in a survey on a computer at home. How do you think children would feel about answering this question in front of other people, their parents, teachers, or friends? What makes you think that?

8. Would you find this question easier to answer with a response scale from 0 to 10 where 0 is "never" and 10 is "all of the time"?

9. Would you feel better answering these questions in school or at home?

10. How important do you think it is to ask children how often they have someone to talk to?

11. Why do you think we might be interested in this question?

12. What do you think the word "companionship" means?

13. What do you think is the difference between "companionship" and "having someone to talk to"?

14. What do you think is a better question to ask? "How often do you feel that you have no one to talk to?" or "How often do you feel that you lack companionship?" Why? Do you think people would answer these questions differently?

How often do you feel left out?

1. What do you think this question is asking you?

2. Can you think of another way of asking this question?

3. What does it mean to be "left out"?

4. Can you give me an example of a time you have felt left out? What made you feel like this? How long did it take to recover from those feelings? How did you recover; what helped?

5. How did you feel after answering this question? Do you think most children would feel that way? Do you think this question could be upsetting for children aged 10 to 15 years to answer?

6. How important do you think it is to ask children how often they feel left out?

7. Why do you think we might be interested in this question about feeling left out?

How often do you feel alone?

1. In your own words, can you tell me what this question is asking you?

2. Can you think of another way of asking this question?

3. Can you give me some examples of when you may have felt alone? What reasons can you think of why someone might feel alone?

4. How do you think children would feel about answering this question in front of other people, their parents, teachers, or friends?

5. How important do you think it is to ask children how often they feel alone?

6. Why do you think we might be interested in this question?

7. What do you think the world "isolated" means?

8. What is the difference between being "isolated" and being "alone"?

9. What do you think is a better question to ask? "How often do you feel alone?" or "How often do you feel isolated?" Why? Do you think people would answer this question differently?

How often do you feel lonely?

1. What do you think this question is asking you?

2. What reasons can you think of why someone might feel lonely?

3. How did you feel after answering this question? Do you think most children would feel that way? Do you think this question could be upsetting for children aged 10 to 15 years to answer?

4. Children would be asked to answer this question in a survey on a computer at home. How comfortable do you think children would feel doing it that way? Why do you say that?

5. Would you find this question easier to answer with a response scale from 0 to 10 where 0 is "never" and 10 is "all of the time"?

6. Would you feel better answering these questions in school or at home?

7. In the question we looked at before this one, we used the word "alone". What do you think the differences are or what is the same between being alone or being lonely?

Section 3: In-depth subject investigation on loneliness

Other people's experiences of loneliness

(Start with other people to lead gently into the topic.)

I want to talk about the subject of loneliness a little more now.

1. So, if you can start by telling me about someone you know who feels lonely or someone who has felt lonely in the past?

2. If yes, do you know why they are lonely or can you think of any reasons for why they are lonely?

3. If yes, did they stop being lonely? How did that happen?

4. Who do you think would be most likely to feel lonely? Why?

5. When do you think people are more or less likely to be lonely? Why do you say that?

6. Do you think it is good to be alone sometimes or not? Why or why not?

7. How important do you think it is it to help young people who are feeling lonely?

8. What could we do to improve things for young people who feel lonely? (for example, at home, at school, in their neighbourhood)

Child's experiences of loneliness

I'd like us to talk about you now. I want to remind you that you do not have to answer any questions that make you feel uncomfortable. If you can tell us as much as you feel able we're very grateful. (If the respondent seems reluctant to talk about their experiences, remind them of the confidentiality clause.)

1. So, let's begin with what loneliness means to you? How would you describe loneliness?

2. Can you tell me about a time you have felt lonely? What were you doing? How long for?

3. How strong was the feeling? (You can use a scale to help respondents, such as 0 to 10 with 0 being "not lonely at all" and 10 being "completely lonely")

4. What caused you to feel lonely? (for example, were you missing somebody? Was it because of something to do with friends, family or people at school?)

5. How did you move on from being lonely? How lonely are you now?

6. What can you tell me about a time when you did not feel lonely at all?

7. If yes, why do you think that was? What was happening then? What were you doing then? Where were you? Were you alone or with other people? What feelings did you have instead?

8. What do you think the opposite of loneliness is?

9. What could we do to improve things for people feeling lonely? What would you find most helpful if you felt lonely? Are there things that you really would not find helpful?

Social networks

1. How close do you live to your friends? (Close, near-by or far away.)

2. How often do you see family members that you do not live with? (Often, sometimes, hardly ever or never.)

3. Is there anything that stops you from seeing friends and family as often as you would like? If so, what? Do you speak with them often in other ways, for example, by telephone, video calls or social media?

4. How much do you feel that you are listened to by family and friends? Why?

5. How well do you know what's happening with family and friends?

6. Can you give me examples of people who you can talk to about your feelings?

7. Would you say that you and/or your family are involved in the community? What sort of community activities are you involved in?

8. Have you and/or your family lived in the area for a long time?

9. How often do you go to after school clubs, youth clubs and sport clubs? (Often, sometimes, hardly ever, or never.)

10. Do you have good relationships with your neighbours, for example, do you spend time with them more than to just say hello?

11. How happy or unhappy are you with your friendships and relationships with other people? Why?

12. Can you give me examples of people who you can ask for help at any time? Why them? What makes them the people you can ask for help from?

13. Who are the people who you can trust? If nobody, why do you think that? How does that feel?

14. Can you give me examples of people who you feel close to? If nobody, who would you like to feel close to? Why?

Section 4: Finishing the interview

1. If there was money to spend in tackling loneliness in children, how could this be best spent to help young adults out of loneliness? What types of activities, help, groups and so on?

(Use these or any others you can think of to bring the child or young person out of the intensity of the subject.) You've told me lots of information. It's been useful. How did it feel for you? Is there anything you want to ask me since I've asked you lots and lots of questions? Thank you very much for answering the questions. We are really grateful. Your answers will help us to understand loneliness and how we can help people who might be feeling lonely. How do you feel? Do you feel OK? It can be an upsetting topic for some people, so I will leave this list of phone numbers with you. (If upset), I understand it can be an upsetting topic. It is totally normal to feel upset sometimes. If you are feeling upset or worried, you might want to talk to your doctor, parent or teacher. Remember, you can always call Childline on 0800 1111.

Section 5: Safeguarding

What to do if the respondent discloses something that makes you concerned for their safety

Listen to what the respondent is saying. Do not offer advice or attempt to provide counselling. Do not try to stop them from speaking about the issue, as it might be the first time they have felt comfortable discussing the issue with somebody. Instead, ask the respondent:

- how does that make you feel?

- what do you think could be done to help?

- what would you like to be done?

- have you spoken to anyone else about this? (for example, a parent or teacher)

(If it is a safeguarding issue that needs to be reported), It is important that you are safe and not in any danger. What you've said makes me think that you might need to speak to someone else who will be able to help you. So, what I suggest is that I will speak to my Project Leader and let them know what you've said, to figure out if this should be mentioned to your teacher, parent or guardian. Does that sound OK?

Following the interview, you should report the issue with the safeguarding team, who will decide about whether action should be taken, and whether there are sufficient grounds for breaking confidentiality. They will decide whether to:

- take no further action

- recommend that the respondent passes on their concerns to the appropriate authority

- pass the concern on to the appropriate authority

- refer the situation to the National Statistician

For more information, please refer to the ONS Safeguarding Policy.

3 . Annex 3: Loneliness topic guide for young adults (aged 16 to 24 years)

Interviewing tips

Use open questions – who, how, what, why, when? Closed questions are not as effective so try to turn closed into open wherever possible.

Do not be afraid to use silence – give respondents enough time to think and say what they want to. Some people need more time than others so be aware of that.

Encouragement – reassure with "umm", "yes" or head nodding, for example. This shows you are listening and interested but do not lead respondents by over-using them. Hanging probes – you can leave a question or statement hanging for respondents to finish such as, "So you think…?".

Summaries – you can recap what respondents have said then ask if you have it right or not to check you've understood. You can also ask them to summarise their thoughts; this can often provide great quotes for reports too!

Paraphrasing – paraphrasing a lot of information is a further way to check you have understood their point.

Do not assume – never think you know what respondents mean. Try your hardest to take nothing at face value. Use probes, paraphrases and summaries to check you have understood what respondents say. As a general rule of thumb, it's good to remember that if the respondent did not say it on the recording, it does not count.

Tone – the interview should be conversational and you should try to sound relaxed so respondents are put at ease. One of the best ways to achieve this is to know the topic guide inside out so you do not sound script-bound. Remember that the probes are not set in stone; a good interviewer finds their own way to ask the probes without changing the meaning of the research objective.

Interview checklist

Topic guide, respondent's contact and address details, two copies of the consent form, the useful contacts list, a dictaphone, cash incentive, pens, notepad, and batteries.

Section 1: Introduction

Loneliness is something we're hearing a lot about lately in the news. It's a normal part of life, but we do not understand enough about it and what we can do to help people in our lives who may feel lonely. That's what we'd like to talk about today. We're speaking to children and young people as well as to adults to understand more about loneliness and what we can do about it. What you have to say will help us advise the Prime Minister on how we can tackle loneliness in the UK.

There are no right or wrong answers. We just want to find out what you think. Your answers will be kept private, and we will not tell anybody what you've said. Just so you are aware, if you tell me something that makes me concerned about your safety or the safety of someone else, then we'll need to talk about it, and I might have to share that with the Project Leader. You do not have to answer any question if you do not want to, and we can stop at any time. We usually record the interviews so that we can listen back to it later and make notes. Does that sound OK to you? Do you have any questions you want to ask before we start?

You also get a £30 cash incentive as a thank you for taking part. (Give them the money and ask the respondent to sign two consent forms, keeping one copy for yourself.)

1. Firstly, can I ask whether you are studying at school or college or university, working or doing something else?

2. Do you live with family, friends or someone else?

Section 2: Cognitive question testing

We are developing some questions about loneliness for our surveys, and we would like to ask you for your thoughts on the survey questions. So, I want to start by asking you four questions and I will ask you to answer these using three response options. Once we have completed this we can discuss your thoughts about the questions.

Interviewer – Read out each question one at a time and give the respondent the three answer options. Wait for a response before delivering the next question. (Try not to engage or answer any questions from the respondent at this time.)

Loneliness questions

a. How often do you feel that you lack companionship?

b. How often do you feel left out?

c. How often do you feel isolated from others?

d. How often do you feel lonely?

Answers:

Hardly ever or never

Some of the time

Often

Loneliness measure questions

How often do you feel that you lack companionship?

1. In your own words, can you tell me what this question is asking you?

2. Can you think of another way of asking this question?

3. Can you give me some examples of who you might have that you can talk to? Who do you think other people might have to talk to?

4. What do you think the word "companionship" means?

5. How important do you think it is to have a companion? Why?

6. How did you feel after answering this question? Do you think most young adults would feel that way? Do you think these questions could be upsetting for respondents?

7. How well do you think young people between 16 to 24 years old would understand this question?

8. Young people could be asked to answer this question in a survey on a computer at home. How do you think young people would feel about answering this question in front of other people, their parents, colleagues or friends? What makes you think that? Do you think there is a best location to answer this question (home, college, university or work)?

9. What do you think is the difference between "companionship" and "having someone to talk to"?

10. What do you think is a better question to ask? "How often do you feel that you have no one to talk to?" or "How often do you feel that you lack companionship?" Why? Do you think people would answer these questions differently?

How often do you feel left out?

1. What do you think this question is asking you?

2. Can you think of another way of asking this question?

3. What does it mean to be "left out"?

4. Can you give me an example of a time you have felt left out? What made you feel like this? How long did it take to recover from those feelings? How did you recover; what helped?

5. How did you feel after answering this question? Do you think most young adults would feel that way? Do you think these questions could be upsetting to answer?

6. How important do you think it is to ask young people how often they feel left out?

7. Why do you think we might be interested in this question about feeling left out?

How often do you feel isolated from others?

1. In your own words, can you tell me what this question is asking you?

2. Can you think of another way of asking this question?

3. Can you give me some examples of when you may have felt isolated from others? What reasons can you think of why someone might feel isolated from others?

4. How important do you think it is to ask young people how often they feel isolated?

5. What do you think the world "isolated" means?

6. What is the difference between being "isolated" and being "alone"?

7. What do you think is a better question to ask? "How often do you feel alone?" or "How often do you feel isolated?" Why? Do you think people would answer these questions differently?

How often do you feel lonely?

1. What do you think this question is asking you?

2. What reasons can you think of why someone might feel lonely?

3. How did you feel after answering this question? Do you think most young adults would feel that way? Do you think this question could be upsetting to answer?

4. Young people could be asked to answer these questions in a survey on a computer at home. How comfortable do you think young people would feel doing it that way? Why do you say that?

5. Would you feel better answering these questions in school or at home?

6. Would you find these questions easier to answer with a response scale from 0 to 10 where 0 is "never" and 10 is "all of the time"?

7. In the question we looked at before this one, we used the word "alone". What do you think the differences are and what is the same between being alone or being lonely?

Section 3: In-depth subject investigation on loneliness

Other people's experiences of loneliness

(Start with other people to lead gently into the topic.)

I want to talk about the subject of loneliness a little more now.

1. So, if you can start by telling me about someone you know who feels lonely or someone who has felt lonely in the past?

2. If yes, do you know why they are lonely or can you think of any reasons for why they are lonely?

3. If yes, did they stop being lonely? How did that happen?

4. Who do you think would be most likely to feel lonely? Why?

5. When do you think people are more or less likely to be lonely? Why do you say that?

6. Do you think it is good to be alone sometimes or not? Why or why not?

7. How important do you think it is it to help young people who are feeling lonely?

8. What could we do to improve things for young people who feel lonely? (for example, at home, at college or university, at work, or in their neighbourhood)

Young person's experiences of loneliness

I'd like us to talk about you now. I want to remind you that you do not have to answer any questions that make you feel uncomfortable. If you can tell us as much as you feel able we're very grateful. (If the respondent seems reluctant to talk about their experiences, remind them of the confidentiality clause.)

1. So, let's begin with what loneliness means to you? How would you describe loneliness?

2. Can you tell me about a time you have felt lonely? What were you doing? How long for?

3. How strong was the feeling? (You can use a scale to help respondents, such as 0 to 10 with 0 being "not lonely at all" and 10 being "completely lonely")

4. What caused you to feel lonely? (for example, were you missing somebody? Was it because of something to do with friends, family, people at college or university, or work?)

5. How did you move on from being lonely? How lonely are you now?

6. What can you tell me about a time when you did not feel lonely at all?

7. If yes, why do you think that was? What was happening then? What were you doing then? Where were you? Were you alone or with other people? What feelings did you have instead?

8. What do you think the opposite of loneliness is?

9. What would you find most helpful if you felt lonely? Are there things that you really would not find helpful?

Social networks

1. How close do you live to your friends? (Close, nearby or far away)

2. How often do you see family members that you do not live with? (Often, sometimes, hardly ever or never.)

3. Is there anything that stops you from seeing friends and family as often as you would like? If so, what? Do you speak with them often in other ways, for example, by telephone, video calls or social media?

4. How much do you feel that you are listened to by family and friends? Why?

5. How well do you know what's happening with family and friends?

6. Can you give me examples of people who you can talk to about your feelings?

7. Would you say that you and/or your family are involved in the community? What sort of community activities are you involved in?

8. How often do you go to after school clubs, youth clubs and sport clubs? (Often, sometimes, hardly ever or never)

9. Have you and/or your family lived in the area for a long time?

10. Do you have good relationships with your neighbours, for example, do you spend time with them more than to just say hello?

11. How happy or unhappy are you with your friendships and relationships with other people? Why?

12. Can you give me examples of people who you can ask for help at any time? Why them? What makes them the people you can ask for help from?

13. Who are the people who you can trust? If nobody, why do you think that? How does that feel?

14. Can you give me examples of people who you feel close to? If nobody, who would you like to feel close to? Why?

Section 4: Finishing the interview

1. If there was money to spend in tackling loneliness in young adults, how could this be best spent to help young adults out of loneliness? What types of activities, help, groups and so on?

(Use these or any others you can think of to bring the young adult out of the intensity of the subject.)

You've told me lots of information. It's been useful. How did it feel for you?

Is there anything you want to ask me since I've asked you lots and lots of questions?

Thank you very much for answering the questions. We are really grateful. Your answers will help us to understand loneliness and how we can help people who might be feeling lonely.

How do you feel? Do you feel OK? It can be an upsetting topic for some people, so I will leave this list of phone numbers with you. (If upset), I understand it can be an upsetting topic. It is totally normal to feel upset sometimes. If you are feeling upset or worried, you might want to talk to your GP, parent, colleague or friend. Remember, you can always call The Samaritans for advice and support on 0845 790 9090.

Section 5: Safeguarding

What to do if the respondent discloses something that makes you concerned for their safety

Listen to what the respondent is saying. Do not offer advice or attempt to provide counselling. Do not try to stop them from speaking about the issue, as it might be the first time they have felt comfortable discussing the issue with somebody. Instead, ask the respondent:

- how does that make you feel?

- what do you think could be done to help?

- what would you like to be done?

- have you spoken to anyone else about this? (for example, a parent or teacher)

(If it is a safeguarding issue that needs to be reported), It is important that you are safe and not in any danger. What you've said makes me think that you might need to speak to someone else who will be able to help you. So, what I suggest is that I will speak to my Project Leader and let them know what you've said, to figure out if this should be reported to someone else. Does that sound OK?

Following the interview, you should report the issue with the safeguarding team, who will decide about whether action should be taken, and whether there are sufficient grounds for breaking confidentiality. They will decide whether to:

- take no further action

- recommend that the respondent passes on their concerns to the appropriate authority

- pass the concern on to the appropriate authority

- refer the situation to the National Statistician

For more information please refer to the ONS Safeguarding Policy.

4 . Annex 4: Children and young persons' loneliness consent form (10- to 15-year-olds)

I understand that I have been asked to take part in an interview, which involves having a conversation with a researcher, about what loneliness means, what I think about loneliness, and whether I have ever been lonely, or if I know people who have been lonely.

I understand that the conversation will be recorded, so that the researcher can listen back to it later and makes notes, and the information I tell them will be used to help reduce loneliness.

I understand that I do not have to take part if I don't want to, and I can stop at any time, without having to give anybody a reason. I understand that I can ask questions at any time.

I understand that everything I say will be kept private. However, if I tell the researcher something that makes them worried about my safety, I understand they might have to report it to somebody else. I understand that the researcher will write a report, or paper, about the interview, but they won't mention my name or any other information about me, so it will all be anonymous.

I know that I will be given a £15 voucher, as a thank you for taking part.

Child's Consent

I, _____(NAME) am happy to take part in the interview about loneliness.

I, _____ (NAME) confirm I have been given a £15 voucher.

Signature of child: _____

Date: _____

Parent/Guardian's Consent

I, _____(NAME) consent to the researcher conducting the interview with my child.

Signature of Parent or Guardian: _____

Date: _____

Interviewer Contact Details

If you have any queries or comments following the interview, please feel free to contact me on (INSERT CONTACT NUMBER) or email me at (INSERT EMAIL). Office for National Statistics, Government Buildings, Cardiff Road, Newport, Wales, NP10 8XG

5 . Annex 5: Young adults' loneliness consent form (16- to 24-year-olds)

I understand that I have been asked to take part in an interview about my understanding, views and experiences of loneliness.

I understand that the interview will be recorded, and following the interview, will be transcribed and analysed. I understand the information I provide will be used to help the Office for National Statistics to produce a national measure for loneliness and help organisations design programmes to reduce loneliness.

I am aware that my participation is voluntary, and that I have the right to withdraw at any time, without giving a reason. I am aware that I have right to ask questions at any time.

I am aware that I will receive £30 as a thank you for taking part.

I understand that my participation and data will be kept confidential and all information will be stored securely and anonymously. However, if I disclose something which makes the researcher concerned for my safety, I understand that the researcher has a duty to report it. I am aware that the final report will not name or identify me in any way, nor will it contain any information which could be used to identify me.

I, _____ (NAME) consent to taking part in the interview.

I, _____ (NAME) confirm I have received £30 as a thank you for taking part.

Signature of Interviewee: _____

Date: _____

Interviewer Contact Details

If you have any queries or comments following the interview, please feel free to contact me on (INSERT CONTACT NUMBER) or email me at (INSERT EMAIL).

Office for National Statistics, Government Buildings, Cardiff Road, Newport, Wales, NP10 8XG

Statistical bulletin

Personal and economic well-being in the UK: February 2019

Estimates of the combined findings for personal well-being (October 2017 to September 2018) and economic well-being (July to September 2018) in the UK. This is part of a new series on people and prosperity.

Contact:
Gueorguie Vassilev and Silvia Manclossi
PeopleAndProsperity@ons.gov. uk
+44 (0)1633 456265 or +44 (0) 1633582486

Release date:
4 February 2019

Next release:
To be announced

Table of contents

1 . Main points

- This is the first time Office for National Statistics (ONS) has brought together its data on both personal and economic well-being to give a fuller picture on the well-being of UK households .

- In the latest quarter, economic indicators such as income and spending continue to increase, however, longer term, there is a slowdown of household conditions, also seen in a levelling off of people's personal well-being and people's perception of the future has been worsening.

- In Quarter 3 (July to Sept) 2018, there was an increase in real household disposable income per head, up 0.7% compared with a year ago, alongside similar rises in earnings, employment and household spending and improved anxiety ratings.

- Since the end of 2017, improvements have levelled off in average happiness, life satisfaction and worthwhile ratings, similar to recent trends in net household financial wealth and household disposable income per head.

- Since Quarter 1 (Jan to Mar) 2013, household debt per head has been increasing, and is now 133% of disposable income; combined with spending per person outgrowing disposable income by £119 since Quarter 2 (Apr to June) 2016, it supports previous analysis suggesting that some households may be living beyond their means.

- People perceive the economy and their personal financial situation will worsen over the next 12 months, continuing more pessimistic views seen since the beginning of 2018.

- These trends may not necessarily be equally distributed across different parts of society; for example, between 2011 and 2016 financial years, average income for the bottom 20% of households increased by 4.8% or £589 while for the top 20% it increased by 6.7% or £4,123.

2 . Dashboard of well-being indicators

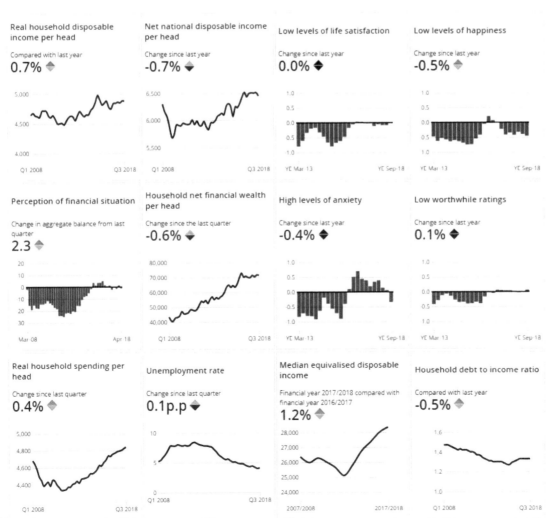

3 . Statistician's comment

Commenting, Head of Inequalities Glenn Everett said:

"Despite high levels of employment, rising incomes and spending across UK households, people are not reporting increases in their well-being. This may be due to worries about rising debt repayments, which could be driving concerns about their future financial situation."

4 . Things you need to know about this release

Measuring "people and prosperity"

Gross domestic product (GDP) is an important economic indicator telling us about the size and shape of national economic output. However, it was never designed to be an all-encompassing measure of social progress and well-being. To better inform policy and public debate, we have developed and analysed a wider range of measures, capturing important aspects of life not included within GDP. This is the basis of our "Beyond GDP" initiative which focuses on sustainable economic, human and environmental well-being. Fundamentally, we define "well-being" as "how we are doing" as individuals, as communities and as a nation, and how sustainable this is for the future. The goal is to support better decision making among policymakers, individuals, communities, businesses and civil society.

In November 2010, we set up the Measuring National Well-being Programme with the aim to monitor and report UK progress by producing accepted and trusted measures of the well-being of the nation. Since then, we have been measuring personal well-being – for example, how people assess their own life satisfaction and happiness, alongside a wider range of other aspects of life. In terms of the economy, we monitor economic well-being, which assesses how households are faring using measures of household wealth and disposable income.

We have pioneered the measurement of well-being in the UK in addition to traditional measures of prosperity, enabling policymakers to make better, more well-informed decisions. As the work matures, its scope is being expanded to better reflect the well-being of the whole population. Traditionally, we have reported our quarterly updates on personal well-being and economic well-being in separate publications. However, a recent user feedback survey suggested the need for more in-depth analysis on the relationship between personal and economic well-being, factors most associated with well-being, and an interest in how the UK's exit from the EU may impact on people's well-being.

To increase the value of our work to decision-makers and in keeping with our aspiration to "leave no one behind", this release aims to provide a fuller picture of well-being in the UK by looking at people's experiences from different perspectives to better understand who is struggling and who is thriving. This will enable us to assess current well-being as well as to monitor changes in the future as we move towards the UK's exit from the EU and beyond.

Quality and methodology

This release is based on the most recent available data as of February 2019. It is important to note that the data underpinning the well-being indicators are often from different sources with different timeliness and coverage. Personal well-being estimates are mainly taken from household surveys and they help understand the well-being of those living in private residential households. People living in communal establishments (such as care homes) or other situations are not represented in these surveys and this may be important in interpreting the findings in relation to those people reporting lower personal well-being.

The Personal well-being in the UK Quality and Methodology Information report contains important information on the strengths and limitations of the data and how it compares with related data, uses and users of the data, how outputs are created and the quality of the output including the accuracy of the data. Also, for more information on personal well-being, please see Personal well-being user guide and Harmonised principles of personal-well-being.

The framework and indicators for economic well-being used in this release were outlined in Economic Well-being, Framework and Indicators, published in November 2014. Also, basic quality and methodology information for all economic well-being indicators included in this statistical bulletin is available from National accounts Quality and Methodology Information report, Consumer Price Indices Quality and Methodology Information report, Wealth and Assets Survey Quality and Methodology Information report, Effects of taxes and benefits Quality and Methodology information report and Labour market Quality and Methodology Information reports.

Your feedback and our next publications

You can help inform our work by sharing your opinions in this short survey: Personal and Economic well-being: Your feedback.

Your feedback will be very valuable in making our results useful and accessible. If you have any questions, please contact us via email at PeopleAndProsperity@ons.gov.uk.

Thank you for taking part!

5 . A mixed well-being picture over the last quarter up to September 2018

The latest quarter's results, looking at both economic and personal well-being indicators, presents a mixed picture for people in the UK.

Figure 1: The four main measures of economic well-being have shown a mixed picture in the latest quarter

UK, Quarter 1 (Jan to Mar) 2008 to Quarter 3 (Jul to Sept) 2018

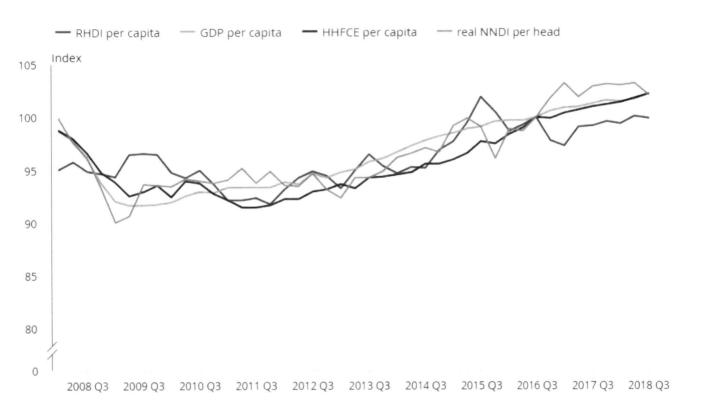

Source: Office for National Statistics - UK National Accounts

Notes:

1. Quarter 3 (July to Sept) 2016 = 100 is the base period

2. Real net national disposable income per head adjusts total domestic output (GDP per head) to account for flows in and out of the country, as well as removing wear and tear in the nation's capital used up in production

3. Household final consumption expenditure (HHFCE) is the amount of expenditure made by households to meet their everyday needs.

4. Real household disposable income (RHDI) is money households have to spend on consumption, or to save and invest after taxes, national insurance, pension contributions and interests have been paid.

5. Chart axis has a break in it.

Real household spending per head increased again, growing by 0.4% in Quarter 3 (July to Sept) 2018 compared with the previous quarter, to be equal to £19,251 per person for the year to September 2018. This has been followed by continued increases in gross domestic product (GDP) per head and is also seen in other household finance data, such as real earnings.

Figure 2: Real wages have continued to grow in 2018

UK, Quarter 1 (Jan to Mar) 2001 to Quarter 3 (Jul to Sept) 2018, seasonally adjusted

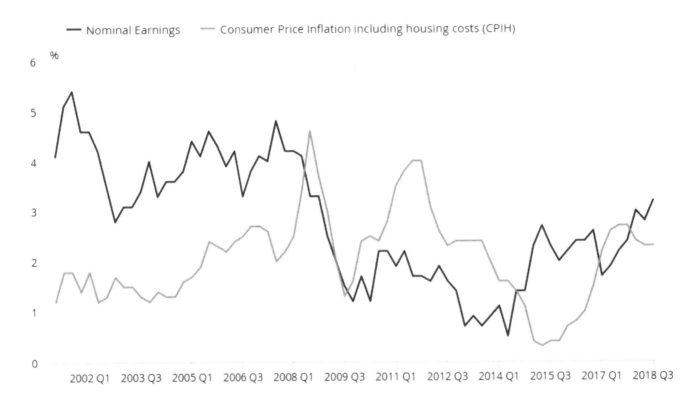

Source: Office for National Statistics

Notes:

1. Nominal earnings is Average Weekly Earnings (regular pay)

2. Consumer Price Inflation including housing costs (CPIH)

3. Annual change in nominal earnings and consumer price inflation including housing costs.

Real earnings grew by 0.8% in the year to Quarter 3 2018. An increase in real earnings – which is nominal earnings adjusted for the rise in the costs of goods and services – allows you to spend more on goods and services such as restaurants and recreation activities then you could previously.

Before the economic downturn, real earnings increased by 0.9% on average, as nominal earnings grew faster than prices over the same period. However, after the economic downturn, nominal earnings growth remained relatively subdued compared with the pre-downturn period, while growth in prices remained volatile and higher than nominal earnings growth for most of the period, leading to a fall in real earnings.

Average anxiety ratings decrease across the UK

Comparing the years ending September 2017 and September 2018, average anxiety ratings decreased across the UK; this replicates the last quarter's release, which also showed an improvement of anxiety ratings. However, this is the only measure of personal well-being to show any significant change during this period.

Figure 3: Average anxiety ratings decrease in the latest year

UK, average ratings of anxiety: year ending March 2012 to September 2018

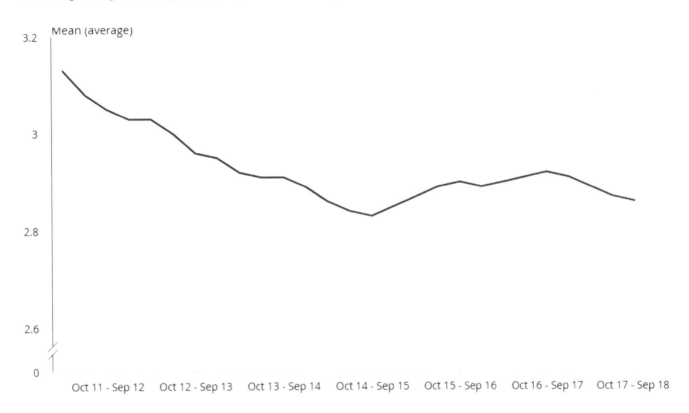

Source: Office for National Statistics - Annual Population Survey

Notes:

1. Chart axis has a break in it.

Among the things that may have been associated with the recent fall in anxiety, the unemployment rate has been falling since Quarter 4 (Oct to Dec) 2011 (as shown in Figure 4). The decline in the unemployment rate slowed in Quarter 1 (Jan to Mar) 2015 but has still largely been falling; it fell 0.2 percentage points in Quarter 3 2018 compared with a year ago. Considering this trend over time, we can see that, on the 0 to 10 scale, the average anxiety rating in the UK has been generally decreasing and has dropped significantly from 3.13 out of 10 in the year ending March 2012 to 2.86 out of 10 in the year ending September 2018. Similarly, looking at unemployment from Quarter 1 2012 to Quarter 3 in 2018, the unemployment rate has been consistently dropping, decreasing from 8.2% to 4.1%.

Considering the wider well-being measures, we have also seen improvements over time in other factors that are strongly associated with personal well-being, such as good health and being in positive relationships. For example, in 2015 to 2016, fewer people reported being in unhappy relationships and more people in the UK reported being "mostly or completely" satisfied with their general health, compared with the previous period.

Figure 4: Unemployment has fallen steadily since 2011

UK, Quarter 1 (Jan to Mar) 2000 to Quarter 3 (Jul to Sept) 2018, seasonally adjusted

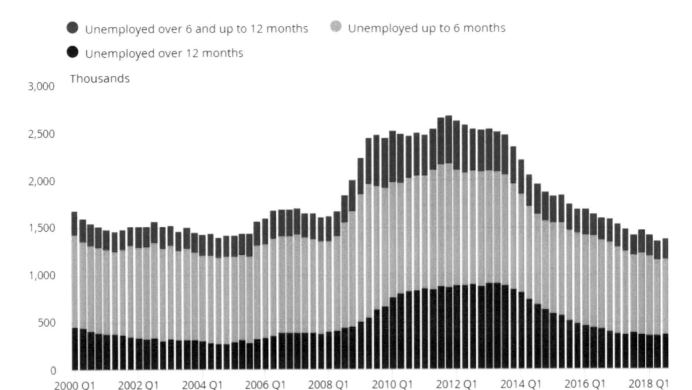

Source: Office for National Statistics – Labour Force Survey

Notes:

1. Aged 16 years and over.

The unemployment rate has continued to fall since 2011, as the labour market continues to strengthen since the economic downturn (Figure 4). Unemployment fell from 2.6 million in 2011 to 1.4 million in Quarter 3 (July to Sept) 2018, where those who have been unemployed for over a year have seen the largest fall (57.2%). As employment is closely associated with a positive personal well-being, an increase in employment and a corresponding fall in unemployment could be partly attributed to the increase in personal well-being indicators between 2011 and 2018. However, in the latest quarter, unemployment rose by 0.1 percentage point, which was led by a 3.7% increase in the number of people unemployed over a year – the first time it increased since Quarter 3 2017.

Figure 5: The number of underemployed people have been steadily falling since 2014, while those overemployed have been increasing since 2012

UK, Quarter 1 (Jan to Mar) 2002 to Quarter 3 (Jul to Sept) 2018, seasonally adjusted

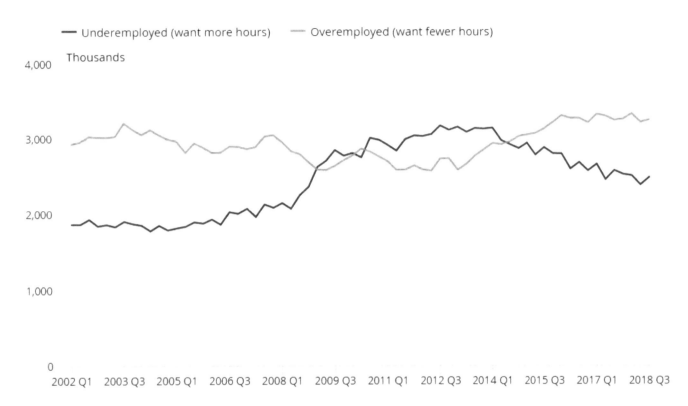

Source: Office for National Statistics – Labour Force Survey

Notes:

1. Underemployment - workers wanting to work more hours than they currently do and available to start in 2 weeks.

2. Overemployment - workers wanting to work less hours than they currently do, even with less pay.

Along with the longer-term fall in the unemployment rate, the number of people saying they would like to work more hours (the underemployed), remained relatively flat between 2011 and 2014, before falling after 2014. In comparison, the number of people saying they would like to work fewer hours even with less pay (overemployed), has been increasing steadily since 2013. By Quarter 3 (July to Sept) 2018, the number of underemployed decreased to 2.5 million, while the number of overemployed increased to 3.3 million. This increase in overemployment and fall in the underemployment rate can be partly attributed to an improvement in the labour market conditions, as firms could be increasing the number of hours worked of their existing workforce, instead of hiring new staff.

While previous analysis has shown that being unemployed has a negative association with personal well-being, the quality of the job may also have a part to play .

The average life satisfaction has increased since September 2012 from 7.45 to 7.69 out of 10, in line with the strengthening of the labour market over the same period.

The rate of change for average happiness, life satisfaction and worthwhile has levelled off recently

The average ratings of the other three measures of personal well-being – life satisfaction, happiness and worthwhileness – have been levelling off, as is seen in Figure 6. The average worthwhile rating (out of 10) across the UK in the year ending March 2012 was 7.67, with this increasing significantly to its highest level of 7.88 for the year ending September 2018.

Similarly to net financial wealth and income, we have seen national ratings of life satisfaction beginning to level off in recent years. Average ratings of life satisfaction in the UK have now been at 7.69 since June 2017. Before this, life satisfaction had been steadily increasing since March 2012, where the average rating was at 7.42. In the same way, increases in worthwhile ratings have slowed down over recent years. Also, self-employment income in the form of mixed income and gross operating surplus has positively contributed to the rise in income over the last year, contributing 1.2 percentage points to growth in the last quarter.

Figure 6: No change in average life satisfaction, worthwhile and happiness ratings in the latest year

UK, average ratings of personal well-being, year ending March 2012 to September 2018

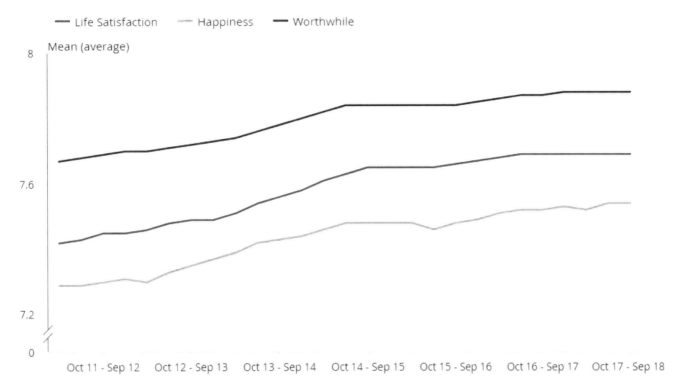

Source: Office for National Statistics - Annual Population Survey

Notes:

1. Chart axis has a break in it.

Considering the recent slowdown in real household disposable income per head next, we show the contributions to growth by different household incomings and outgoings in Figure 7.

Figure 7: Property income has been the main contributor to growth in real household disposable income per head over the last four quarters

Contributions to growth of RHDI per head, UK, Quarter 1 (Jan to Mar) 2014 to Quarter 3 (Jul to Sept) 2018

Source: Office for National Statistics - UK National Accounts

Notes:

1. Contributions may not sum due to rounding.

2. Contributions to growth compared with same quarter a year ago.

3. "Other" includes net other current transfers and net social benefits minus contributions.

Over the last four quarters, property income received has been the main contributor to positive growth in household income per head. Property income includes investment income from interest and dividends. The biggest contributor was from dividend receipts (which contributed 36% to the growth in total property income in Quarter 3 2018 compared with the same quarter a year ago), followed closely by the income payable from pensions, which contributed 31% in the latest quarter compared to Quarter 3 2017. Also, self-employment income in the form of mixed income and gross operating surplus has positively contributed to the rise in income over the last quarters, contributing 1.2 percentage points to the growth.

At the same time, there are some continuing pulls on household income growth. The biggest is current taxes on income and wealth, which includes taxes for employment, which have now reached £3538 per person in the UK for the year ending September 2018. This is the highest amount ever recorded. This reflects a larger number of people in work than at any point since records began in 1971, contributing their employment taxes. In addition, income paid out on loans (property income paid out) is continuing to rise. The amount we pay out for interest is now the highest seen since Quarter 1 2009. Over the last four quarters, these increases in the amount of interest paid has been due to the interest on unsecured loans such as on credit cards and overdrafts, as opposed to increases in mortgage interest payments, despite mortgage interest being a large proportion of total interest paid.

As seen in Figure 8, since Quarter 2 2016 spending has outgrown income (by £119 per head in real terms). This links to previous analysis showing households are spending beyond their means, and is also reflected in a low household savings ratio, the joint third lowest ratio seen since 1963.

Figure 8: Savings ratio continues to stay flat since Quarter 2 2017, after the falls seen since Quarter 3 2015

UK, Quarter 1 (Jan to Mar) 2008 to Quarter 3 (July to Sept) 2018, seasonally adjusted

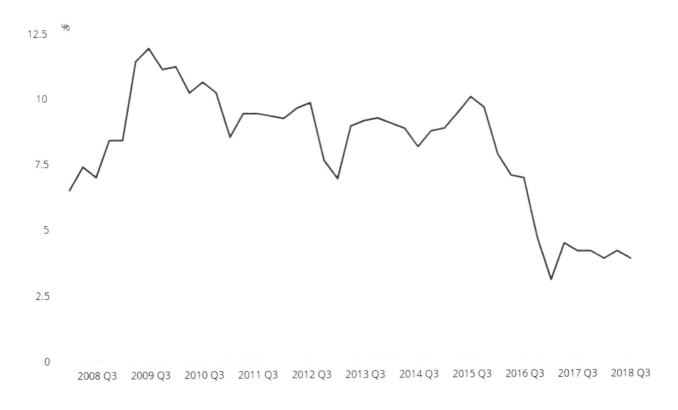

Source: Office for National Statistics - UK National Accounts

Another indicator of economic well-being is net financial wealth per head. This is calculated as the financial assets people hold (such as current and savings accounts and investments) less the liabilities they owe (for example, loans and mortgages) per average person in the UK. This is one of the types of wealth people hold, along with property and physical wealth, such as cars and jewellery. In the latest quarter, net financial wealth per head fell by 0.6%. This follows eight quarters of a slowdown, which has been observed since Quarter 3 2016. Previously, average wealth per head grew consistently. It is important to note that financial wealth is unequally distributed across society, with 61% of net financial wealth held by 10% of the population in the latest period known.

The growths of the types of assets and types of liabilities can be seen in Figure 9. Since Quarter 3 2016, insurance, pension and standardised guarantee schemes per head has largely remained at a similar level. This includes the current value of assets held by pension funds. This is a trend similar to that seen in the equity and investment fund shares (shares people hold as well as investment individual savings accounts (ISAs)) and currency and deposits (current and savings accounts). Liabilities (including loans) have, however, shown a general increase since 2013 – from £23,280 per head in Quarter 3 2013 to £26,800 per head in Quarter 3 2018. So, as well as higher interest payments, household debt for the average person continues to rise.

Figure 9: Average personal net financial wealth growth has stalled since the end of 2016

Net financial wealth per head, UK, Quarter 1 (Jan to Mar) 2008 to Quarter 3 (Jul to Sept) 2018

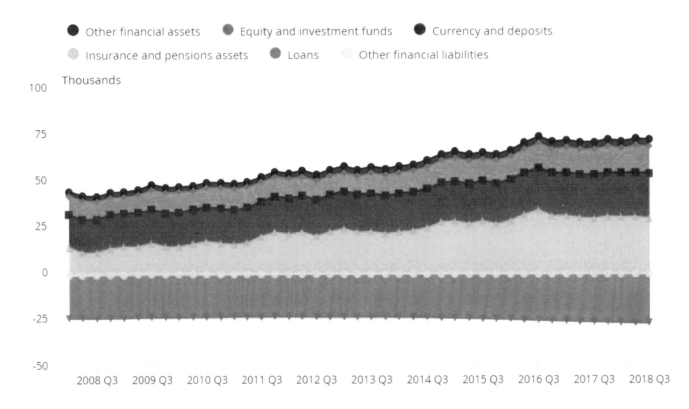

Source: Office for National Statistics - UK National Accounts

Household debt – which is comprised of secured (mortgages) and unsecured lending (credit cards and overdrafts) – has been increasing steadily since 2013. Because of this, the unsecured lending to household disposable income ratio increased by 27.2% between Quarter 1 (Jan to Mar) 2013 and Quarter 3 (July to Sept) 2018, as growth in unsecured lending grew faster (1.9%) than household disposable income (0.8%) over the period.

Figure 10: Unsecured lending per person has been steadily increasing since 2013.

UK, Quarter 1 (Jan to Mar) 2001 to Quarter 3 (Jul to Sept) 2018, seasonally adjusted

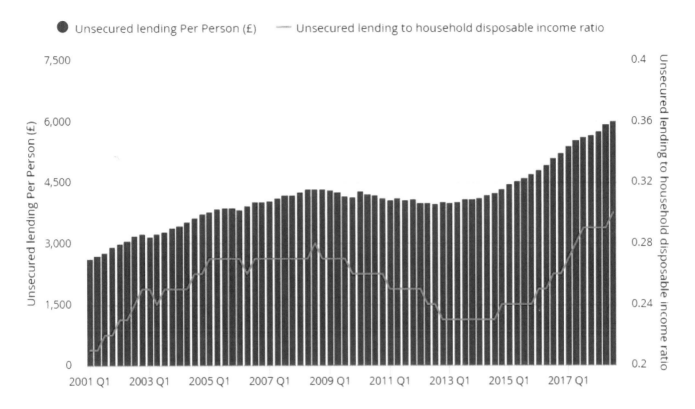

Source: Office for National Statistics

What are we spending our money on?

Figure 11 shows the cumulative increases in different types of spending since 2016.

Figure 11: Household goods and services, housing and miscellaneous spending accounts for 65% of the increase in real spending over the last 3 years

UK, Chain Volume Measures,cumulative contributions to total household spending per head increase, Quarter 1 (Jan to Mar) 2016 to Quarter 3 (Jul to Sept) 2018

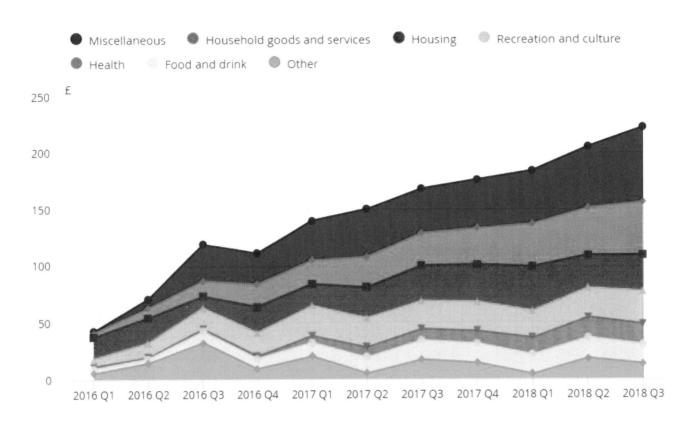

Source: Office for National Statistics

Notes:

1. Other includes: net tourism, alcohol, tobacco and narcotics, clothing and footwear, transport, communication, education, restaurants and hotels.

The increase in real spending is largely accounted for through a selection of goods and services, such as furniture and furnishings, personal care products, major household appliances and jewellery, clocks and watches, while also due to increasing average home rentals and financial services excluding insurance. This is in contrast to the small real increases in food and drink spending, accounting for 8% of the increase in spending since Quarter 4 2015.

Putting all this evidence together, since Quarter 2 2016, household spending has been increasing, helped by all-time-high unsecured borrowing, while household income has stayed flat. This is reflected in flatter life satisfaction, happiness and worthwhile ratings in the UK.

6 . What's the situation for different parts of society?

It is important to highlight that national economic indicators may mask different experiences for different parts of the population. Types of spending differ depending on the gross income of the household. As can be seen in Figure 12, those in the poorest 20% of households spend over 43% of their total spending on food, housing and utilities, much more than other categories. In contrast, those in the top 20% of households spend over 26% on recreation and culture, as well as hotels and restaurants.

Figure 12: The poorest 20% of households spent over 43% of their total spending on food, housing and utilities

Financial year ending 2016 to financial year ending 2018, UK

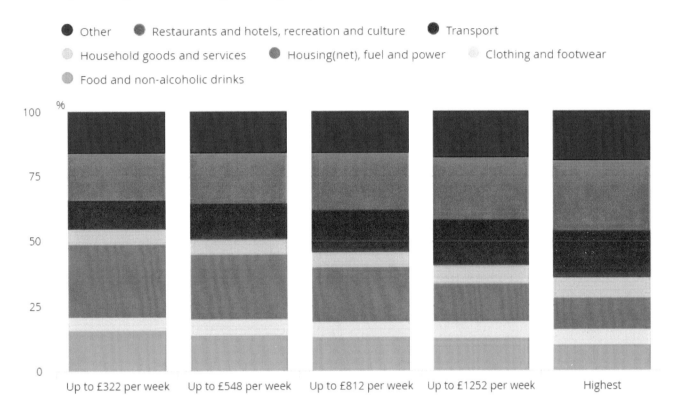

Source: Office for National Statistics

Notes:

1. Three-year average across 2016 – 2018 financial years

2. The income measure used to create the deciles or quintiles is consistent with previous Family Spending reports. However, this differs from our preferred measure of income. For more details please see the methodology section of the Family Spending bulletin.

3. Lower boundary of 2017 to 2018 gross income quintile groups (£ per week).

4. Housing spending excluding mortgage interest payments, council tax and Northern Ireland rates.

5. X-axis represents maximum weekly income per quintile of household income.

The growth in spending (and unsecured debt) at the national level may reflect important disparities in daily life for people in households across the income distribution.

Additionally, recent inflation changes will be experienced differently by households which spend on different categories. For example, food prices have generally grown slower than overall inflation, though some categories, such as bread, have grown quicker. Some of these price changes can be seen in the next graph.

Figure 13: Since 2016, food prices have grown slower than inflation, while prices for transport, hotels and restaurants have grown quicker than overall inflation

UK, Quarter 1 (Jan to Mar) 2016 to Quarter 4 (Oct to Dec) 2018

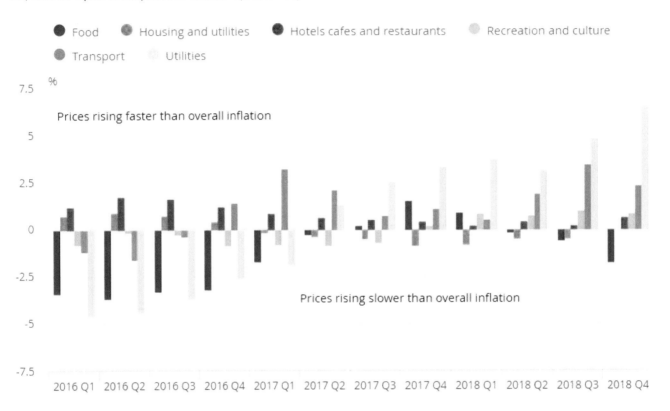

Source: Consumer Prices Index including owner occupiers' housing costs (CPIH)

Notes:

1. A positive figure means the price of the good or service has increased more than overall inflation. A negative figure means the price of the good or service has increased slower than overall inflation.

2. Latest bulletin can be found here: https://www.ons.gov.uk/economy/inflationandpriceindices/bulletins/consumerpriceinflation/december2018

3. Housing and utilities refers to Classification of individual consumption by purpose (COICOP) item 04, which includes housing, water and fuel

4. Values are calculated as annual changes minus the annual change of CPIH.

Generally, prices for hotels and restaurants have been increasing higher than overall inflation. Since Quarter 3 2017, recreational and culture goods and services have also grown more quickly, while food has grown slower than overall inflation, as has housing and utilities. Hence, inflation may be affecting the richest households more than the poorest, though it is important to note that within these higher level spending categories, there is a lot of variation in price changes reflecting people's wide spending habits. For example, there has been a sharp rise in utility prices, such as for electricity and gas, since Quarter 2 2017, which will likely affect the poorest the most adversely, as they spend a larger proportion of their spending on utilities.

Similarly, seeing average household income per head grow might not apply for people across the income distribution. This is why we show median disposable income, which for financial year 2018 grew by 1.2%. Median disposable income reflects the income received by the household in the middle of the distribution, that is, 50% of households have higher disposable income in the UK, while 50% have less. Looking within the distribution shows further differences in experiences. For example, between 2011 to 2012 and 2016 to 2017, average income for the bottom 20% of households has increased by £589, while for the top 20% it has increased by £4,123. Further detail can be found in the last analysis published on household income.

In addition to this, it is worth seeing which types of income are more likely to be received by poorer and richer households.

Figure 14: Those who own their houses are the main recipients of pensions income while those renting in social housing receive the majority of their income from benefits.

2016 financial year, UK

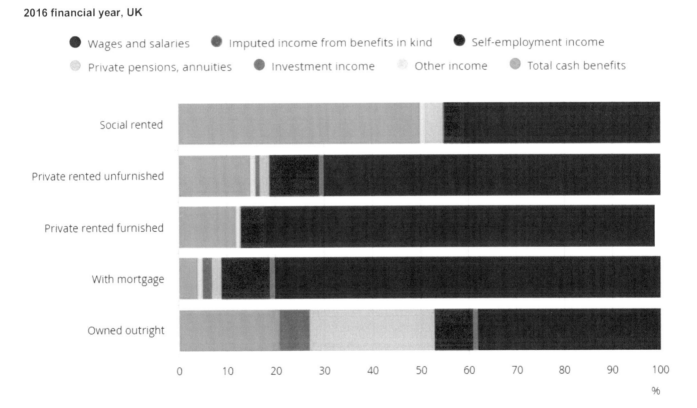

Source: Office for National Statistics

Notes:

1.May not sum to 100 due to rounding.

As can be seen in Figure 14, people in different types of households receive their income from very different sources. Those in social renting households received 50% of their income from cash benefits in 2016 financial year and we have seen much slower increases in total benefit income since then. In contrast, those who own their house outright receive 25% of their income from private pensions and annuities, which has seen a rise in the last four quarters.

People's personal well-being ratings may also vary across parts of the population, even if average national-level scores are remaining flat and average anxiety ratings are falling.

Very good" personal well-being ratings have been rising faster than "poor" ratings", suggesting that the improvement for those people struggling the most has been slower over time.

In addition to looking at average ratings, potential inequalities in personal well-being have also been monitored by comparing those rating each aspect of their well-being at a very high level or very low level within the UK. Observing these inequalities may help to explain some of the variance in the relationship between personal and economic well-being.

Figure 15: Increases in the share of those reporting "very good" ratings of personal well-being have slowed since year ending September 2015

UK, average percentage changes, October 2012 to September 2015 and October 2015 to September 2018

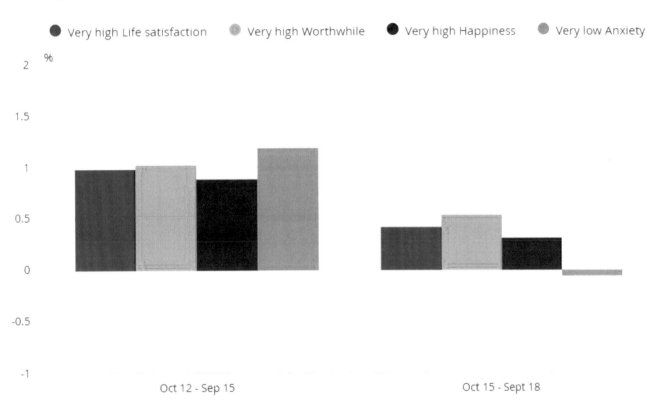

Source: Office for National Statistics - Annual Population Survey

Notes:

1. Statistically significant differences have been determined on the basis of non-overlapping confidence intervals.

2. "Very good" well-being refers to those providing a rating of 0 to 1 for anxiety and 9 to 10 for happiness, life satisfaction and worthwhile.

Figure 16: Decreases in the share of those reporting "poor" ratings of personal well-being have slowed and show slight change since year ending September 2015

UK, average percentage changes, October 2012 to September 2015 and October 2015 to September 2018

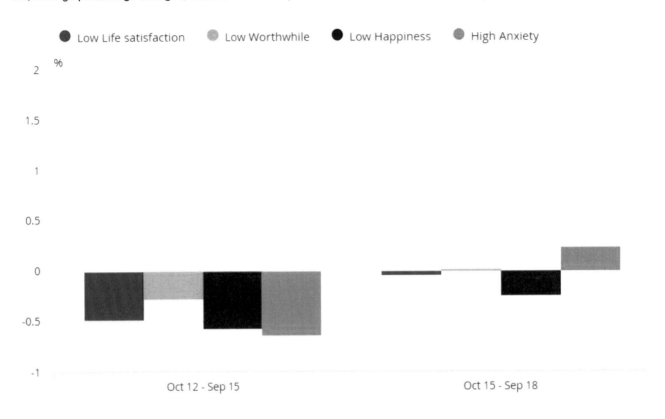

Source: Office for National Statistics - Annual Population Survey

Notes:

1. Statistically significant differences have been determined on the basis of non-overlapping confidence intervals.

2. "Poor" well-being refers to those providing life satisfaction, worthwhile, and happiness ratings of 0 to 4 on an 11-point scale, and anxiety ratings of 6-10.

In relation to the change over the last six years, the proportion of people reporting "poor" personal well-being (that is, low levels of life satisfaction, worthwhile and happiness ratings, and high anxiety) decreased (Figure 15). The proportion of those reporting "very good" well-being (that is, very high levels of life satisfaction, worthwhile and happiness ratings, and very low anxiety) increased for all measures since the year ending September 2012 (Figure 16). However, the increases at the positive end of the scale are larger than the decreases at the negative end, suggesting that the improvement for those people struggling the most has been slower over time.

Between the years ending September 2017 and 2018, in particular, the proportion of people reporting very low ratings of anxiety has increased from 39.89% to 41.10%, while the proportion of people who reported low levels of happiness decreased from 8.44% to 7.98% across the UK. So, we have seen that "very good" ratings (i.e. very low scores) of anxiety have increased (by 1.21% in the latest year) faster than the decrease in "poor" happiness ratings (by 0.46% in the latest year), as shown in Figures 17 and 18 below.

Figure 17: "Very low" ratings of anxiety increase by 1.21% in the latest year

UK, yearly percentage change of "very good" well-being: year ending September 2013 to 2018

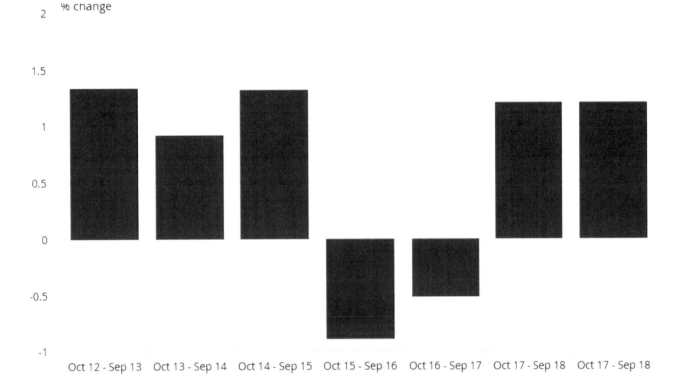

Source: Office for National Statistics - Annual Population Survey

Notes:

1. Statistically significant differences have been determined on the basis of non-overlapping confidence intervals.

2. "Very low" ratings of anxiety refer to ratings of 9 to 10 on an 11-point scale.

Figure 18: Percentage of people reporting "poor" happiness ratings decreases by 0.46% in the latest year

UK, yearly percentage change of "very good" well-being: year ending September 2013 to 2018

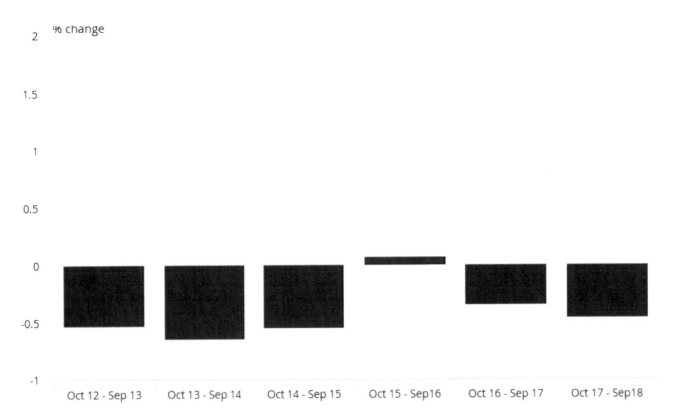

Source: Office for National Statistics - Annual Population Survey

Notes:

1. Statistically significant differences have been determined on the basis of non-overlapping confidence intervals.

2. "Poor" happiness ratings refer to ratings of 0 to 4 on an 11-point scale.

Looking ahead, people expect the next 12 months to be worse, both for the economy and their personal financial situation

In line with objective economic well-being measures, it is important to consider people's subjective expectations about the economy and their own financial situation. Figure 19 shows that since Quarter 1 2018, people's levels of optimism about perceptions of their future financial situation in the next 12 months declined at its fastest rate since Quarter 2 2016. Also, people's expectations of the general economic situation over the next 12 months are worsening.

Figure 19: Perceptions of the future 12 months of the economy and the financial situation have worsened since 2018.

Perception rating for the UK, Quarter 1 (Jan to Mar) 2008 to Quarter 4 (Oct to Dec) 2018

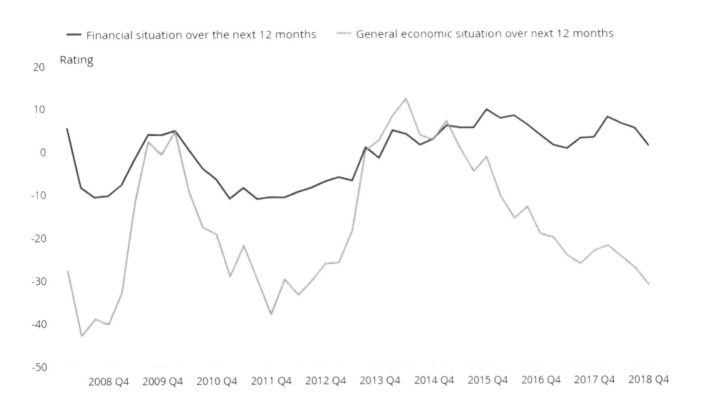

Source: Eurobarometer Consumer survey, European Commission

Notes:

1. The Eurobarometer Consumer Survey, conducted by GFK on behalf of the European Commission, provides information regarding perceptions of the economic environment. A positive balance means that consumers perceived an improvement within the economy, a zero balance indicates no change and a negative balance indicates a perceived worsening.

2. The Eurobarometer Survey results are also available for Quarter 4 2018 across the measures presented here. The perceived financial situation over the next 12 months drops dramatically whereas the general economic situation perceptions remain at a perceived worsening.

7 . Next steps

This bulletin has aimed to provide a fuller picture of well-being in the UK by looking at the relationship between personal and economic well-being and how households are faring across society.

In the future we plan to provide insights into well-being inequalities and a range of factors that might have an impact on people's personal well-being such as personal characteristics, household circumstances and household income and expenditure. We will also monitor changes in well-being levels going forward, especially assessing whether and how the UK's exit from the EU will have an impact on how we feel about our lives and our daily emotions.

8 . Authors

Gueorguie Vassilev, Silvia Manclossi, David Tabor, Sunny Sidhu, Meera Parmar, Jack Yull, Ed Pyle, Chris Payne, Rhian Jones from the Economic Well-being and Quality of Life Teams, Office for National Statistics.

Office for
National Statistics

Statistical bulletin

Personal and economic well-being in the UK: April 2019

Estimates looking across both personal well-being (January to December 2018) and economic well-being (October to December 2018) in the UK. This bulletin is part of a new series on "people and prosperity" introduced in February 2019.

Contact:
Sunny Sidhu or Jack Yull
PeopleAndProsperity@ons.gov. uk
+44 (0)1633651701

Release date:
11 April 2019

Next release:
To be announced

Table of contents

1 . Main points

- Most economic well-being indicators such as real household disposable income and spending per head continued to improve in the final quarter (October to December) of 2018, similar to recent trends; although other aspects of personal well-being remained flat, anxiety ratings improved in the year ending December 2018.

- Real household disposable income per head grew quicker than real household spending per head, compared with the same quarter a year ago for only the third time in the past 12 quarters.

- Looking beneath the aggregate picture, up to the financial year ending 2018, the richest fifth of individuals saw a 4.7% annual increase in their real equivalised household disposable income compared with a 1.6% contraction for the poorest fifth, resulting in increased income inequality.

- Prices on essentials such as food and non-alcoholic beverages grew by 0.7% up to December 2018, slower than prices for non-essentials such as recreation and culture, which grew by 2.9%.

- Although average anxiety ratings reached a three-year low in 2018, about 10.3 million people or around a fifth of the population continued to report high anxiety, and this proportion has remained similar since 2014.

2 . Dashboard of well-being indicators

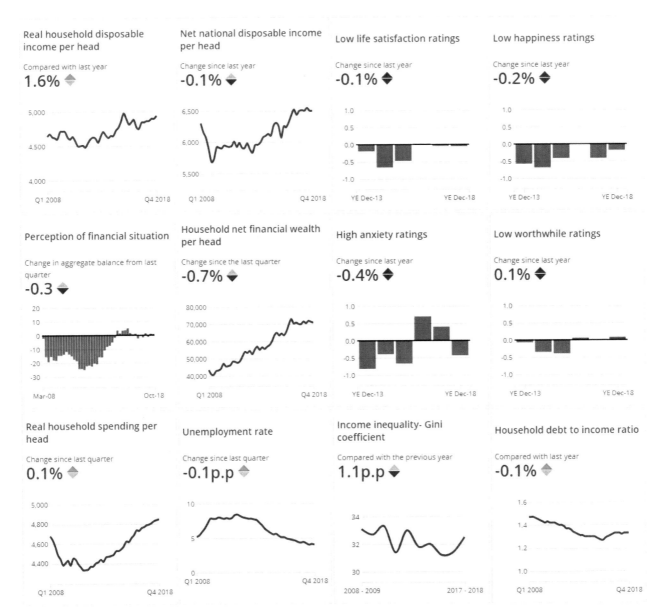

3 . Real household disposable income per head grew faster than real household spending per head, for only the third time in 12 quarters

Figure 1: All four main measures of economic well-being increased in the latest quarter ending December 2018

UK, Quarter 1 (Jan to Mar) 2008 to Quarter 4 (Oct to Dec) 2018, index, 2008 Quarter 1 = 100

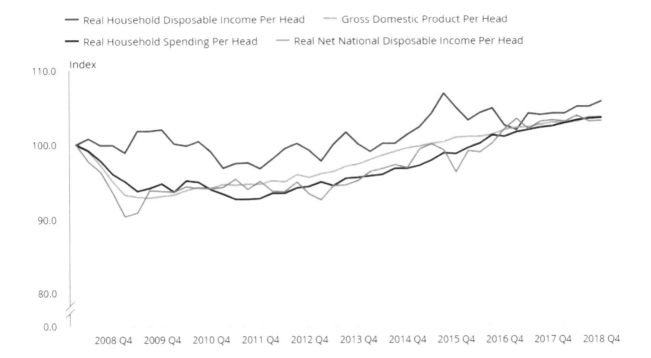

Source: Office for National Statistics - UK National Accounts

Notes:

1. Quarter 1 (Jan to Mar) 2008 = 100 is the base period.

2. Real net national disposable income per head adjusts total domestic output (GDP per head) to account for flows in and out of the country, as well as removing wear and tear in the nation's capital used up in production.

3. Real household spending per head is the amount of expenditure by households to meet their everyday needs.

4. Real household disposable income is the money households have, which they can spend on consumption, or to save and invest after taxes, National Insurance, pension contributions and interest have been paid.

5. Gross domestic product (GDP) is the amount of goods and services produced during a period. GDP per person is an indicator of the trend in an economy's output controlling for population growth.

Real household disposable income per head – which is the money households in the UK have available to spend, save or invest after taxes, adjusted for inflation – increased by 1.6% in Quarter 4 (Oct to Dec) 2018, compared with the same quarter a year ago.

This was higher than the increase in real household spending per head, which is the amount of spending by households and individuals for their everyday needs, such as buying food and toiletries as well as non-essentials, adjusting for inflation.

Real spending per head increased by 1.1% in Quarter 4 (Oct to Dec) 2018, compared with the same quarter a year ago, and changed by 0.1% from the previous quarter. This was reflected in a slight increase to the savings ratio, though the debt to income ratio remains at 1.33, similar to its recent flattening off since Quarter 2 (Apr to June) 2017.

Figure 2: Real household spending per head on household furnishings, equipment, and routine household maintenance grew more than any other spending category

UK, Quarter 4 (Oct to Dec) 2017 to Quarter 4 (Oct to Dec) 2018, annual percentage change

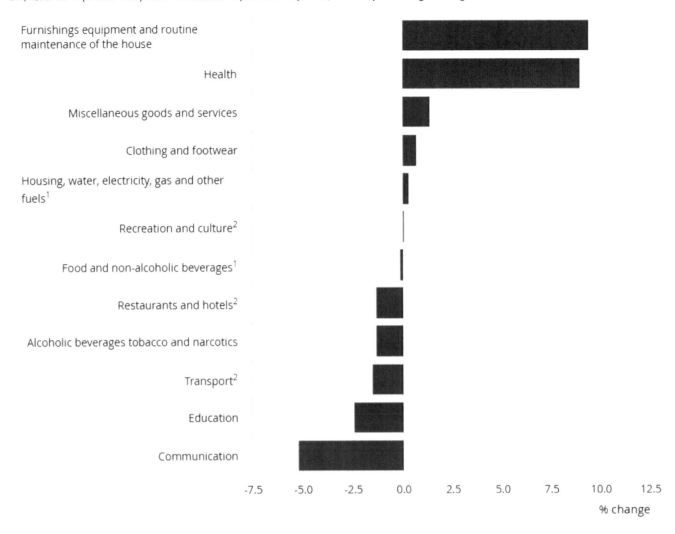

Source: Office for National Statistics – Consumer Trends.

Notes:

1. Represent household spending categories that the bottom 20% of households spend more on, on average.

2. Represent household spending categories that the top 20% of households spend more on, on average.

The increase in real household spending per head in Quarter 4 (Oct to Dec) 2018, compared with the same quarter a year ago, was driven mainly by spending on items such as furnishings, equipment and routine household maintenance, health and miscellaneous goods, and services such as insurance.

Real spending per head on furnishings, equipment, and routine household maintenance increased by 9.4% over the period, since Quarter 4 (Oct to Dec) 2017 and contributed most (0.5 percentage points) to the overall change in real per head spending.

Figure 3: Lower income households spent a higher proportion of their spending on essentials, such as food and non-alcoholic drinks and housing, fuel and power

UK, financial year ending 2018

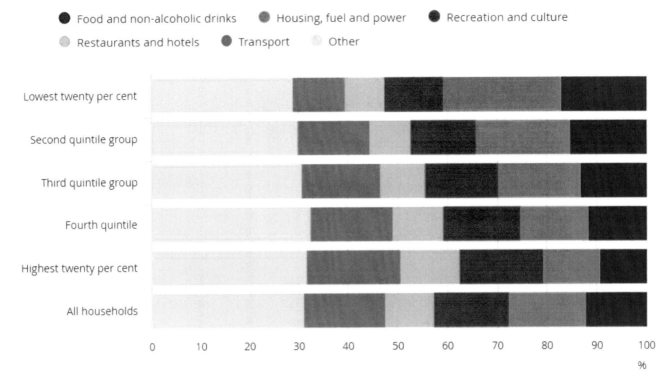

Source: Office for National Statistics – Living Costs and Food Survey

Notes:

1. "Other" spending category includes alcohol and tobacco, clothing and footwear, household goods and services, health, communication, education, and miscellaneous goods and services.

As shown in Figure 3, for the financial year ending 2018 (April 2017 to March 2018) the poorest fifth of households spent 17% of their overall expenditure on food, and 24% on housing, water, electricity, gas and other fuels. At the other end of the distribution, those at the top 20% of the income distribution spent a bigger share on transport (19%), recreation and culture (17%), and restaurants and hotels (12%).

Bringing this back to the average spending per head seen in Figure 2, real household spending per head on food and non-alcoholic beverages, and housing, fuel and power increased respectively by negative 0.1% and 0.3% in Quarter 4 (Oct to Dec) 2018, compared with the same quarter a year ago.

On the other hand, spending on items that those in the top 20% of the income distribution spend more on, increased more slowly. For example, spending on recreation and culture increased by 0.1% in Quarter 4 (Oct to Dec) 2018 compared with the same quarter a year ago, and spending on transport, and restaurants and hotels decreased over the same period. It is worth noting that spending on more discretionary items and leisure experiences, such as recreation and culture, and hotels and restaurants, is positively associated with personal well-being.

4 . Prices on essentials such as food and non-alcoholic beverages grew more slowly up to December 2018 than prices for non-essentials such as recreation and culture

Figure 4: Prices for food and non-alcoholic beverages grew slower and prices for housing, fuel and power grew faster than average inflation over the year to Quarter 4 2018

UK, annual percentage change, Quarter 4 (Oct to Dec) 2017 to Quarter 4 (Oct to Dec) 2018

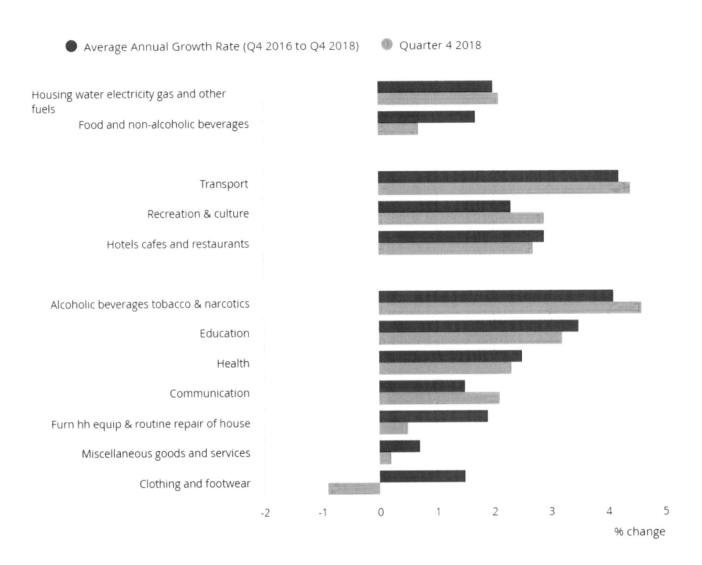

Source: Office for National Statistics – Consumer Price Inflation

Notes:

1. Consumer Prices Index including owner occupiers' housing costs (CPIH).

Nominal spending is important in determining spending priorities for households. However, an increase in prices for goods and services may lead to households spending more on certain items for the same quantity, if they do not switch to buying other products. For example, an increase in the prices of essentials such as food, may lead to households spending more on food to consume the same amount they did previously. This means that they would have proportionally less to spend on other discretionary spending, such as recreation and culture.

Consumer price inflation including owner occupiers' housing costs (CPIH) – which is a measure of price change based on the cost of a fixed basket of goods and services consumed by households, such as transportation and food – was 2.0% in Quarter 4 (Oct to Dec) 2018, compared with the same quarter a year ago. This is the slowest increase in consumer prices over the last two years.

Prices for food and non-alcoholic beverages increased by 0.7% in Quarter 4 (Oct to Dec) 2018, compared with the same quarter a year ago. This growth was at a much slower rate compared with the average for the past year (1.7%). Prices for housing, water, electricity, gas and other fuels have instead increased by 2.1% up to Quarter 4 (Oct to Dec) 2018, slightly quicker than the average increases seen over the past two years (2.0%) (Figure 4).

Discretionary spending on recreation and culture, as well as restaurants and hotels, has increased by 2.9% and 2.7% respectively in Quarter 4 (Oct to Dec) 2018 compared with Quarter 4 (Oct to Dec) 2017.

Given these different trends in recent prices, it is likely that they impact on households' spending habits disproportionately across the income distribution. For the bottom 20%, the prices of some of their main spending categories such as food and non-alcoholic beverages, increased more slowly in the three months up to December 2018 than over the past year, while the reverse was true for spending on housing and utilities, which increased more than average inflation.

On the other hand, transport, recreation and culture, as well as restaurants and hotels prices all rose higher than inflation. Their prices have continued to increase in the three months up to December 2018 at rates close to their average for the past two years and these categories are the largest-spending categories for those at the top 20% of the income distribution.

It is important to highlight the relationship between price expectations and household spending. If consumers expect higher prices tomorrow, they may decide to make more purchases today rather than wait for prices to rise. On the other hand, if consumers expect lower prices tomorrow, they may withhold spending on purchases today and wait for prices to fall.

Figure 5: People continue to expect prices over the next 12 months to increase, at a similar rate seen since Quarter 4 2016 for the average individual

UK, positive balance means that consumers perceive an increase in prices and a negative balance shows perception of a decrease in prices, Quarter 1 2008 to Quarter 1 2019

Source: Eurobarometer

Notes:

1. The Eurobarometer Consumer Survey, conducted by GFK on behalf of the European Commission, provides information regarding perceptions of prices. A positive balance means that consumers perceive or expect an increase in prices, a zero balance indicates no perceived change to prices and a negative balance indicates a perceived or expected decrease in prices.

The slower increase in overall consumer prices in Quarter 4 2018, compared with the same quarter a year ago corresponds with households' perceptions of price trends over the same period (Figure 5). People have perceived consumer prices to have grown, albeit at a slower rate. In contrast, individuals' expectations for the next 12 months continued to be that prices will increase, at a rate similar to the one seen since Quarter 4 2016. For Quarter 1 (Jan to Mar) 2019, the expectations for higher prices over the next year increased.

5 . While average real household disposable income increased in the latest period, income inequality also increased for the financial year ending 2018

Figure 6: The increase in real household disposable income per head has been driven by contributions from employment income

Quarter 4 (Oct to Dec) 2015 to Quarter 4 (Oct to Dec) 2018

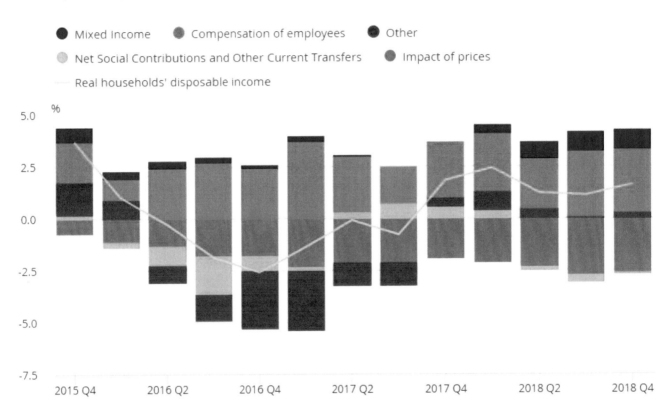

Source: Office for National Statistics – National Accounts

Notes:

1. Other contains gross operating surplus, net property income, and current taxes on income, wealth and so on.

Compensation of employees – which is the wages and salaries received by employees, along with employer's social contributions – contributed the most to the change in household income per head, contributing 3.0 percentage points in Quarter 4 (Oct to Dec) 2018, compared with the same quarter a year ago (Figure 6). These larger contributions from compensation of employees in Quarter 4 (Oct to Dec) 2018 and the previous quarter coincide with stronger wage growth in the labour market, with average weekly earnings (excluding bonuses) continuing to grow at a faster pace (3.6% over the same period).

Alongside the stronger contributions from compensation of employees, mixed income – which is the income earned by the self-employed – contributed 1.0 percentage point to the increase in real household disposable income per head for the same period. This could be partly attributed to the increase in the number of self-employed workers, which grew by 1.3% in the year to Quarter 4 (Oct to Dec) 2018, compared with the same quarter the previous year, with part-time workers making up most of the increase in self-employed workers.

Though mean real household income has increased, this has differed across the income distribution, seen in a rise in income inequality up to the financial year ending 2018

The average income of the richest fifth of the population – when ranked by equivalised household disposable income – increased by 4.7% due largely to increases in average household earnings from employment. The average income of the poorest fifth, on the other hand, contracted by 1.6%, driven mainly by a fall in the average value of cash benefits their households receive.

Further analysis can be seen in the Average household income, UK: financial year ending 2018 release, published on 26 February 2019. These are the latest available data, but we will be monitoring how this compares with income inequality over the financial year ending March 2019 in subsequent releases.

6 . While average anxiety levels reached a three-year low in 2018, about 10.3 million people continued to report high anxiety scores

Figure 7: In the year ending December 2018, the average rating of anxiety in the UK reached its lowest level since the year ending December 2015

UK, average ratings of anxiety for the year ending December 2012 to December 2018

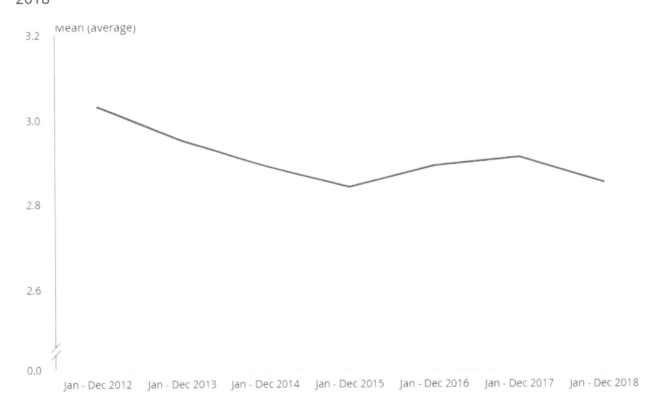

UK, average ratings of anxiety for the year ending December 2012 to December 2018

Source: Office for National Statistics - Annual Population Survey

Alongside increases in real household disposable income, there has been an improvement in the average ratings of anxiety. Between the years ending December 2017 and December 2018, anxiety scores fell across the UK from 2.91 to 2.85 measured on a scale from 0 to 10 (Figure 7). This was the lowest average rating of anxiety since the year ending December 2015 and represents a decrease of 2.1% in the average anxiety across the UK. This was replicated in the average anxiety ratings across England, also showing similar improvements in reported levels of anxiety.

However, this is the only measure of personal well-being to show any significant change during this period. For the other measures of personal well-being – life satisfaction, feeling that the things done in life are worthwhile, and happiness – average ratings remained level with no significant changes since the year ending December 2016.

In addition to looking at average ratings, we also monitor potential inequalities in personal well-being by comparing those rating each aspect of their well-being either at a very high level or a very low level (Figure 8).

Figure 8: About 10.3 million people continue to report "high" levels of anxiety for the year ending December 2018

UK, yearly percentage change of "very low" and "high" ratings of anxiety since year ending December 2012

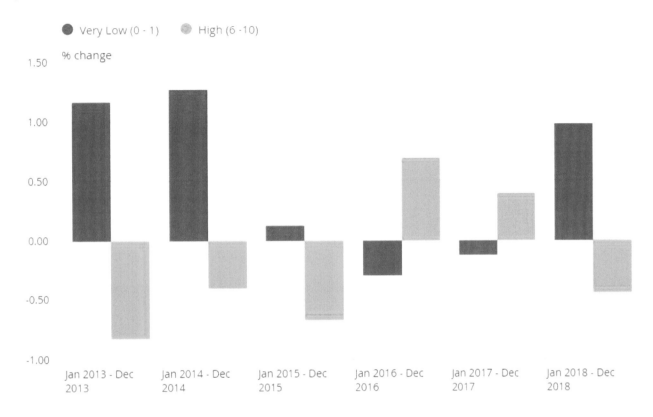

UK, yearly percentage change of "very low" and "high" ratings of anxiety since year ending December 2012

Source: Office for National Statistics – Annual Population Survey

Notes:

1. "Very low "anxiety refers to those providing a rating of 0 to 1, "high" anxiety refers to those reporting a score of 6 to 10 (on an 11-point scale from 0 to 10).

During the years ending December 2017 and 2018, there was an increase in the people reporting very low levels of anxiety in the UK, from 40.2% to 41.2% of the population. This improvement in anxiety was driven by an increase in the very low ratings in England, rising from 39.9% to 41.1%. This change in the proportion of respondents reporting very low levels of anxiety is the biggest improvement since the year ending December 2014.

However, in the year ending December 2018, among the UK population 19.7% or about 10.3 million people reported high levels of anxiety. There was no significant change compared with the year ending December 2017 (20.1%). The proportion of respondents reporting "high" levels of anxiety has not seen an improvement since the year ending December 2013.

7 . Conclusion and next steps

As suggested by the user feedback provided for our first personal and economic well-being publication in February 2019, this bulletin looked at how households are faring across society by focusing on those indicators that have changed the most over the period up to December 2018.

In the next few months, we plan to provide insights into well-being inequalities and a range of factors that might have an impact on people's personal well-being, such as personal characteristics, household circumstances and household income and expenditure – as these are clear areas of interest identified by our users.

We also intend to focus more on the environmental aspects of well-being, both in terms of how the environment affects our living standards now and the extent to which growth is environmentally sustainable. In doing this, we will move a step closer to looking holistically at "people, prosperity and planet".

8 . Quality and methodology

The Personal well-being in the UK Quality and Methodology Information report contains important information on the strengths and limitations, uses of the data as well as how outputs are created and the quality and accuracy of those outputs. For more information on personal well-being, please see the Personal well-being user guide and Harmonised principles of personal-well-being.

The framework and indicators for economic well-being used in this release were outlined in Economic Well-being, Framework and Indicators, published in November 2014. Basic quality and methodology information for all economic well-being indicators included in this statistical bulletin is available from Gross domestic product Quality and Methodology Information report, Consumer Price Indices Quality and Methodology Information report, Wealth and Assets Survey Quality and Methodology Information report, Effects of taxes and benefits Quality and Methodology information report and Labour Force Survey Quality and Methodology Information report.

Measuring "people and prosperity"

In November 2010, we set up the Measuring National Well-being programme to monitor and report UK progress by producing accepted and trusted measures of the well-being of the nation. We have pioneered the measurement of well-being in the UK in addition to traditional measures of prosperity, enabling policy-makers to make better, more well-informed decisions. We have also been monitoring economic well-being by assessing how households are faring using measures of household wealth and disposable income.

Traditionally, we reported our quarterly updates on personal well-being and economic well-being in separate publications; however, a recent user feedback survey suggested the need for more in-depth analysis on the relationship between personal and economic well-being.

In February 2019, we introduced a new series on "people and prosperity" as part of our "Beyond GDP" initiative bringing together personal and economic well-being for the first time. The aim is to provide timely, quarterly indicators and analysis of household financial health as well as personal well-being. In measuring economic growth, we want to know the extent to which it affects different groups in society. This will make it easier for policy-makers and other users to consider questions such as whether changes in the size of the economy, and the distribution of that income, are reflected in our personal well-being.

Data quality

This release is based on the most recent data available as of April 2019. It is important to note that the data underpinning the personal and economic well-being indicators come from various sources with different timeliness and coverage.

The personal well-being estimates are from the Annual Population Survey (APS), which provides a representative sample of those living in private residential households in the UK. People living in communal establishments (such as care homes) or other non-household situations are not represented in this survey and this may be important in interpreting the findings in relation to those people reporting lower personal well-being. Most of the economic indicators capture the full coverage of the UK regardless of people's economic status.

APS data reweighting

Weighting answers to survey questions ensures that estimates are representative of the target population. Each person in the survey data has a "weight", the number of people that person represents in the population, which is used to produce estimates for the population.

More accurate weighting is based on the latest available population estimates for that time-period. When new population estimates become available, data can be reweighted to ensure better representation and so precision of estimates. For greater accuracy, it is common practice to revise previously published estimates when new weights become available.

Based on new population estimates, new well-being weights are now available for the APS data. We have used this reweighted data to produce annual personal well-being estimates for the UK and its countries for January to December 2012 to 2018. We plan to produce the quarterly UK, regional and local authority level estimates based on most recent weightings later in the year.

Your feedback

In February 2019, alongside our previous publication, we launched a survey to gather user feedback about our personal and economic well-being outputs.

Users told us that our work fitted their requirements well – the language used, analytical detail and visual analyses met their needs. But the feedback also highlighted ways in which we could improve the quality and usability of our outputs such as shortening the length of bulletins. Additionally, there were requests to focus on more in-depth analysis, such as more insights into regional data and inequalities, and providing more information or explanation of more technical aspects.

Over the coming months, we will continue to address feedback and engage further with our users to improve the usability and usefulness of our work. Our feedback identified a demand for further analysis of other factors associated with well-being and this will be explored in a regression analysis to be published in May. We also aim to better promote our well-being dashboard and explore opportunities to improve our interactive tools.

Your feedback will be very valuable in making our results useful and accessible. If you have any questions, please contact us at PeopleAndProsperity@ons.gov.uk. Thank you!

9 . Authors

Gueorguie Vassilev, Silvia Manclossi, Sunny Sidhu, Jack Yull, and Ed Pyle from the Economic Well-being and Quality of Life Teams, Office for National Statistics.

Office for
National Statistics

Statistical bulletin

Personal and economic well-being in the UK: August 2019

Estimates looking across both personal well-being (April 2018 to March 2019) and economic well-being (January to March 2019) in the UK. This bulletin is part of a new series on "people and prosperity" introduced in February 2019.

Contact:
Gueorguie Vassilev or Silvia Manclossi
PeopleAndProsperity@ons.gov. uk

+44 (0)1633 456265 or +44 (0) 1633 582486

Release date:
12 August 2019

Next release:
14 November 2019

Table of contents

1 . Main points

- While all economic well-being measures improved in the latest quarter ending March 2019, people's personal well-being showed very little change in the UK in the year ending March 2019; however, people's expectations for the economy for the year ahead are that it will worsen.

- While people in the UK reported slightly higher happiness ratings on average, about 4.2 million people continued to report "low" levels of happiness in the year ending March 2019.

- Net financial wealth per head increased by 3.0% for the quarter ending March 2019 compared to the same quarter a year ago, led by increases in equity and investment fund shares.

- Anxiety in the UK remained stable in the year ending March 2019, with no significant decrease in the proportion of people who reported the highest anxiety ratings.

- Expectations for higher unemployment for the year ahead have been climbing and are now higher than at any point for the past five and a half years.

2 . Dashboard of well-being indicators

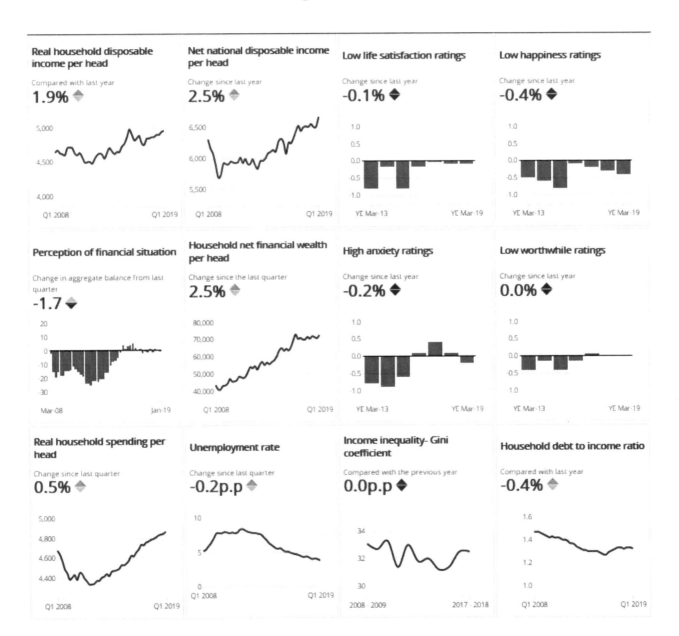

3 . Overall, objective economic well-being has increased

Figure 1: All measures of economic well-being have increased in the latest period up to March 2019

UK, Quarter 2 (Apr to June) 2014 to Quarter 1 (Jan to Mar) 2019, index, 2016 Quarter 3 = 100

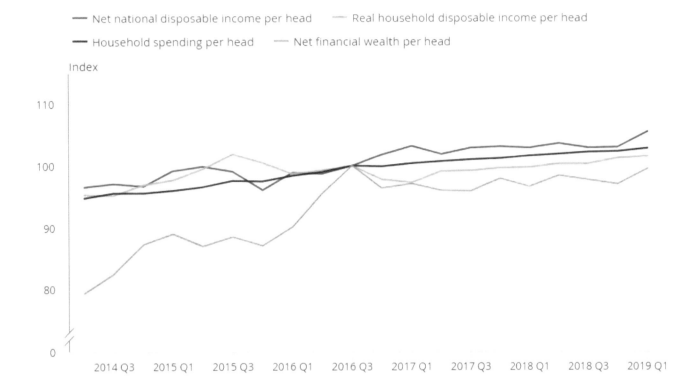

UK, Quarter 2 (Apr to June) 2014 to Quarter 1 (Jan to Mar) 2019, index, 2016 Quarter 3 = 100

Source: Office for National Statistics – UK National Accounts

Notes:

1. Quarter 3 (July to Sep) 2016 = 100.

2. Real net national disposable income per head adjusts total domestic output (GDP per head) to account for monetary flows in and out of the country, as well as removing wear and tear in the nation's capital used up in production.

3. Real household disposable income is the money households have, which they can spend on consumption, or to save and invest after taxes, National Insurance, pension contributions and interest have been paid.

4. Real household spending per head is the amount of expenditure by households to meet their everyday needs, adjusted for the prices of goods and services.

5. Net financial wealth per head is the financial assets people hold (such as current and savings accounts and investments) less the liabilities they owe (for example, loans and mortgages) per average person in the UK.

6. Chart axis has a break in it.

As shown in Figure 1, all main measures of economic well-being increased in the latest quarter. Net financial wealth per head increased the most, at 3.0% compared to the same quarter a year ago. This was mostly driven by an increase in the value of equity and investment fund shares and pension schemes. It is worth noting that net financial wealth is more disproportionately spread out than income and other types of wealth. For the period between April 2014 and March 2016, for example, 61.4% of the total financial wealth of households was owned by the top 10%, according to the latest Wealth in Great Britain release.

Household spending per head also continued to increase – it grew consecutively for nine quarters and is at an all-time high. It should be noted that 43% of the latest quarter's growth was driven by an increase in real terms spending on life insurance. However, it is unclear what drove this increased spending and whether it was linked to changes in mandatory cover requirements (such as cover for larger mortgages).

This was offset by a decrease in spending on restaurants and cafés, 1.7% per head less than for the last quarter. Our previous analysis looked at the relationship between household finances and personal well-being, and showed that expenditure on restaurants and cafés was related to higher life satisfaction. At the same time, spending on other services (such as life insurance) was associated with lower life satisfaction. Because of the potential impact on personal well-being, this change in expenditure patterns is something important to track in future well-being releases.

4 . Overall, people's personal well-being shows very little change in the UK

Figure 2: People in the UK report a slightly higher average happiness rating than a year ago

UK, average ratings of life satisfaction, feeling that the things done in life are worthwhile, and happiness for the years ending March 2012 to March 2019

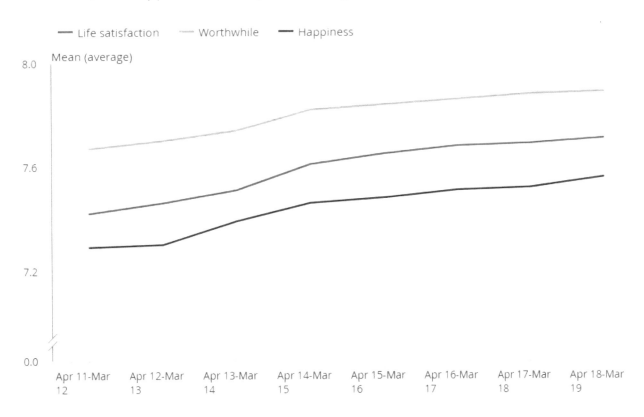

UK, average ratings of life satisfaction, feeling that the things done in life are worthwhile, and happiness for the years ending March 2012 to March 2019

Source: Office for National Statistics - Annual Population Survey

Notes:

1. Chart axis has a break in it.

Although there were improvements in all measures of economic well-being, there was very little change in ratings of personal well-being. The only slight improvement in the year to March 2019 was in the average rating of happiness. Between the years ending March 2018 and March 2019, happiness scores increased slightly across the UK from 7.52 to 7.56, measured on a scale from 0 to 10 (Figure 2). This represents an increase of 0.53% in the average reported happiness across the UK.

Happiness is the only measure of personal well-being to show any significant change in the year ending March 2019. For the other measures of personal well-being – life satisfaction, feeling that the things done in life are worthwhile (Figure 2), and anxiety (Figure 4) – average ratings remained level with no significant changes over this period.

In addition to looking at average ratings, we also monitor potential inequalities in personal well-being by comparing those rating each aspect of their well-being either at a "very high" or "low" level (Figure 3).

Figure 3: About 4.2 million people continue to report "low" levels of happiness in the year ending March 2019

UK, proportion of people reporting "low" and "very high" ratings of happiness since the year ending March 2012

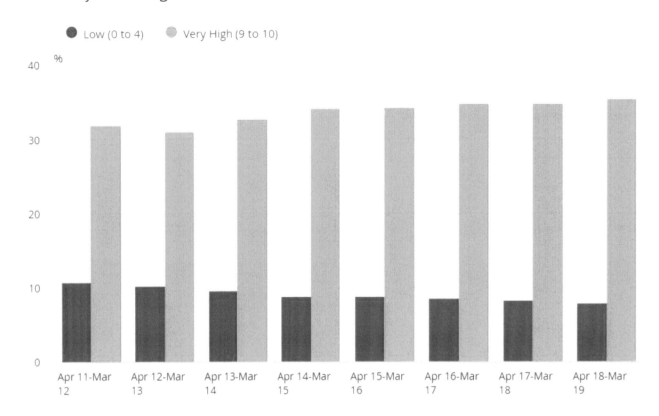

Source: Office for National Statistics – Annual Population Survey

Notes:

1. "low" happiness refers to those reporting a rating of 0 to 4 and "very high" happiness refers to those reporting a score of 9 to 10 (on an 11-point scale from 0 to 10).

Between the years ending March 2012 and March 2019, the proportion of people reporting "low" happiness ratings decreased by 2.8 percentage points and the proportion of those reporting "very high" ratings increased by 3.5 percentage points. Since the proportion of people reporting "very good" ratings rose slightly faster than the one reporting "low" ratings, the improvement for those people struggling the most has been slower over time.

Over the short-term, there were no changes in the proportions of people reporting either the highest or the lowest levels of happiness between the years ending March 2018 and March 2019. The slight improvement in the average happiness rating was driven by people reporting marginally higher scores in the middle range of the scale. Approximately 7.9%, or about 4.2 million people (out of a population aged 16 and over of nearly 53.1 million), continued to report low levels of happiness in the year ending March 2019.

Figure 4: The average anxiety in the UK remains flat in the year ending March 2019 with no significant decrease in the proportion of people reporting the highest anxiety ratings

UK, average anxiety ratings and proportions of people reporting "high (6-10)" anxiety for the years ending March 2012 to March 2019

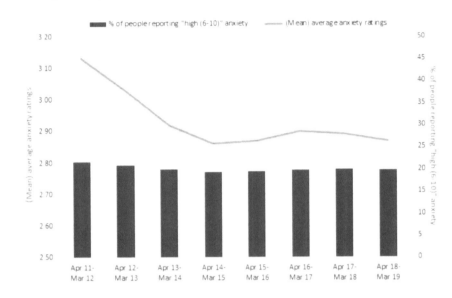

Source: Office for National Statistics - Annual Population Survey

Looking at the long-term trend, average anxiety ratings continued to improve in the UK up to the year ending March 2015. After this period, anxiety ratings reached a plateau, with a small fluctuation year on year and no significant changes for the latest year up to March 2019.

Similarly to people's happiness levels, also for this measure, there was no significant decrease in the proportion of people who reported the highest anxiety ratings and who might be struggling the most. As highlighted in our last release, about 19.8% or 10.4 million (out of a population aged 16 and over of nearly 53.1 million) people continued to report high levels of anxiety.

5 . Looking ahead, economic expectations about the next 12 months continue to decline

Figure 5: Expectations for the year ahead for unemployment trends and the general economic situation continue to decline

UK, Quarter 1 (Jan to Mar) 2011 to Quarter 1 (Jan to Mar) 2019, aggregate balance

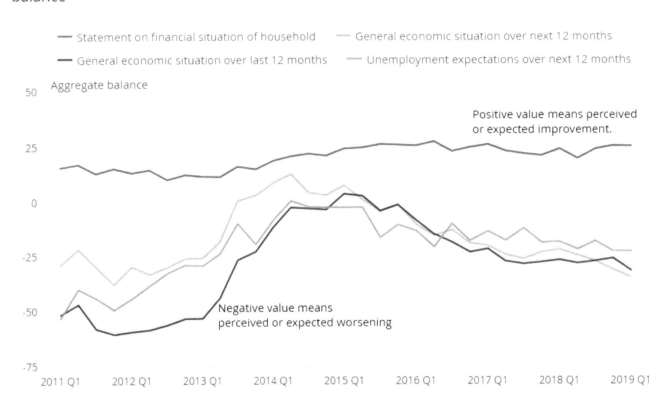

Source: European Commission – Eurobarometer Consumer Survey

Notes:

1. The source is the Eurobarometer Consumer Survey, which is collected by GFK for the European Commission.

2. A negative balance means that, on average, respondents reported the general economic situation worsened. A positive balance means they reported it improved and a zero balance indicates no change.

As discussed in section 3, objective household finance measures have improved. This is reflected in people's perception of their personal financial situation remaining positive. However, subjective expectations about the general economy continue to be negative:

- expected general economic situation for the year ahead is worse than at any point since the last quarter of 2011

- expectations for higher unemployment for the year ahead have been climbing, and are now higher than at any point since the quarter ending June 2013, despite <u>record-low unemployment rates</u>

6 . Next steps

Our users have expressed strong interest in additional analysis of well-being at local level. In the Autumn, we are planning to present estimates for the UK countries, regions and local authorities and to provide insights into how local circumstances might affect well-being, to enable better decision-making at local level. In November, we will be releasing the estimates looking across personal well-being and economic well-being in the UK for the period April to June 2019.

We also intend to focus more on the environmental aspects of well-being, both in terms of how the environment affects our living standards now and the extent to which growth is environmentally sustainable. In doing this, we will move a step closer to looking holistically at "people, prosperity and planet".

7 . Quality and methodology

The Personal well-being in the UK Quality and Methodology Information report contains important information on the strengths and limitations and uses of the data as well as how outputs are created and the quality and accuracy of those outputs. For more information on personal well-being, please see the Personal well-being user guidance and Harmonised principles of personal well-being.

The framework and indicators for economic well-being used in this release were outlined in Economic Well-being, Framework and Indicators, published in November 2014. Basic quality and methodology information for all economic well-being indicators included in this statistical bulletin is available from:

- the Gross domestic product (GDP) Quality and Methodology Information report

- Consumer Price Indices Quality and Methodology Information report

- Wealth and Assets Survey Quality and Methodology Information report

- Effects of taxes and benefits on household income Quality and Methodology information report

- Labour Force Survey (LFS) Quality and Methodology Information reports

Measuring "people and prosperity"

In November 2010, we set up the Measuring National Well-being programme to monitor and report UK progress by producing accepted and trusted measures of the well-being of the nation. We have pioneered the measurement of well-being in the UK in addition to traditional measures of prosperity, enabling policy-makers to make better, more well-informed decisions. We have also been monitoring economic well-being by assessing how households are faring, using measures of household wealth and disposable income.

Traditionally, we reported our quarterly updates on personal well-being and economic well-being in separate publications; however, a recent user feedback survey suggested the need for more in-depth analysis on the relationship between personal and economic well-being. In February 2019, we introduced a new series on "people and prosperity" as part of our "Beyond GDP" initiative, bringing together personal and economic well-being for the first time. The aim is to provide timely, quarterly indicators and analysis of household financial health as well as personal well-being. In measuring economic growth, we want to know the extent to which it affects different groups in society. This will make it easier for policy-makers and other users to consider questions such as whether changes in the size of the economy, and the distribution of that income, are reflected in our personal well-being.

Data quality

This release is based on the most recent data available as of August 2019. It is important to note that the data underpinning the personal and economic well-being indicators come from various sources with different timeliness and coverage.

The personal well-being estimates are from the Annual Population Survey (APS), which provides a representative sample of those living in private residential households in the UK. People living in communal establishments (such as care homes) or other non-household situations are not represented in this survey. This may be important in interpreting the findings in relation to those people reporting lower personal well-being. Most of the economic indicators capture the full coverage of the UK regardless of people's economic status.

APS data reweighting

Weighting answers to survey questions ensures that estimates are representative of the target population. Each person in the survey data has a "weight", the number of people that person represents in the population, which is used to produce estimates for the population.

More accurate weighting is based on the latest available population estimates for that time period. When new population estimates become available, data can be reweighted to ensure better representation and so precision of estimates. For greater accuracy, it is common practice to revise previously published estimates when new weights become available.

Based on new population estimates, new well-being weights have been available for the APS data since March 2019. We have used this reweighted data to produce annual personal well-being estimates for the years ending March 2012 to 2019, as we did for our previous publication for the years ending December 2012 to 2018. We plan to produce the UK country, regional and local authority level estimates for the years ending March 2012 to 2019 based on the most recent weightings in the Autumn this year. The reweighted data for the years ending June 2012 to 2019 and September 2012 to 2019 will be available in our upcoming publications later this year or early next year.

Your feedback

In February 2019, alongside our previous publication, we launched a survey to gather user feedback about our personal and economic well-being outputs. Users told us that our work fitted their requirements well – the language used, analytical detail and visual analyses met their needs. But the feedback also highlighted ways in which we could improve the quality and usability of our outputs such as by shortening the length of bulletins. Additionally, there were requests to focus on more in-depth analysis, such as more insights into regional data and inequalities and providing more information or explanation of more technical aspects.

Over the coming months, we will continue to address feedback and engage further with our users to improve the usability and usefulness of our work. We also aim to better promote our well-being dashboard and explore opportunities to improve our interactive tools. Your feedback will be very valuable in making our results useful and accessible. If you have any questions, please contact us at PeopleAndProsperity@ons.gov.uk. Thank you!

Statistical bulletin

Personal and economic well-being in the UK: November 2019

Estimates looking across personal well-being and economic well-being in the UK for Quarter 2 (April to June) 2019. This bulletin is part of a new series on "people and prosperity" introduced in February 2019.

Contact:
Silvia Manclossi, Gueorguie Vassilev,
Mark Hamilton, Khloe Evans
PeopleAndProsperity@ons.gov.uk
+44 (0)1633 582486 or +44 (0) 1633 45626

Release date:
14 November 2019

Next release:
6 February 2020

Table of contents

1 . Main points

- All of the economic well-being measures, including real household income, spending and financial wealth per head, grew in the three months to June 2019 compared with the same quarter last year.

- In terms of how we are feeling about our lives, average anxiety ratings increased in Quarter 2 2019 compared with the same quarter last year, while average ratings of life satisfaction, perceptions that the things we do in life are worthwhile, and happiness remained unchanged.

- The proportion of people reporting levels of high anxiety in Quarter 2 2019 was 21.2%, which was an increase of 1.7 percentage points compared with the same quarter last year.

- In the quarter ending June 2019, the household debt to income ratio increased, driven by the value in outstanding long-term loans such as mortgages.

- Although people's views of their own personal finances remained positive, expectations for both the general economic outlook and concerns about unemployment in the year ahead worsened compared with the same quarter last year.

This is the first time that we are publishing quarterly data for the personal well-being figures as Experimental Statistics, providing a more timely picture comparable with economic well-being statistics.

2 . Dashboard of well-being indicators

The dashboard below provides information on the main changes and historical trends over time for the main personal and economic well-being measures.

Notes:

1.p.p refers to percentage point change.

2."Compared with last year" refers to Q2 (Apr to June) 2019 compared with Q2 (Apr to June) 2018.

3."Change in aggregate balance compared with last year" refers to June 2019 compared with June 2018.

4."Compared with previous year" refers to 2018 to 2019 compared with 2017 to 2018.

3 . Economic well-being

Figure 1: Most measures of economic well-being increased in the quarter ending June 2019

Index (Quarter 3 2016 = 100), UK, Quarter 2 (April to June) 2014 to Quarter 2 2019

Index (Quarter 3 2016 = 100), UK, Quarter 2 (April to June) 2014 to Quarter 2 2019

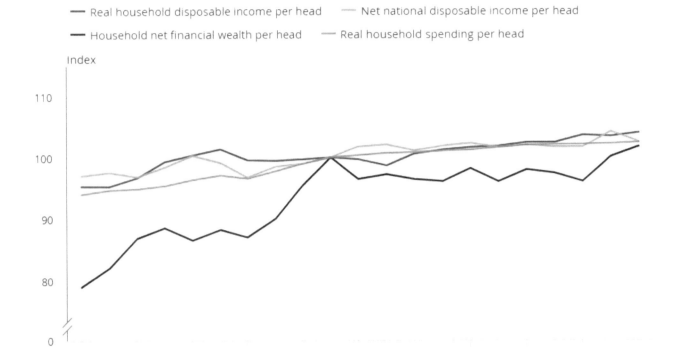

Source: Office for National Statistics – UK National Accounts

Notes:

1. Quarter 3 2016 = 100.

2. Net national disposable income per head is similar to GDP but it takes into account the depreciation of assets – such as the day-to-day wear and tear on vehicles and machinery – and the income generated by foreign-owned businesses in the UK, but includes the money made by UK companies based in other countries.

3. Real Household disposable income per head is the total amount of money that households have to spend on consumption, or to save and invest, after taxes, national insurance, pension contributions and interest have been paid, divided by the number of people.

4. Real household spending per head is household spending adjusted for the prices of goods and services, divided by the total population.

5. Household net financial wealth per head is the financial assets people hold (such as current and savings accounts and investments) less the liabilities they owe (for example, loans and mortgages) per average person in the UK.

As shown in Figure 1, all main measures of economic well-being increased in Quarter 2 (Apr to June) 2019 when compared with the same quarter a year ago. Net financial wealth per head increased the most, at 3.8%, compared with the same quarter a year ago. This was mostly driven by an increase in holdings of currency and deposits, the value of equity and investment fund shares, and pension schemes. It is worth noting that net financial wealth is more unequally distributed across the UK than income and other types of wealth such as property, physical, or private pension wealth. According to our latest Wealth in Great Britain release, net financial wealth was the wealth component with the highest inequality in the latest period of July 2014 to June 2016, with a Gini coefficient of 0.91. This means that, although this measure increased for UK households as a whole, only a small proportion of households will be impacted directly.

Real household disposable income per head also increased by 0.5% over the same period, and this was predominantly driven by an increase in wages and salaries, in line with recent labour market data.

Household spending per head has grown consecutively over the past fourteen quarters, although at a slower rate in recent periods. The latest quarter's growth, of 0.2% when compared with Quarter 1 (Jan to Mar) 2019, was driven by an increase in real terms spending on household running costs such as utility bills and rent, and an increase in real terms spending on clothes and footwear. These increases were offset by a decrease in spending on restaurants and cafés, which has now decreased for two consecutive quarters. Previous analysis has shown that spending on restaurants and cafés is linked to higher life satisfaction.

Figure 2: Household debt has increased in the quarter ending June 2019

Contribution to quarterly growth in UK debt, UK, Quarter 2 (Apr to Jun) 2011 to Quarter 2 2019

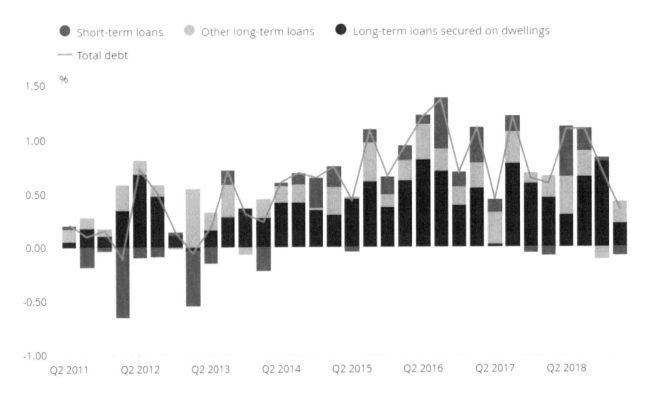

Contribution to quarterly growth in UK debt, UK, Quarter 2 (Apr to Jun) 2011 to Quarter 2 2019

Notes:

1. Short-term loans are loans with an original maturity of one year or less.

2. Long-term loans are loans with an original maturity of one year or more.

3. Original maturity is defined as period from the issue date until the final scheduled payment date.

The household debt to income ratio also showed an increase of 0.4% compared with the previous quarter which was driven by an increase in household debt. Figure 2 shows a breakdown of total household debt showing that the increase in the quarter ending June 2019 was driven by an increase in the value of long-term loans secured on dwellings which is predominantly made up of mortgages. Household debt can fluctuate, however this is the first time that the household debt to income ratio has increased since Quarter 3 (July to Sept) 2017. Although it remains in line with the overall trend of the series, we will continue to monitor this measure.

4 . Personal well-being

Figure 3: Most measures of personal well-being showed little change in the quarter ending June 2019

Average ratings of life satisfaction, feeling that the things done in life are worthwhile, and happiness, UK, Quarter 2 (Apr to June) 2011 to Quarter 2 2019

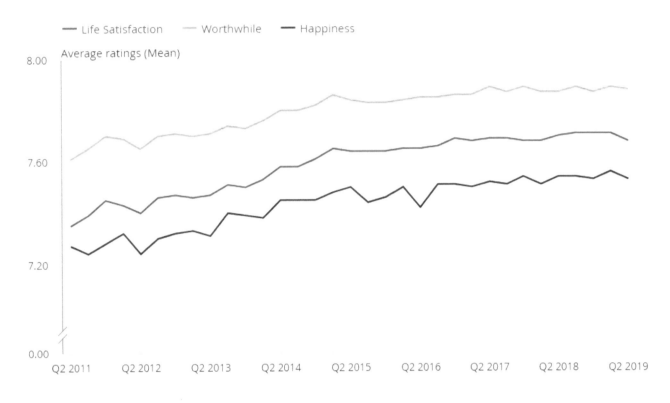

Average ratings of life satisfaction, feeling that the things done in life are worthwhile, and happiness, UK, Quarter 2 (Apr to June) 2011 to Quarter 2 2019

Source: Office for National Statistics - Annual Population Survey

Notes:

1. Chart axis has a break in it.

2. The data have been seasonally adjusted – see <u>Personal well-being quarterly estimates technical report</u> for more information.

Although there were improvements in measures of economic well-being in Quarter 2 (Apr to June) 2019, there was little change in ratings of life satisfaction, feeling that things done in life are worthwhile, and happiness in Quarter 2 2019 compared with the same quarter a year ago. Looking at the longer-term trends, average ratings for these three measures continued to improve in the UK up to Quarter 1 (Jan to Mar) 2015. After this period, they reached a plateau, with fluctuations quarter on quarter but no significant changes in Quarter 2 2019 compared with the same quarter a year ago.

In addition to looking at average ratings, we also monitor potential inequalities in personal well-being by comparing those rating each aspect of their well-being either at a very high level or a very low level. In Quarter 2 2019, the proportion of people rating their happiness at a low level increased by 0.6 percentage points (from 7.8% to 8.4%) compared with the same quarter a year ago. None of the other measures showed any significant change over this period.

Figure 4: Average anxiety levels in the UK increased by 4.9% in the quarter ending June 2019

Average anxiety ratings, UK, Quarter 2 (Apr to June) 2011 to Quarter 2 2019

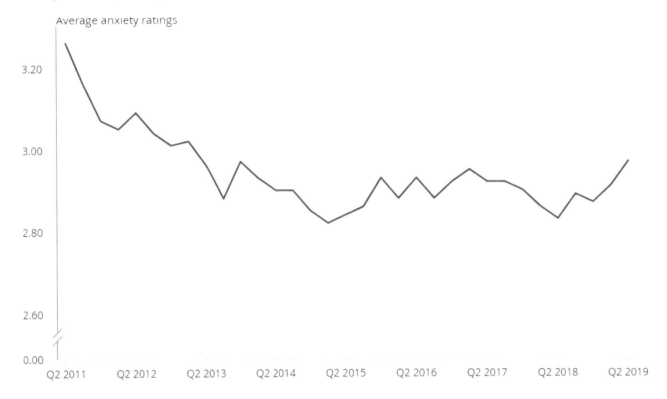

Average anxiety ratings, UK, Quarter 2 (Apr to June) 2011 to Quarter 2 2019

Source: Office for National Statistics - Annual Population Survey

Notes:

1. Chart axis has a break in it.

2. The data have been seasonally adjusted – see Personal well-being quarterly estimates technical report for more information.

In Quarter 2 2019, average anxiety ratings increased by 4.9% (from 2.83 to 2.97 out of 10) when compared with the same quarter a year ago. Looking at the longer-term, anxiety reached its highest average rating in Quarter 2 2019 in more than five years, since Quarter 4 (Oct to Dec) 2013 at 2.97 out of 10.

Figure 5: More people reported "high" anxiety and fewer people reported "very low" anxiety in the quarter ending June 2019

Proportion of people reporting "low" and "very high" ratings of anxiety, UK, Quarter 2 (Apr to June) 2011 to Quarter 2 2019

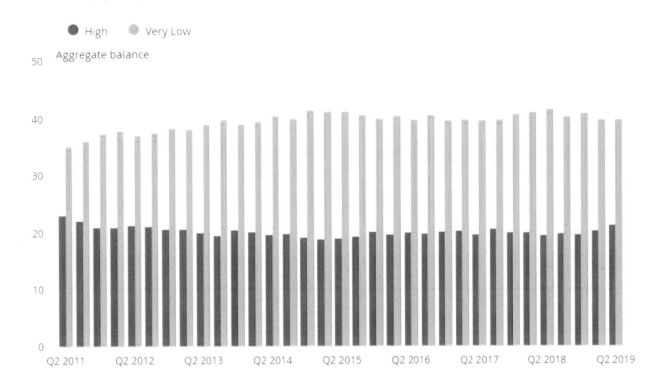

Proportion of people reporting "low" and "very high" ratings of anxiety, UK, Quarter 2 (Apr to June) 2011 to Quarter 2 2019

Source: Office for National Statistics - Annual Population Survey

Notes:

1. "High" anxiety refers to those reporting a rating of 6 to 10 and "very low" anxiety refers to those reporting a score of 0 to 1 (on an 11-point scale from 0 to 10).

2. The data has been seasonally adjusted – see Personal well-being quarterly estimates technical report for more information.

In Quarter 2 2019, the proportion of people reporting "very low" anxiety decreased from 41.6% to 39.8% compared with the same quarter a year ago. Over the same period, the proportion of people reporting "high" anxiety increased from 19.6% to 21.2%.

5 . Economic expectations for the next 12 months

Figure 6: Expectations for the year ahead for unemployment trends and the general economic situation remained negative

Aggregate balance, UK, Quarter 1 (January to March) 2011 to Quarter 2 (April to June) 2019

Aggregate balance, UK, Quarter 1 (January to March) 2011 to Quarter 2 (April to June) 2019

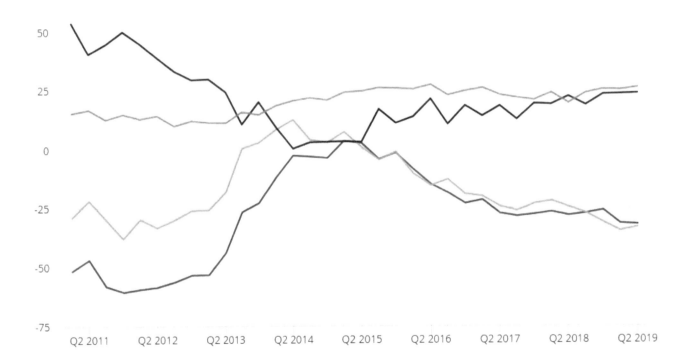

Source: European Commission - Eurobarometer Consumer Survey

Notes:

1. The source is the Eurobarometer Consumer Survey, which is collected by GFK (Growth from Knowledge) for the European Commission.

2. A negative balance means that, on average, respondents expected the general economic situation to worsen. A positive balance means they expect it improved and a zero balance indicates no change.

People's perceptions of their personal financial situation remained positive in the second quarter of 2019. This is in keeping with the continued improvement in a range of household finance measures as seen in Section 3. Despite this, expectations of the general economic situation for the next year continued to be negative as they have been since Quarter 3 (July to Sept) 2015.

Although the unemployment rate increased slightly in Quarter 2 (Apr to June) 2019 compared with the previous quarter (by 0.1 percentage points), it remained at historically low levels. This was not reflected in people's own subjective assessments, as expectations for increasing unemployment in the year ahead continued to climb and reached their highest level since Quarter 2 (Apr to June) 2013.

6 . Personal and economic well-being data

Quarterly personal well-being estimates - Seasonally Adjusted

Dataset | Released 14 November

Experimental seasonally adjusted quarterly estimates of life satisfaction, worthwhile, happiness and anxiety in the UK.

Quarterly personal well-being estimates - Non-seasonally Adjusted

Dataset | Released on 14 November 2019

Experimental quarterly statistics of life satisfaction, feeling that the things done in life are worthwhile, happiness and anxiety in the UK.

Quality information for quarterly personal well-being estimates

Dataset | Released on 14 November 2019

Confidence intervals and sample sizes for experimental quarterly statistics of life satisfaction, feeling that the things done in life are worthwhile, happiness and anxiety in the UK.

Annual personal well-being estimates

Dataset | Released on 14 November 2019

Annual estimates of life satisfaction, feeling that the things done in life are worthwhile, happiness and anxiety in the UK.

Quality information for annual personal well-being estimates

Dataset | Released on 14 November 2019

Confidence intervals and sample sizes for annual estimates of life satisfaction, feeling that the things done in life are worthwhile, happiness and anxiety in the UK.

Economic well-being estimates

Dataset | Released on 14 November 2019

Estimates of economic well-being, including household income, spending and wealth, distribution of wealth and income, whole economy wealth, and unemployment.

7 . Glossary

Economic well-being

Our economic well-being measures present a rounded and comprehensive basis for assessing changes in economic well-being through indicators that adjust or supplement more traditional measures such as gross domestic product (GDP).

Personal well-being

Our personal well-being measures ask people to evaluate, on a scale of 0 to 10, how satisfied they are with their life overall, whether they feel they have meaning and purpose in their life, and about their emotions (happiness and anxiety) during a particular period.

Thresholds

Thresholds are used to present dispersion in the data. For the life satisfaction, worthwhile and happiness questions, ratings are grouped in the following way:

- 0 to 4 (low)

- 5 to 6 (medium)

- 7 to 8 (high)

- 9 to 10 (very high)

For the anxiety question, ratings are grouped differently to reflect the fact that higher anxiety is associated with lower personal well-being. The ratings for anxiety are grouped as follows:

- 0 to 1 (very low)

- 2 to 3 (low)

- 4 to 5 (medium)

- 6 to 10 (high)

8 . Measuring the data

Data sources

The data underpinning the personal and economic well-being indicators come from various sources with different timeliness and coverage. This release is based on the most recent data available as of November 2019. The personal well-being estimates are from the Annual Population Survey (APS), which is a continuous household survey, covering the UK, with the aim of providing estimates between censuses of important social and labour market variables at a local area level.

The economic well-being estimates are from the UK Economic Accounts, which aim to provide detailed estimates of national product, income and expenditure, UK sector accounts and UK balance of payments. The economic expectations estimates are sourced from the Eurobarometer Consumer Survey, which is collected by GFK (Growth from Knowledge) for the European Commission. The questions included in the survey (PDF, 285KB) provide information on the general perception of the financial and economic situation.

Measuring "people and prosperity"

In November 2010, we set up the Measuring National Well-being programme to monitor and report UK progress by producing accepted and trusted measures of the well-being of the nation. We have pioneered the measurement of well-being in the UK in addition to traditional measures of prosperity, enabling policymakers to make better, well-informed decisions. We have also been monitoring economic well-being by assessing how households are faring using measures of household wealth and disposable income.

Traditionally, we reported our quarterly updates on personal well-being and economic well-being in separate publications; however, a recent user feedback survey suggested the need for more in-depth analysis on the relationship between personal and economic well-being.

In February 2019, we introduced a new series on "people and prosperity" as part of our "Beyond GDP" initiative bringing together personal and economic well-being for the first time. The aim is to provide timely, quarterly indicators and analysis of household financial health as well as personal well-being. In measuring economic growth, we want to know the extent to which it affects different groups in society. This will make it easier for policymakers and other users to consider questions such as whether changes in the size of the economy, and the distribution of that income, are reflected in our personal well-being.

Quality and methodology information

The Personal well-being in the UK Quality and Methodology Information report contains important information on the strengths and limitations and uses of the data as well as how outputs are created, and the quality and accuracy of those outputs. For more information on personal well-being, please see the Personal well-being user guidance and Harmonised principles of personal well-being.

The framework and indicators for economic well-being used in this release were outlined in Economic Well-being, Framework and Indicators, published in November 2014. Basic quality and methodology information for all economic well-being indicators included in this statistical bulletin is available from:

- Gross domestic product (GDP) Quality and Methodology Information report

- Consumer Price Indices Quality and Methodology Information report

- Wealth and Assets Survey Quality and Methodology Information report

- Effects of taxes and benefits on household income Quality and Methodology information report

- Labour Force Survey (LFS) Quality and Methodology Information report

Interpreting the term "aggregate balance"

Aggregate balance is a measure which shows the difference between positive and negative answering options, measured as percentage points of total answers. For example, if there are six options: "very positive", "positive", "stayed the same", "negative", "very negative" and "don't know", with PP, P, S, N, NN and D representing the respective percentages of respondents choosing these options, the aggregate balance (AB) is calculated as follows:

$$AB=(PP+0.5*P)-(0.5*N+NN)$$

Therefore, the aggregate balance is a scale from negative 100 (where all respondents chose "very negative") to positive 100 (where all respondents chose "very positive"). See section 3.3 of the Eurobarometer User Guide for more information.

Feedback and future publications

In February 2019, alongside our previous publication, we launched a survey to gather user feedback about our personal and economic well-being outputs. Users told us that our work fitted their requirements well – the language used, analytical detail and visual analyses met their needs. But the feedback also highlighted ways in which we could improve the quality and usability of our outputs such as shortening the length of bulletins. Additionally, there were requests to focus on more in-depth analysis, such as more insights into regional data and inequalities, and providing more information or explanation of more technical aspects.

Over the coming months, we will continue to address feedback and engage further with our users to improve the usability and usefulness of our work. We also aim to better promote our well-being dashboard and explore opportunities to improve our interactive tools. Your feedback will be very valuable in making our results useful and accessible. If you have any questions, please contact us at PeopleAndProsperity@ons.gov.uk.

9 . Strengths and limitations

Data quality

This is the first time that we are publishing quarterly data for the personal well-being figures as Experimental Statistics. The aim is to use the quarterly data to explore short-term changes in personal well-being by looking at fluctuation over the years and comparisons over quarters one year apart. Additionally, using quarterly estimates has the benefit of being more comparable with the economic well-being estimates which use quarterly data for its indicators.

Seasonal adjustment

The data published for our quarterly personal well-being figures are all seasonally adjusted (although non-seasonally adjusted estimates are also available). This aids interpretation by removing recurring fluctuations caused, for example, by holidays or other seasonal patterns. Further information on the seasonality in the quarterly personal well-being can be found in the accompanying Technical report: personal well-being quarterly estimates.

Annual Population Survey data reweighting

Weighting answers to survey questions ensures that estimates are representative of the target population. Each person in the survey data has a "weight", the number of people that person represents in the population, which is used to produce estimates for the population. More accurate weighting is based on the latest available population estimates for that time period. When new population estimates become available, data can be reweighted to ensure better representation and so precision of estimates. For greater accuracy, it is common practice to revise previously published estimates when new weights become available. Based on new population estimates, new well-being weights have been available for the Annual Population Survey (APS) data since March 2019. We have used this reweighted data to produce our quarterly personal well-being estimates and our annual personal well-being estimates for the years ending June 2012 to 2019 at the UK level. The reweighted data for the years ending September 2012 to 2019 will be available in our upcoming publication early next year.

Statistical significance

Please note that:

- any changes mentioned in this publication are "statistically significant"

- the statistical significance of differences noted within the release are determined based on non-overlapping confidence intervals

- comparisons have been based on unrounded data

10 . Related links

Personal well-being quarterly estimates technical report

Methodology | Released on 14 November 2019

Description of the statistical methods and techniques used to create and analyse quarterly estimates for personal well-being in the UK. This is the first time that we are publishing quarterly data for the personal well-being figures as Experimental Statistics, providing a more timely picture comparable with economic well-being statistics.

Personal well-being in the UK: April 2018 to March 2019

Bulletin | Released on 23 October 2019

Estimates of life satisfaction, feeling that the things done in life are worthwhile, happiness and anxiety at the UK, country, regional, county and local authority level.

Personal and economic well-being: what matters most to our life satisfaction?

Article | Released on 15 May 2019

Examines how socio-demographic and economic factors are associated with life satisfaction. These factors include sex, age, health, marital and economic status as well as household income and expenditure.

Article | 4 February 2019

A summary of how ONS is continuing to develop new ways of measuring and reporting the UK's economic and social progress and an introduction to the Personal and economic well-being publication.

Beyond GDP: How ONS is developing wider measures of well-being

Article | 4 February 2019

A summary of how ONS is continuing to develop new ways of measuring and reporting the UK's economic and social progress and an introduction to the Personal and economic well-being publication.

Office for
National Statistics

Article

Measuring national well-being in the UK: international comparisons, 2019

This article explores how the UK is faring in important areas of well-being compared with the member states of the European Union (EU) and the member countries of the Organisation for Economic Co-operation and Development (OECD).

Contact:
Chris Randall, Abbie Cochrane,
Rhian Jones and Silvia Manclossi
qualityoflife@ons.gov.uk
+44 (0) 1633 58 2486

Release date:
6 March 2019

Next release:
To be announced

Table of contents

1 . Main points

- Overall, personal well-being levels have improved in the UK, as have mental well-being scores – the latter increasing by 4.6 percentage points between 2011 and 2016 to 63.2%, close to the EU-28 average of 64.0%.

- The proportion of people in the UK reporting feeling close to those in their neighbourhood increased by 3.6 percentage points to 62.0% between 2011 and 2016, compared with an average decrease of 4.0 percentage points across the EU-28 to 63.0%.

- In the UK, 14.1% of people reported struggling to make ends meet in 2017, below the EU-28 average of 21.6%, and one-fifth reported that they were "very satisfied" with their household income in 2018, above the EU-28 average.

- In the UK, people had a lower level of trust in the EU in 2018 than the average across the 28 countries of the EU (30.0% and 42.0% respectively).

- In 2017, 9.6% of the UK's total primary energy supply came from renewable sources; this proportion has increased year-on-year since 2010, but it is still below the OECD average (10.2%).

- In the UK, health and social security (33.0%) and housing (22.0%) were the most important concerns; while across the EU-28, the most frequently cited issues in 2018 were unemployment (25.0%) and health and social security (23.0%).

2 . Things you need to know about this release

Measuring "people, prosperity and the planet"

In November 2010, we set up the Measuring National Well-being Programme to monitor and report UK progress by producing accepted and trusted measures of the well-being of the nation. We have pioneered the measurement of well-being in the UK in addition to traditional measures of prosperity, enabling policy-makers to make better, more well-informed decisions.

In February 2019, we introduced a new series on "people and prosperity" as part of our "Beyond GDP" initiative bringing together personal and economic well-being for the first time. In measuring economic growth, we want to know the extent to which it benefits different groups in society. This will make it easier for policy-makers and other users to consider questions such as whether changes in the size of the economy are reflected in our incomes or our life satisfaction.

Our recent user feedback survey suggested the need for more in-depth analysis and an interest in how the UK's exit from the EU may impact on people's well-being. To increase the value of our work to decision-makers and in keeping with our aspiration to "leave no one behind", this release aims to provide a comparative picture of well-being in the UK and other countries across the European Union (EU) or the Organisation for Economic Co-operation and Development (OECD) by looking at people's experiences from different perspectives to better understand who is struggling and who is thriving.

Understanding the well-being of individual people and communities both within and across countries can help identify inequalities from more than one angle and compare strengths and weaknesses in different areas of life over time. In this article, we cover the traditional national well-being domains, such as personal well-being, our relationships and health. Additionally, we look at opinions of civic engagement, trust in civic institutions and the most frequently reported concerns of people in the UK and EU. This will enable us to assess current well-being as well as to monitor changes in the future.

Quality and methodology

The article uses the latest data available from sources including the OECD, Eurobarometer, European Quality of Life Survey, Eurostat, Gallup World Poll, the International Institute for Democracy and Electoral Assistance, the United Nations and the World Health Organisation.

Most of the data used in this article are for adults aged 15 years and over (unless otherwise stated) and cover different survey dates, which are defined in the text.

This release is based on the most recent available data as of February 2019. It is important to note that the data underpinning the indicators are often from different sources with different timeliness and coverage. A lot of the data come from household surveys so people not living in households are not included in the data (for example, people who live in communal establishments such as nursing homes, homelessness hostels, care homes, barracks or prisons) and accordingly, these findings are unlikely to accurately reflect their quality of life.

This article includes data for the UK or Great Britain. It is worth noting that different groups or different areas of the UK may feel very differently about their lives and have different experiences. Also, for this article, we have used the more recent data available at an international level. We will be publishing an update of the UK national well-being measures later in 2019, which will use the latest data available for the UK and allow comparisons across groups and geographies in the UK.

Comparisons have been made with the previous year's data, or the previously published figures where year-on-year data are not available. Additionally, where further previous data were available, longer-term comparisons and trends have been reported. To assess change between the two most recent data points, the overall average change across available countries was calculated. When the UK change was more than 1 percentage point away from the overall average, this was reported as a change over time. When only a single data point for an indicator is available, the measure has not been assessed over time.

Bar charts showing where the UK stands in comparison with other OECD or EU-28 countries have been included for a selection of indicators, using the most recent data point. On these charts, the top- and bottom-ranking countries have been presented alongside the UK and the countries scoring most similarly to the UK. Where possible, the OECD average or EU-28 average have also been included on these charts to show the position of the UK and other countries in relation to the average.

This article only covers a selection of national well-being indicators, for more information on all the data and sources, please see Measuring national well-being international comparisons dataset.

3 . Personal well-being

Personal well-being is a subjective assessment of how people feel about their own lives. Our measures of personal well-being focus on overall satisfaction with life, the extent to which we feel the things we do are worthwhile and daily emotions such as happiness and anxiety. These measures are strongly related to other important aspects of quality of life such as our health, relationships and employment.

Overall, personal well-being levels have increased in the UK.

Mental well-being improved by 4.6 percentage points between 2011 and 2016, compared with the EU-28 average change of 2.2 percentage points.

Feelings of worthwhile increased by 4.1 percentage points between 2011 and 2016 in the UK, compared with the EU-28 average decrease of 0.5 percentage points.

There was little change in ratings of happiness between 2011 and 2016, but the UK remains similar to the EU-28 average of 7.4 out of 10.

It is important to note that figures for personal well-being only cover the period up to 2016 because these are the latest internationally-comparable data. For users interested in more recent UK estimates, please see our latest release.

Life satisfaction

According to data from the Organisation for Economic Co-operation and Development (OECD), the average (mean) rating of life satisfaction of people aged 15 years and over in the UK was 6.7 out of 10 from 2014 to 2016 (Figure 1).

This figure was the same as Chile and similar to the Czech Republic and Mexico (6.6 out of 10). The UK was slightly higher than the OECD average, which was 6.5 out of 10.

The highest-ranked countries for life satisfaction were Denmark, Finland, Iceland, Norway and Switzerland (all 7.5 out of 10), while the lowest-ranked countries were Greece and Portugal (both 5.2 out of 10).

OECD countries, 2014 to 2016

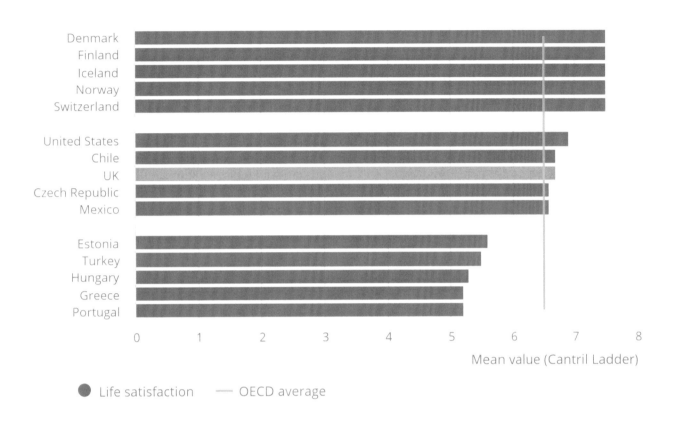

Figure 1: The UK's mean rating of life satisfaction was slightly higher than the OECD average

OECD countries, 2014 to 2016

Source: Gallup World Poll

Notes:

1. The reference period is the three-year average 2014 to 2016 for all the countries. Chart shows the countries with the highest and lowest values along with the countries that have the same or similar values to the UK.

2. Respondents were asked to: "Imagine an 11 rung ladder where the bottom (0) represents the worst possible life for you and the top (10) represents the best possible life for you. On which step of the ladder do you feel you personally stand at the present time?"

Feeling worthwhile

According to 2016 data from the European Quality of Life Survey (EQLS), 86% of adults aged 18 years and over in the UK agreed or strongly agreed that they generally felt that what they did in life was worthwhile. This was a 4.1-percentage point increase from 2011, where 82% agreed or strongly agreed.

The proportion in the UK in 2016 was higher than the EU-28 average of 78% in 2016 and was similar to Austria and Luxembourg (85%). The highest-ranked countries in 2016 were both Ireland and the Netherlands, where 9 in 10 (90%) people agreed or strongly agreed that what they did in life was worthwhile. The lowest-ranked country in 2016 was Greece (53%).

Happiness

When the EQLS asked adults aged 18 years and over to rate how happy they were, the average happiness rating for the UK was 7.8 out of 10 in 2016.

This was the same as Ireland, the Netherlands and Sweden, and was slightly higher than the EU-28 average of 7.4 out of 10. The highest-ranked country in 2016 was Finland (8.2 out of 10). Greece was the lowest-ranked country in 2016 (6.0 out of 10).

Mental well-being

The EQLS also asked adults aged 18 years and over the questions on the World Health Organisation's (WHO-5)'s mental well-being index. This comprises five questions about feeling cheerful, calm, active, rested, and interested. A higher percentage score on the index indicates better mental well-being.

The UK scored an average of 63.2% on the scale in 2016; an increase from 58.6% in 2011.

In 2016, the UK was similar to the EU-28 average of 64.0% and the Czech Republic (63.4%), Latvia and Poland (both 62.6%). The highest-ranking country for mental well-being was Ireland, scoring 70.5%, and the lowest-ranking country was Croatia, scoring 57.3%.

4 . Our relationships

Our previous research has shown that having positive relationships is one of the most important factors shaping people's personal well-being. To explore how people in the UK and EU compare on the quality of their relationships, we consider the extent to which people feel they have someone to rely on in times of trouble and whether they feel lonely.

There was little change between 2011 and 2016 in the proportion of people in the UK saying they were lonely most or all of the time, with the UK remaining on par with the EU-28 average of 6%.

It is important to note that figures for our relationships only cover the period up to 2014 to 2016 because these are the latest internationally-comparable data. For users interested in more recent UK estimates, please see our Measuring national well-being dashboard.

Loneliness

Inadequate social connectedness, or poor relationships, may lead to people experiencing loneliness. However, the feeling of loneliness is subjective and related to personal expectations about relationships. A person may feel lonely even in the company of family and friends.

As of January 2018, the UK was the first country to have a Minister for Loneliness, highlighting its importance as an important social issue with a range of implications for people's health and well-being, as well as for societal and community well-being (PDF, 2.8MB). Some research suggests that persistent loneliness may be as bad for your health as smoking 15 cigarettes a day (PDF, 160KB).

Loneliness was measured on the European Quality of Life Survey (EQLS) by asking adults aged 18 years and over to rate how often they felt lonely in the past two weeks.

In 2016, of respondents in the UK, 5% reported that they felt lonely most or all of the time (Figure 2), compared with 7% in 2011.

For 2016, the proportion of people reporting frequent loneliness was the same as in Austria, the Czech Republic, Estonia and Germany, and was similar to the EU-28 average of 6%. The highest-ranking countries were both Denmark and Finland, where only 2% of people reported feeling lonely most or all of the time. Greece was the lowest-ranking country with 11% of people reporting frequent loneliness.

Figure 2: The proportion feeling lonely all or most of the time in the UK was similar to the EU-28 average

EU-28, 2016

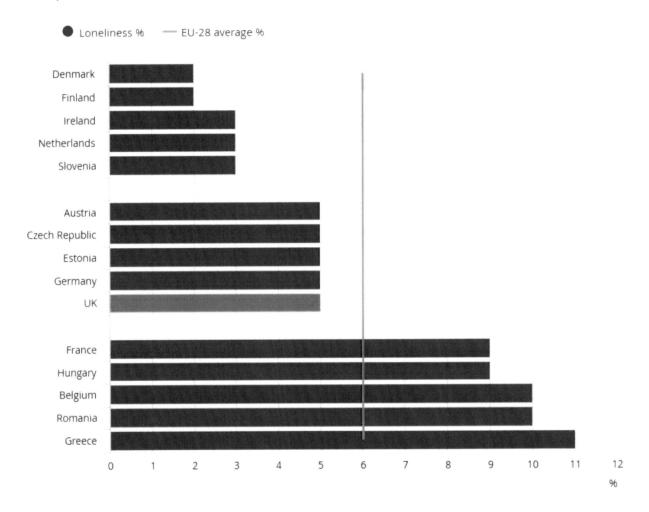

EU-28, 2016

Notes:

1. Based on the question "Which is closest to how you have been feeling lonely over the last two weeks".

2. Chart shows the countries with the highest and lowest values along with the countries that have the same or similar values to the UK.

Perceived social network support

An average of 93% of respondents in the UK (aged 15 years and over) from 2014 to 2016 answered positively to the question "If you were in trouble, do you have relatives or friends you can count on to help you whenever you need them, or not?", saying that they did have a relative or friend they could count on.

This was the same proportion as Canada and was higher than the Organisation for Economic Co-operation and Development (OECD) average of 89%. The highest-scoring country was Iceland, where 98% of respondents reported having someone to count on. The lowest-scoring country was Korea, where only 76% of respondents reported having someone to count on.

5 . Health

Our previous research has shown that how people view their health is one of the most important factors contributing to overall personal well-being. Despite increases in estimated health-adjusted life expectancy at birth of males and females in the UK (between 2000 and 2016), there has been a decrease in self-reported health in the UK since 2010, suggesting that more people in the UK are believing themselves to be in worse health despite the fact that World Health Organisation (WHO) estimates showed we were living longer, healthier lives on average over this period.

It is important to note that the WHO estimates used here for the sake of international comparisons use a different method of calculation to the Office for National Statistics (ONS) estimates of healthy life expectancy and produce a slightly different picture for the UK. The figures also only cover the period up to 2016 because these are the latest internationally-comparable data. For users interested in more recent UK estimates of healthy life expectancy , please see our latest release.

Health-adjusted life expectancy (HALE) at birth

Health-adjusted life expectancy at birth is an estimate of the average number of years babies born in a particular year would live in a state of good general health if mortality levels at each age and the level of good health at each age, remain constant in the future.

According to data from the WHO, males in the UK had an estimated health-adjusted life expectancy of 70.9 years at birth in 2016, an increase of 3.5 years in good health since 2000. In 2016, this was the same as Austria and was similar to Denmark and Korea (both 70.7 years) and to Ireland and Luxembourg (both 71.1 years).

Females in the UK had an average health-adjusted life expectancy of 72.9 years at birth in 2016 , gaining 2.5 extra years in good health on average since 2000. This was a similar expectancy to the Netherlands (72.8 years) and to Belgium, Denmark and Germany (all 73.0 years). Japan was the highest-ranking country for health-adjusted life expectancy at birth in 2016 for both males (72.6 years) and females (76.9 years). Latvia was the lowest-ranking country for males (62.4 years) and Turkey was the lowest-ranking country for females (67.6 years).

This means that, compared with the highest-ranking country (Japan), females in the UK can expect to live 4.0 fewer years in good health, while males will live 1.7 fewer years in good health. However, the UK has much higher health-adjusted life expectancy at birth than the lowest-ranking countries, with females in the UK expected to live 5.3 years longer in good health on average than those in Turkey and males 8.5 years longer in good health than those in Latvia.

Percentage reporting to be in good or better than good health

Data from the Organisation for Economic Co-operation and Development (OECD) showed that just over two-thirds (69.0%) of adults aged 15 years and over in the UK reported being in very good or good health in 2016.

This proportion peaked at 79.4% in 2010 and has been decreasing each year since, suggesting more people in the UK believe themselves to be in worse health. The UK decrease (10.4 percentage points) between 2010 and 2016 compares with an average decrease of 0.4 percentage points across the EU-28.

The deterioration in our assessments of our health is at odds both with improvements in objective measures of health like average health-adjusted life expectancy at birth and in improvements in our mental well-being, as measured by the WHO-5 mental well-being index.

In 2016, the UK had around the same proportion (69.0%) as Luxembourg (69.1%) and Turkey (69.4%) reporting good or better than good health (Figure 3). The highest-ranking country was Canada (88.4%), while the lowest-ranking was Korea (32.5%).

Interestingly, in 2016, only 35.5% of respondents in Japan regarded themselves as being in good or better health, making it the second-lowest ranking country, despite being the country with the highest health-adjusted life expectancy at birth for both males and females.

Figure 3: Around 7 in 10 people in the UK reported very good or good health

OECD countries, 2016

OECD countries, 2016

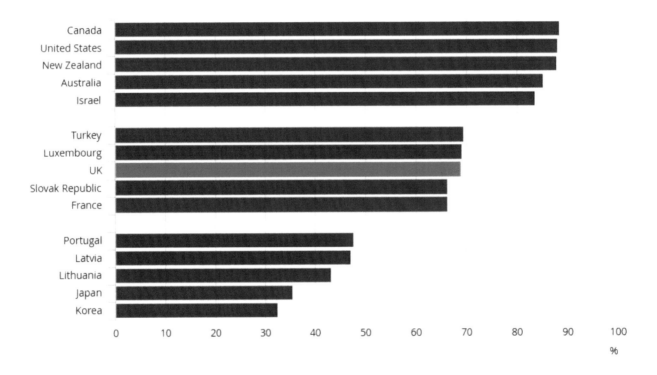

Source: Organisation for Economic Co-operation and Development

Notes:

1. Results for Australia, Canada, Chile, Israel, New Zealand and the United States are not directly comparable with those for other countries, due to differences in reporting scales, which may lead to an upward bias in the reported estimates.

2. The reference period for Australia is 2014.

3. Chart shows the countries with the highest and lowest values along with the countries that have the same or similar values to the UK.

Prevalence of depressive and anxiety disorders

Another important aspect of health is good mental health. According to data from WHO, the prevalence of depressive disorders in the UK in 2015 was 4.5% (PDF, 1.6MB). This was a similar proportion to Turkey (4.4%) and Israel (4.6%). The country with the lowest prevalence of depressive disorders was Korea (3.7%), while the countries with the highest prevalence were Australia, Estonia and the United States (all 5.9%).

The prevalence of anxiety disorders in the UK in 2015 was 4.2%. This was similar to Spain (4.1%) and Turkey (4.0%). The country with the lowest prevalence of anxiety disorders in 2015 was Israel (2.8%) while the country with the highest was Norway (7.4%).

6 . What we do

What we do in life shapes our lifestyles, our relationships with others and our well-being. People have many different lifestyles based on individual choices, characteristics, personal preferences and circumstances. Individuals divide their time between various tasks and activities, including paid or unpaid employment, volunteering and numerous leisure activities.

In the UK, the unemployment rate has continued to fall since 2011, as the labour market continues to strengthen since the economic downturn. Along with the longer-term fall in the unemployment rate, the number of people saying they would like to work more hours (the underemployed) remained relatively flat between 2011 and 2014, before falling after 2014. In comparison, the number of people saying they would like to work fewer hours even with less pay (overemployed) has been increasing steadily since 2013.

This increase in overemployment and fall in the underemployment rate can be partly attributed to an improvement in the labour market conditions, as firms could be increasing the number of hours worked of their existing workforce, instead of hiring new staff. In the UK, analysis has shown that the quality of the job may also have a part to play in well-being. For other countries across the EU-28, such as Greece and Spain, where there are higher unemployment rates, we can see that unemployment is more of a main concern than it is in the UK.

Although volunteering, participating in cultural activities and sports participation are not discussed in this section, they are included in the Measuring national well-being: international comparisons dataset.

It is important to note that figures for what we do only cover the period up to 2016 to 2017 because these are the latest internationally comparable data. For users interested in more recent UK estimates, please see our Measuring national well-being dashboard and recent UK estimates for unemployment rates.

Harmonised unemployment rates

There is strong evidence showing that being in work is generally good for physical and mental health and well-being, though the extent of the benefits may depend on job quality and job satisfaction. Worklessness, on the other hand, is associated with poorer physical and mental health and well-being (PDF, 1.2MB) (Waddell and Burton, 2006) and also has important implications for living standards.

Looking first at unemployment, harmonised unemployment rates refer to the number of people of working age who are available to work and have taken specific steps to find work, but who are not currently in employment.

In the UK, harmonised unemployment rates have been improving year-on-year since 2011, from 8.1% in 2011 to 4.4% in 2017, according to data from the Organisation for Economic Co-operation and Development (OECD). In 2017, the harmonised unemployment rate in the UK was the same as in the United States and similar to the rate in Israel (4.2%) (Figure 4).

The countries with the lowest harmonised unemployment rates in 2017 were Japan and Iceland (both 2.8%), while those with the highest rates were Greece (21.5%) and Spain (17.2%).

Given the very high unemployment rates in 2017 in countries like Italy (11.2%), Spain (17.2%) and Greece (21.5%) compared with the OECD average (5.8%), it is perhaps not surprising that unemployment was most frequently cited as a main concern facing their country by people in the EU in both 2016 and 2018.

Meanwhile, the unemployment picture in the UK has been much more positive and improving, as reflected in the fact that unemployment was only the fifth most frequently cited concern in the UK in 2016, falling back to seventh-ranked concern in 2018 (see section 13).

Figure 4: The harmonised unemployment rate in the UK was lower than the OECD average

OECD countries, 2017

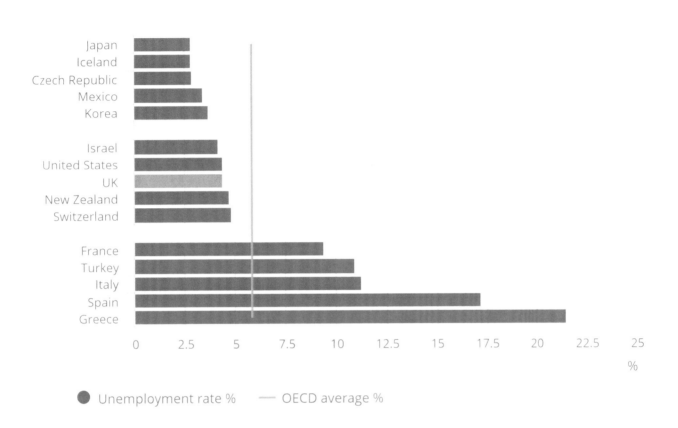

Figure 4: The harmonised unemployment rate in the UK was lower than the OECD average

OECD countries, 2017

● Unemployment rate %　　— OECD average %

Source: Organisation for Economic Co-operation and Development

Notes:

1. Harmonised unemployment rates define the unemployed as people of working age who are without work, are available for work, and have taken specific steps to find work. The uniform application of this definition results in estimates of unemployment rates that are more internationally comparable than estimates based on national definitions of unemployment. This indicator is measured in numbers of unemployed people as a percentage of the labour force and it is seasonally adjusted. The labour force is defined as the total number of unemployed people plus those in civilian employment.

2. Chart shows the countries with the highest and lowest values along with the countries that have the same or similar values to the UK.

Job satisfaction

Work can be a very important part of our lives, providing structure, routine and a sense of self-worth, which are all important to well-being. This section considers how satisfied people in the UK are with their jobs compared with those in other European countries.

According to data from the European Quality of Life Survey (EQLS), the average rating of job satisfaction in the UK for those aged 18 years and over in 2016 was 7.4 out of 10, similar to 2011 levels (7.5 out of 10). This was the same as the EU-28 average, as well as Bulgaria, Czech Republic and France.

Austria and Finland had the highest levels of job satisfaction (both 8.1 out of 10), closely followed by Denmark (8.0 out of 10). Greece had the lowest levels of job satisfaction in 2016 (6.4 out of 10), followed by Spain and Croatia (both 7.0 out of 10). Coupled with the fact that Greece and Spain also had the highest rates of unemployment, this suggests that those in work were not particularly satisfied with their jobs.

Views about citizens from the EU working in their country

People in the UK became more favourable towards EU citizens working in the UK between the spring of 2016 and spring of 2018. Figure 5 shows how different countries compare in views about EU citizens working in their country.

Overall, it was perceived as a good thing by at least half of people in the 28 EU member states in 2018, led by Luxembourg (91%) and Ireland, Spain and Sweden (all 87%). People were least likely to think that this was a good thing in Italy (50%), Cyprus (57%) and Croatia and Austria (both 58%).

Between spring 2016 and spring 2018, support for EU citizens working in their country increased in 18 countries, led by the UK (up 11 percentage points) and Poland (up 10 percentage points). It decreased in seven countries, led by Croatia (down 7 percentage points) and was unchanged in three countries.

Figure 5: At least half of respondents reported it was a good thing for EU citizens to have the right to work in the respondent's country in spring 2018

EU-28, spring 2016 and spring 2018

EU-28, spring 2016 and spring 2018

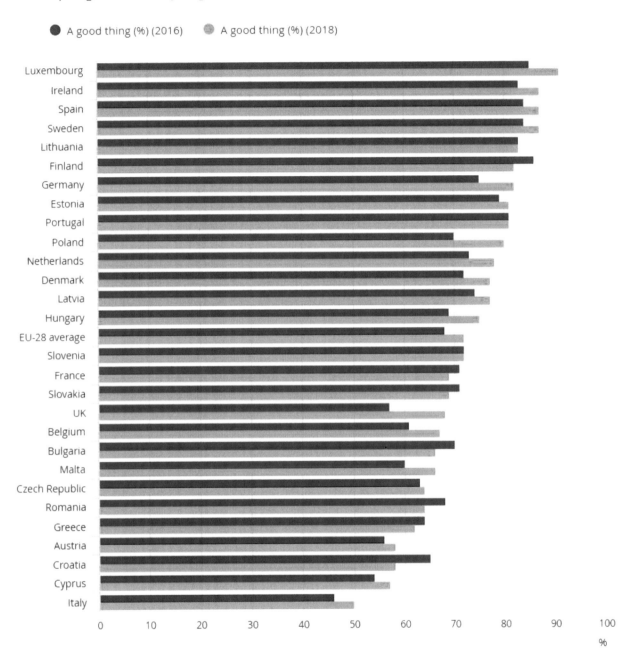

● A good thing (%) (2016) ○ A good thing (%) (2018)

Source: Standard Eurobarometer 85 and 89

Notes:

1. Respondents were asked "For the following statement, please tell me if you think that it is a good thing, a bad thing or neither a good or a bad thing - The right for EU citizens to work in (Our Country)". This chart contains only those that reported "A good thing".

7 . Where we live

Where we live can have a significant impact on our sense of well-being. Homes that meet our individual needs and provide us with shelter and security are made all the better by having positive relationships with people who live in the local area.

Overall, this area of life has improved in the UK since 2011. The proportion of people in the UK reporting feeling close to those in their neighbourhood increased by 3.6 percentage points between 2011 and 2016, compared with an average decrease of 4.0 percentage points across the EU-28.

There was little change in people's satisfaction with their accommodation in the UK during the same period, though we remain slightly above the EU-28 average of 7.7 out of 10.

It is important to note that figures for where we live only cover the period up to 2014 to 2016 because these are the latest internationally comparable data. For users interested in more recent UK estimates, please see our Measuring national well-being dashboard and recent UK figures on household income.

Feeling safe walking alone at night in the area where living

Feeling safe in and around our homes is an essential aspect of leading a healthy, happy life. The Gallup World Poll collected data on Organisation for Economic Co-operation and Development (OECD) countries, assessing the percentage of people aged 15 years and over who felt safe walking home alone at night in the city or area where they lived.

Between 2014 and 2016, of people in the UK, 77.4% said they felt safe walking alone at night. This was similar to Germany and Sweden (both 75.9%) and to Austria (80.7%), and was higher than the OECD average of 68.6%.

People in Norway were most likely to say they felt safe (87.7%), while people in Mexico least likely to say this (45.9%).

Feeling close to people in the local area

Feeling close to others in the area where you live is another aspect of social connectedness and belonging. According to the European Quality of Life Survey (EQLS) in 2016, 62% of people aged 18 years and over in the UK reported that they agreed or strongly agreed that they felt close to the people in the area in which they lived. This was similar to the EU-28 average of 63%, and Austria and Belgium (also 63%).

The lowest-ranked countries in 2016 were Germany and Finland (both 54%), while the highest-ranking country was Latvia (83%).

Satisfaction with accommodation

According to the EQLS, on average, people aged 16 years and over in the UK rated their satisfaction with their accommodation as 8.1 out of 10 in 2016. This was similar to 2011 (7.9 out of 10) and similar to Sweden and Malta (both 8.2 out of 10) (Figure 6). This was also higher than the EU-28 average of 7.7 out of 10.

The highest-ranking countries in 2016 were Austria, Denmark and Ireland, all with an average rating of 8.4 out of 10, while the lowest-ranking country was Latvia (6.8 out of 10).

Figure 6: The mean rating of satisfaction with accommodation was higher than the EU-28 average

EU-28, 2016

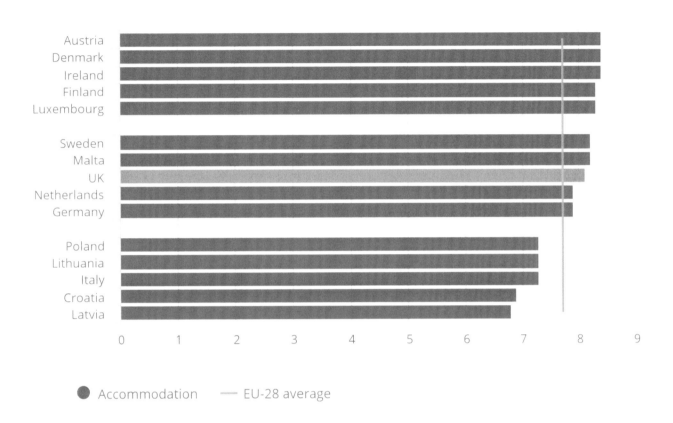

Figure 6: The mean rating of satisfaction with accommodation
was higher than the EU-28 average

EU-28, 2016

Source: European Quality of Life Survey

Notes:

1. Based on the question "Could you please tell me on a scale of 1 to 10 how satisfied you are with your accommodation, where 1 means you are very dissatisfied and 10 means you are very satisfied?".

2. Chart shows the countries with the highest and lowest values along with the countries that have the same or similar values to the UK.

Housing has become a more frequently cited concern for people in the UK recently. Respondents to the Eurobarometer Survey aged 15 years and over were asked what the two most important issues facing their country were. In 2018, over one in five (22%) reported housing was an important issue in the UK (compared with 11% for the EU-28 average) (see section 13).

Factors that can affect people's satisfaction with their accommodation in the UK could be <u>younger people living with parents more</u>, <u>housing quality and energy efficiency (XLS, 279KB)</u> and <u>affordability</u>. There are a few possible reasons for this; for example, the costs of both renting and buying homes have increased and the introduction of stricter mortgage lending rules after the 2008 economic downturn. There are <u>significant relationships between owning or renting and well-being</u> and <u>loneliness</u>; those that <u>own outright or with a mortgage have higher life satisfaction (XLS, 421KB)</u>.

8 . Personal finance

Office for National Statistics research in 2015 showed that <u>individuals in households with higher incomes report higher life satisfaction and happiness (PDF, 215KB)</u> and lower anxiety, holding other factors constant.

In 2017, the UK had a similar proportion of people defined as at risk of poverty as the EU-28 average and, in 2018, a higher proportion of people in the UK expressed satisfaction with their household financial situation than the EU average. In 2017, the UK had a lower proportion of people saying their household was struggling to make ends meet than the EU average. Overall, this is quite a positive picture when comparing the UK with other EU countries.

When we switch the focus to look at personal finance measures within the UK, there are indications of important disparities in how we are faring financially. In 2017, the UK had a similar proportion of people defined as at risk of poverty (17.0%) as the EU-28 average (16.9%) and, in 2018, a higher proportion of people in the UK expressed satisfaction with their household financial situation (20.0%) than the EU average (12.0%). In 2017, the UK had a lower proportion of people saying their household was struggling to make ends meet (14.1%) than the EU average (21.6%). Overall, this is quite a positive picture when comparing the UK with other EU countries.

In the UK, the proportion of people reporting satisfaction with their financial situation decreased by 3.0 percentage points between 2017 and 2018, compared with an average increase of 0.2 percentage points across the EU-28. There was little change to the levels of those at-risk-of-poverty between 2016 and 2017, but the UK remained in line with the EU-28 average of 16.9%.

There was little change to the proportion of people struggling to make ends meet between 2016 and 2017, though the UK scored 7.5 percentage points lower than the EU-28 average of 21.6%. The UK's median equivalised income remained stable between 2016 and 2017.

One of the measures in this domain, namely median household income, is not discussed in this section, but is included in the <u>Measuring national well-being international comparisons dataset</u>. "Median household income" is the income of the middle household if all households are ranked from the lowest income to the highest.

It is important to note that figures for personal finance only cover the period up to 2017 to 2018 because these are the latest internationally comparable data. For users interested in more up-to-date UK estimates, please see our <u>Measuring national well-being dashboard</u>.

At-risk-of-poverty rate

The well-being of people who are at-risk-of-poverty may be low as they face important challenges in many aspects of life, including having more limited resources and, therefore, choices. They may be at greater risk of being in debt, suffer poorer health, experience educational disadvantage and may live in poorer housing in less-safe neighborhoods.

An individual is considered to be in poverty if they live in a household with an equivalised disposable income below 60% of the national median. Equivalisation adjusts the income to consider the size and composition of the household. This type of relative indicator does not measure absolute wealth or poverty, but low income in comparison with other residents in that country, which does not necessarily imply a low standard of living.

According to data from the EU Statistics on Income and Living Conditions (EU-SILC) survey, in the UK, 17.0% of people were at risk of living in poverty in 2017, which was very similar to the EU-28 average of 16.9% and that of Malta (16.8%). This proportion has remained generally stable in the UK since 2009 (range: 15.9% to 17.3%).

The lowest-ranking country in 2017 was Romania, with 23.6% of people at risk of living in poverty, while the highest-ranking country was the Czech Republic, with 9.1% of people at risk of poverty.

Satisfaction with household financial situation

Eurobarometer asked people aged 15 years and over how satisfied they were with the financial situation of their household. In the spring of 2018, of people in the UK, 20% reported that the financial situation of their household was very good. This was the same proportion as Austria and Luxembourg, and is higher than the EU-28 average of only 12%. The UK has scored 7 to 12 percentage points above the EU-28 average each year since 2014.

In spring 2018, Denmark had the highest proportion of people rating their household financial situation as very good (43%), while Greece showed the lowest proportion (1%).

Households making ends meet with difficulty or great difficulty

In 2017, of households in the UK, 14.1% were making ends meet with difficulty or great difficulty, according to the EU-SILC survey data (Figure 7). This was a similar proportion to Estonia (14.3%) and was lower than the EU-28 average of 21.6%. In the UK, this proportion has decreased each year since 2013 (21.1%).

The highest-ranking country was Germany, with 6.1% of households reporting making ends meet with difficulty or great difficulty. The lowest-ranking country, with the highest proportion of households struggling to make ends meet, was Greece (77.2%), as has been the case each year since 2011.

Figure 7: The proportion in the UK who find it difficult to make ends meet was lower than the EU-28 average

EU-28, 2017

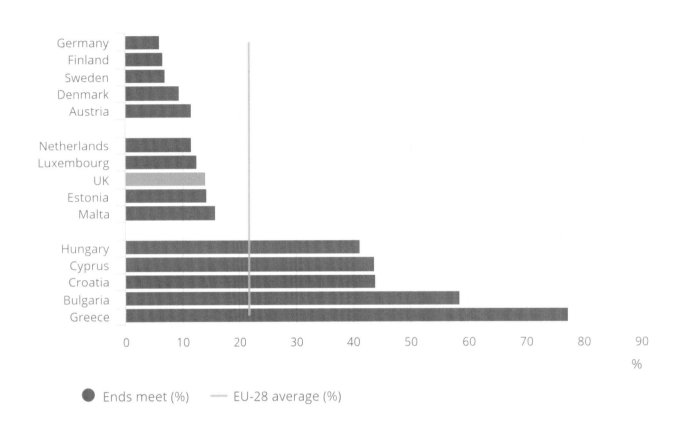

Figure 7: The proportion in the UK who find it difficult to make ends meet was lower than the EU-28 average

EU-28, 2017

Source: Eurostat

Notes:

1. Chart shows the countries with the highest and lowest values along with the countries that have the same or similar values to the UK.

9 . Economy

The UK's government debt increased by 0.9 percentage points between 2016 and 2017. This compared with an average decrease of 0.4 percentage points across the Organisation for Economic Co-operation and Development (OECD).

Net national income (2015 to 2016) and inflation rates (Quarter 1 (Jan to Mar) 2018 to Quarter 3 (July to Sept) 2018) all remained similar. Inflation in the UK is similar to the average inflation rate of 2.3% across OECD countries.

For more detailed information, please see the Measuring national well-being international comparisons dataset.

It is important to note that figures for "economy" only cover the period up to 2016 to 2018 (Quarter 3) because these are the latest internationally comparable data. For users interested in more up-to-date UK estimates, please see Measuring national well-being dashboard and recent UK figures on inflation rates and government debt.

10 . Education and skills

Equipping current and future generations with the necessary skills to keep the UK in a strong and favourable position is an important part of sustaining both our personal and societal well-being into the future.

The proportion of young people not in education, employment or training has declined in the UK year-on-year since 2012 and in 2017 was below the Organisation for Economic Co-operation and Development (OECD) average of 15.6%. At the same time, when comparing with other countries, the UK had a higher proportion of those aged 25 to 64 years that attained less than an upper secondary level of education (18.8%), whilst Japan had the lowest at 0.5%.

It is important to note that figures for education and skills only cover the period up to 2017 because these are the latest internationally-comparable data. For users interested in more up-to-date UK estimates, please see our Measuring national well-being dashboard and recent UK figures on those not in employment, education or training .

20- to 24-year-olds not in employment, education, or training

A young person identified as not in employment, education, or training (NEET) is either unemployed or economically inactive and is either looking for work or is inactive for reasons other than being a student, an apprentice or a carer at home.

In 2017, in the UK, 12.9% of people aged 20 to 24 years were NEET. This was a similar proportion to Austria (11.8%) and was lower than the OECD average of 15.6%. The proportion of NEETs in the UK has decreased each year since 2012, down from 20.2%.

The highest-ranking countries, with the lowest proportions of NEETs in 2017, were Iceland (5.6%) and the Netherlands (7.7%). The lowest-ranking country, with the highest proportion of 20- to 24-year-olds NEETs was Turkey (32.9%), followed by Italy (30.1%), which have alternated bottom two ranking countries each year since 2013.

Educational attainments below upper secondary education

Educational attainment may be a predictor of an individual's future financial well-being. For example, people who have completed higher levels of education are more likely to achieve economic success than those who have not.

According to data from the OECD, in 2017, nearly one in five people (18.8%) aged 25 to 64 years in the UK had attained less than an upper secondary level of education (equivalent to UK "A" Levels). This means their highest level of qualification was only up to lower secondary education (Figure 8). This was similar to Australia (19.0%) and the OECD average (21.8%).

The highest-ranking countries in 2017 were Japan (0.5%) and the Czech Republic (6.2%). Conversely, the lowest-ranking countries were Turkey (60.7%) and Mexico (58.8%).

Figure 8: Proportion of those aged 25 to 64 years with below upper secondary education was lower than the OECD average

OECD countries, 2017

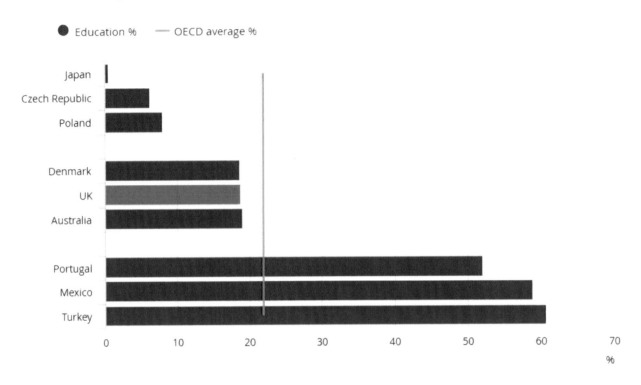

OECD countries, 2017

● Education %   — OECD average %

Source: Organisation for Economic Co-operation and Development

Notes:

1. Chart shows the countries with the highest and lowest values along with the countries that have the same or similar values to the UK.

11 . Governance

Political engagement and voicing political opinions matters to national well-being as it helps shape government activities, which in turn help build strong and resilient communities. People's quality of life may be affected by the functioning of the EU, the national government or parliament, and devolved and local governments, all of which exert an influence over different areas of life.

It is important to note that figures for governance only cover the period up to 2016 to 2017 because these are the latest internationally-comparable data. For users interested in more up-to-date UK estimates, please see Measuring national well-being dashboard.

Confidence in national government

Having confidence in government is essential for social cohesion and well-being. It represents the confidence of citizens and businesses in the actions of the government.

In Great Britain, 41% of people aged 15 years and over reported having confidence in the national government in 2016, according to data from the Organisation for Economic Co-operation and Development (OECD). This was an increase of 5 percentage points since 2007 and was similar to the OECD average of 42% and the findings for Belgium and the Czech Republic (both also 42%).

In Switzerland, four-fifths (80%) of people reported feeling confidence in their national government in 2016, making it the highest-ranked country. Greece had the lowest proportion reporting confidence in their national government (13%).

Although voting turnout is not discussed in this section, it is included in the Measuring national well-being international comparisons dataset.

To provide further insight into how the views of people in the UK compare with those of people in other European countries on matters of governance we look in greater detail at findings on trust in public institutions, perceptions of having a voice and feeling attached to the EU, satisfaction with democracy and views about a possible future outside the EU.

The data are from the Standard Eurobarometer Survey and focus on differences between people aged 15 years and over in the UK and the EU. Two Standard Eurobarometer surveys have been used to compare changes over time, spring 2016 (fieldwork carried out May 2016) and spring 2018 (fieldwork carried out March 2018).

Trust in institutions

Figure 9 compares the views of people in the UK and the EU-28 average on the extent to which they have trust in important civic institutions.

Compared with the EU-28 average, people in the UK are less likely to trust the EU. Looking at the proportion in the UK who said that they did not trust the EU, a similar proportion also said they did not trust the UK Parliament and government. On the other hand, people in the UK tended to trust the army, police and judicial system more than the EU-28 average.

In spring 2016, the percentage of people in the UK saying they trusted the EU was very similar to the EU-28 average (30% and 33% respectively). By the spring of 2018, people in the UK remained unchanged in their level of trust in the EU, while across the EU-28, trust in the EU had increased on average by 9 percentage points.

In spring 2018, Lithuania (66%), Portugal and Denmark (both 57%) led the EU-28 on reporting that they tended to trust the EU. Conversely, Greece (69%), the UK (57%) and the Czech Republic (56%) reported that they tended not to trust the EU.

A similar pattern emerged in relation to trust in the UK government or Parliament with these remaining stable over the period or falling slightly, while the EU-28 averages for trust in these national institutions increased over the period. In spring 2018, Luxembourg (72%) and the Netherlands (67%) led the EU-28 on reporting that they tended to trust their national government. Conversely, Greece (87%), Croatia (82%) and Spain (81%) reported that they tended not to trust their national government.

Figure 9 also shows the tendency to trust institutions such as the army, police and legal systems. In spring 2018, the majority of people in the UK reported that they tended to trust the army (84%), the police (76%) and the UK legal system (61%). A higher proportion of people in the UK tended to trust these institutions when compared with the EU-28 average.

Figure 9: People in the UK trusted the army, police and judicial system more than the EU, government and Parliament in spring 2018

EU-28 average and UK, spring 2016 and spring 2018

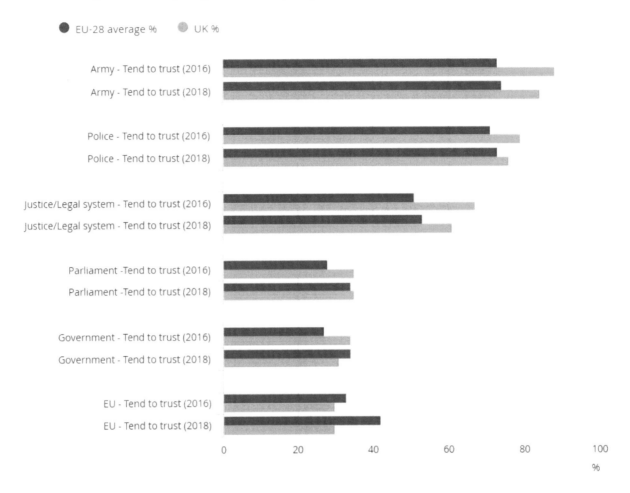

EU-28 average and UK, spring 2016 and spring 2018

Source: Standard Eurobarometer 85 and 89

Notes:

1. Respondents were asked "For each of the following institutions, please tell me if you tend to trust it or tend not to trust it." The chart includes only those who reported "Tend to trust".

Having a voice and feeling attached

Civic engagement and governance are essential for democracies. OECD stated in 2011 that "Civic Engagement allows people to express their voice and to contribute to the political functioning of their society. In turn, in well-functioning democracies, civic engagement shapes the institutions that govern people's lives."

In spring 2018, nearly 6 in 10 people in the UK (59%) disagreed that their voice counted in the EU, compared with 35% who agreed their voice counted in the EU. In the same period, the EU average of those who agreed that their voice counted in the EU reached a new high of 45% (up 7 percentage points since spring 2016). However, the proportion of people in the UK who agreed or disagreed that their voice counted in the EU remained the same as in 2016.

Figure 10 shows an even split across all the EU-28 countries as to whether the majority of people feel their voice counts in the EU or not – with the UK being one in which people were more likely to say that their voice did not count.

Other countries in which a greater proportion of people also disagreed that their voice counts in the EU include Greece (73%), Estonia (70%) and the Czech Republic (67%) all having higher percentages of people than the UK disagreeing they have a voice in the EU. A majority of respondents agreed that their voice counts in the European Union in 14 member states led by Denmark (66%) and Germany and Sweden (both 65%).

Figure 10: Over half of respondents in 13 member states agreed that their voice counted in the EU

EU-28, spring 2016 and spring 2018

EU-28, spring 2016 and spring 2018

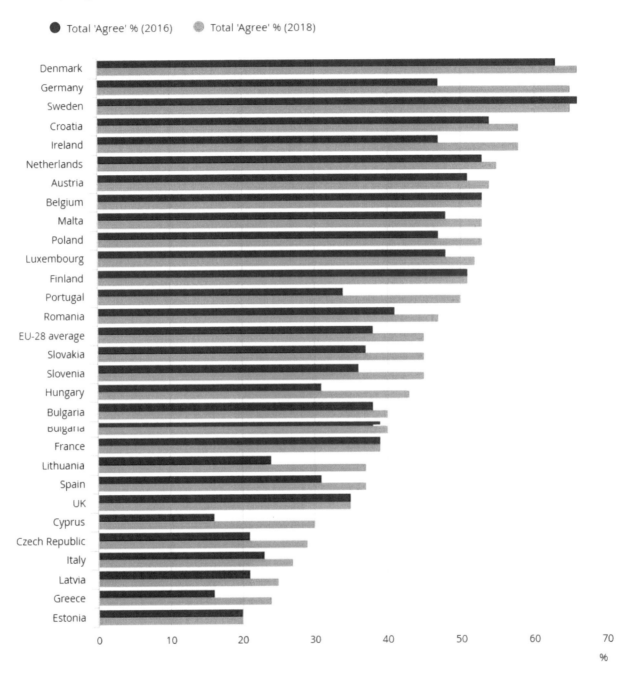

● Total 'Agree' % (2016)　　◐ Total 'Agree' % (2018)

Source: Standard Eurobarometer 85 and 89

Notes:

1. Respondents were asked "Please tell me to what extent you agree or disagree with each of the following statement - My voice counts in the EU". This chart includes only those that agreed with the statement.

In 2018, over half of people (53%) aged 15 years and over in the UK reported that they were "not attached" to the EU compared with 44% that reported that they were. Interestingly, when asked about an attachment to "Europe", over half (57%) reported an "attachment", while 40% reported a "non-attachment". This may be evidence that people in the UK might see themselves as European without connecting strongly to EU governance.

Satisfaction with democracy

People were also asked about their satisfaction with democracy in their own country and in the EU. Democracy can be measured in many ways, for example: regular, free and fair elections; open public debate on major policies and legislation; and citizens' rights to information about the national government and the way it functions. People, themselves, also may have different interpretations of what democracy is or should be.

In spring 2018, just over 6 in 10 people in the UK (61%) reported that they were satisfied with the way democracy works in the UK, a similar proportion to spring 2016 (62%). However, when asked if they were satisfied with the way democracy works in the EU, the proportion was lower at 42% (up from 38% in spring 2016).

Figure 11 shows a comparison of satisfaction with democracy (in their own country and the EU) among people in the EU member states in spring 2018.

Of the 18 countries where a majority of people were satisfied with the way democracy works in their respective countries, Denmark (90%) and Luxembourg (88%) ranked the highest, while Greece ranked the lowest (23%).

Of the 20 countries where a majority of people were satisfied with the way democracy works in the EU, Ireland ranked the highest (75%), while Greece again ranked the lowest (30%).

It is also interesting to note, that some countries, such as Croatia, Italy, Greece and Latvia among others, were more satisfied with democracy in the EU than in their own country while other EU countries, such as Belgium, Denmark, Ireland and Finland, were more satisfied with how democracy works in their own country than in the EU. This suggests people in the UK are not alone in having greater faith in democracy in their own country than in the EU, but equally, people in many other countries have more faith in the EU than in their own democracy.

Figure 11: UK are not alone in having greater faith in democracy in their own country than in the EU

EU-28, spring 2018

EU-28, spring 2018

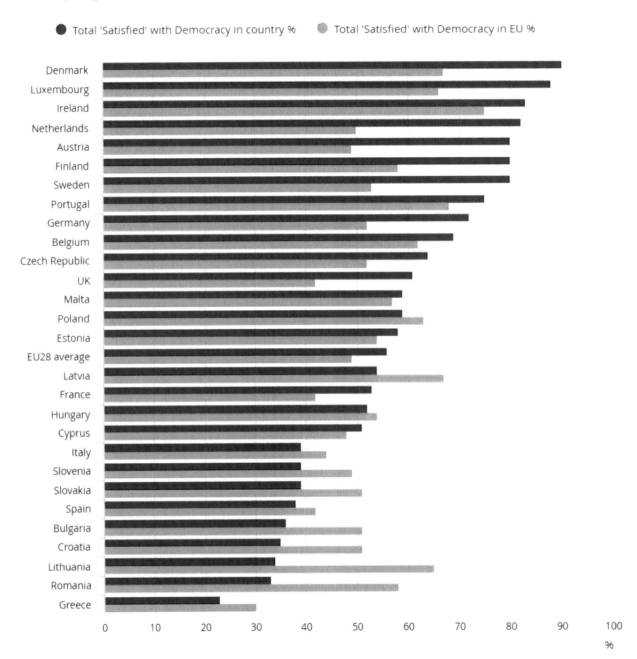

● Total 'Satisfied' with Democracy in country %   ● Total 'Satisfied' with Democracy in EU %

Source: Standard Eurobarometer 89

Respondents were asked whether they agreed or disagreed with the statement that their country could face a better future outside the EU. In 2018, a similar proportion of people in the UK either agreed (44%) or disagreed (43%) with the statement, with 13% reporting that they did not know. This compared with an EU average of 30% and 61% respectively. In 2018, the proportion of people who agreed that the UK could better face the future outside the EU hardly changed from the proportion in spring 2016 (45%).

Although the UK had the highest proportion of people among the 28 EU member states agreeing that their country faced a better future outside the EU in spring 2018, the proportion in the UK disagreeing that the country faced a better future outside the EU increased by 6 percentage points since spring 2016.

Figure 12 shows that, after the UK, the countries in which the highest proportions of people agreeing their country faced a better future outside the EU in spring 2018 were Slovenia (43%), Austria and Italy (both 41%). Countries in which the smallest proportions of people agreed with this were the Netherlands (12%), Denmark (14%) and Germany (15%).

Figure 12: The UK had the highest proportion of people that agreed that their country faced a better future outside the EU in spring 2018

EU-28, spring 2016 and spring 2018

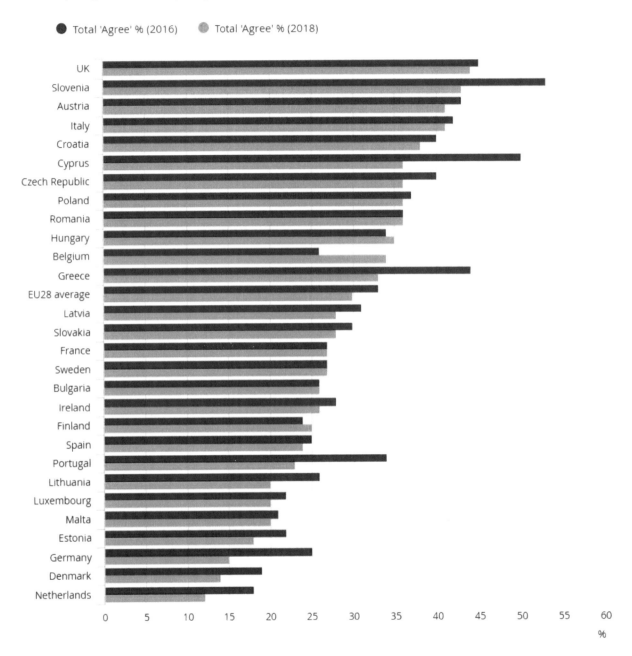

EU-28, spring 2016 and spring 2018

● Total 'Agree' % (2016)　　● Total 'Agree' % (2018)

Source: Standard Eurobarometer 85 and 89

Notes:

1. Respondents were asked "Please tell me to what extent you agree or disagree with each of the following statement - (Our Country) could better face the future outside the EU". The chart includes only those who agreed with the statement.

12 . Natural environment

Well-being is determined by physical and non-physical factors. The ability of a society to produce and consume goods and services determines its standard of living, but in the long-run even more critical is its ability to build and maintain the natural environment that meets basic needs like food, water and clean air, and preserving this for future generations.

Overall, some indicators of environmental quality suggest improvements in the UK. For example, the proportion of marine and terrestrial protected areas increased by 6.1 percentage points between 2010 and 2014, although this is lower than the average increase of 7.5 percentage points across Organisation for Economic Co-operation and Development (OECD) countries. Recycling and composting, and renewable energy usage remained stable between 2015 and 2016 in the UK.

Although protected areas are not discussed in this section, it is included in the Measuring national well-being international comparisons dataset.

It is important to note that figures for natural environment only cover the period up to 2014 to 2016 because these are the latest internationally-comparable data. For users interested in more up-to-date UK estimates, please see Measuring national well-being dashboard.

Greenhouse gas emissions

To mitigate climate change, countries around the world are developing policies to enhance environmental sustainability in areas such as transportation, housing and energy use, to reduce greenhouse gas emissions. In addition to their effects on greenhouse gas emissions, these policies are likely to have consequences, such as accessing high-quality, natural spaces close to where they work and live, encouraging people to spend more time in them benefitting health and well-being.

Figures from the OECD show that the UK's greenhouse gas emissions were 486.3 million tonnes of carbon dioxide equivalent (MtCO2e) in 2016, making it the ninth-highest among OECD countries. Greenhouse gas emissions in the UK have been declining each year since 2008, down from 657.0 MtCO2e. In 2016, this figure was similar to Turkey (496.1 MtCO2e).

The countries with the highest total emissions in 2016 were the United States (6,511.3 MtCO2e) and Japan (1,304.6 MtCO2e), while Iceland had the lowest emissions (4.7 MtCO2e).

Energy from renewable sources

Using renewable sources for supplying energy may enhance human welfare in terms of health and environmental improvements, and contribute to a climate safe future.

In 2017, renewable energy sources accounted for 9.6% of the UK's total primary energy supply, according to data from the OECD (Figure 13). This proportion has been increasing each year, up from 3.6% in 2010. A similar proportion of renewable energy usage in 2017 was seen in Slovakia (9.5%) and France (9.8%), although all were lower than the OECD average of 10.2%.

The lowest shares of renewable energy as a percentage of primary energy supply in 2017 were found in Korea (2.0%) and Israel (2.4%). The highest proportions were found in Iceland (88.5%) and Norway (52.8%).

Figure 13: The UK's renewable contribution to the total primary energy supply was just under the OECD average

OECD countries, 2017

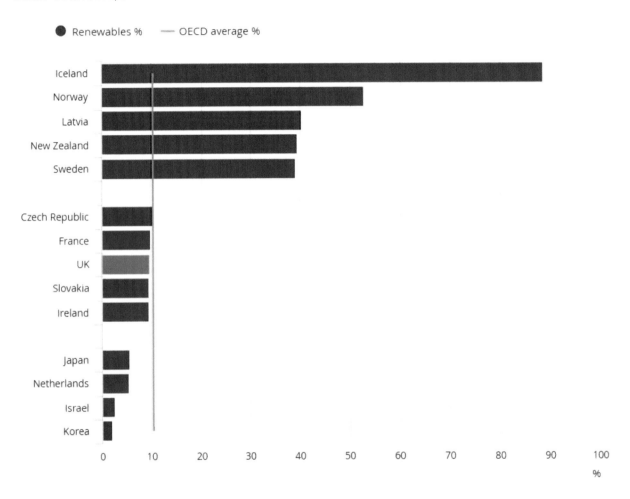

OECD countries, 2017

● Renewables %   — OECD average %

Source: Organisation for Economic Co-operation and Development

Notes:

1. Renewable energy is defined as the contribution of renewables to total primary energy supply (TPES). Renewables include the primary energy equivalent of hydro (excluding pumped storage), geothermal, solar, wind, tide and wave sources. Energy derived from solid biofuels, biogasoline, biodiesels, other liquid biofuels, biogases and the renewable fraction of municipal waste are also included. Municipal waste comprises wastes produced by the residential, commercial and public service sectors that are collected by local authorities for disposal in a central location for the production of heat and/or power.

2. The reference period for Greece is 2016.

3. Chart shows the countries with the highest and lowest values along with the countries that have the same or similar values to the UK.

Material recovery (recycling and composting)

According to data from the OECD, 44% of the UK's municipal waste was recycled or composted in 2016, a proportion that has remained stable since 2010 (range: 40% to 44%). This was the same proportion as Poland and higher than the OECD average of 36%.

In Germany, two-thirds (66%) of municipal waste was recycled or composted in 2016, making it the highest-ranking of the OECD countries, followed by Slovenia (60%). The lowest-ranking country in 2016 was Turkey, where only 10% of waste was recycled or composted.

13 . What are our main concerns at national level?

To set the full range of well-being indicators in context, it is crucial to understand people's priorities and concerns. In response to user feedback requesting more timely and detailed analysis on important issues that may affect well-being, we have analysed data from the Standard Eurobarometer Survey comparing the views and priorities of people aged 15 years and over in the UK and the EU.

Two Standard Eurobarometer surveys have been used for comparison, spring 2016 (fieldwork carried out in May 2016) and spring 2018 (fieldwork carried out March 2018). People aged 15 years and over were asked what the two most important issues facing their country were in spring 2016 and again in spring 2018.

Figure 14 shows the top concerns for the UK and the EU-28 in spring 2016. Unemployment and immigration were the two most frequently reported concerns across the EU-28 (33% and 28% respectively). For the UK, the issues that people said they were most concerned about were immigration at 38% and health and social security at 26%.

Figure 14: The most important issue facing the UK in spring 2016 was immigration

EU-28, spring 2016

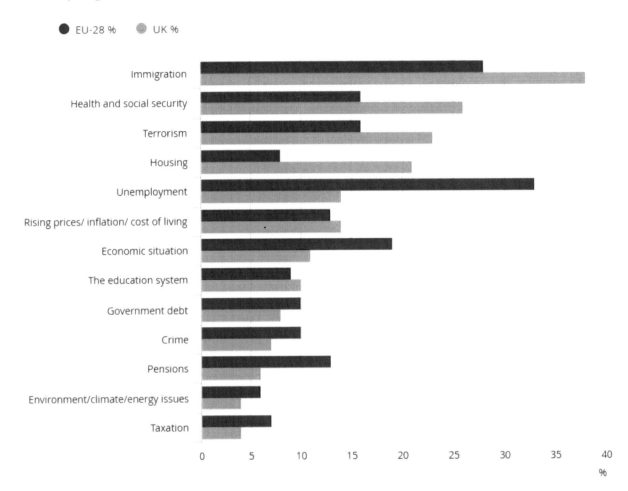

EU-28, spring 2016

● EU-28 %   ○ UK %

id="1"

Immigration	
Health and social security	
Terrorism	
Housing	
Unemployment	
Rising prices/ inflation/ cost of living	
Economic situation	
The education system	
Government debt	
Crime	
Pensions	
Environment/climate/energy issues	
Taxation	

0   5   10   15   20   25   30   35   40

%

Source: Standard Eurobarometer 85

Notes:

1. Respondents were asked "What do you think are the two most important issues facing in your country at the moment? " A maximum of two issues were allowed. The chart does not include those who stated "Other", "None" and "Don't know".

As shown in Figure 15, by the spring of 2018, unemployment (25%) remained the top concern on average across the EU-28 but health and social security (23%) had become the next most important concern, with immigration dropping back to third place (21%). Over the same period, concerns about health and social security became the top concern for people in the UK, followed by housing (33% and 22% respectively).

Figure 15: The most important issue facing the UK in spring 2018 was health and social security

EU-28, spring 2018

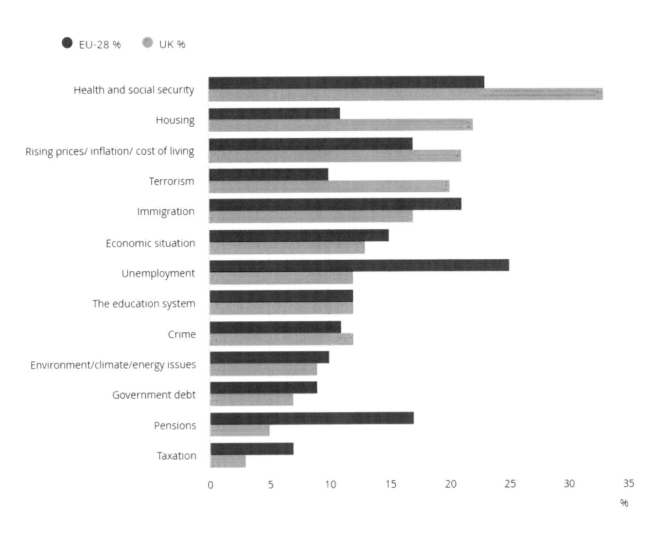

Source: Standard Eurobarometer 89

Notes:

1. Respondents were asked "What do you think are the two most important issues facing in your country at the moment? " A maximum of two issues were allowed. The chart does not include those who stated "Other", "None" and "Don't know".

14 . Next steps

This article has explored how quality of life and well-being in the UK compares with that in other countries of the Organisation for Economic Co-operation and Development (OECD) or the European Union (EU) countries, using measures similar to those adopted as part of the UK's national well-being measures. Looking at the measures within these areas of life from an international perspective gives us a sense of whether quality of life in the UK is better or worse than in other countries.

We plan to explore well-being inequalities, particularly in relation to personal and household circumstances and we will continue to monitor changes in well-being to assess how we feel about our lives and our daily emotions. We also intend to focus more on the environmental aspects of well-being, both in terms of how the environment affects our living standards now and the extent to which growth is environmentally sustainable. In doing this, we will move a step closer to looking holistically at "people, prosperity and the planet".

15 . Technical notes

Sources used in International comparisons, 2019

Eurobarometer
European Quality of Life Survey
Eurostat
Gallup World Poll
International Institute for Democracy and Electoral Assistance
Organisation for Economic Co-operation and Development
United Nations Statistics Division
World Health Organisation

The Organisation for Economic Co-operation and Development (OECD)

The OECD is an international economic organisation of 36 countries, founded in 1961 to stimulate economic progress and world trade. It is a forum of countries describing themselves as committed to democracy and the market economy, providing a platform to compare policy experiences, seeking answers to common problems, identify good practices and coordinate domestic and international policies of its members.

OECD member countries are: Australia, Austria, Belgium, Canada, Chile, Czech Republic, Denmark, Estonia, Finland, France, Germany, Greece, Hungary, Iceland, Ireland, Israel, Italy, Japan, Korea (South Korea), Latvia, Lithuania, Luxembourg, Mexico, the Netherlands, New Zealand, Norway, Poland, Portugal, Slovakia, Slovenia, Spain, Sweden, Switzerland, Turkey, the UK and the United States.

The European Union (EU)

The EU was created on 1 November 1993, when the Maastricht Treaty came into force. It encompasses the old European Community (EC) together with two intergovernmental "pillars" for dealing with foreign affairs and with immigration and justice. The European Union consists of 28 member states (EU-28); where the EU-27 is referred to in this article, Croatia is not included.

The 28 member states are: Austria, Belgium, Bulgaria, Croatia, Cyprus, Czech Republic, Denmark, Estonia, Finland, France, Germany, Greece, Hungary, Ireland, Italy, Latvia, Lithuania, Luxembourg, Malta, the Netherlands, Poland, Portugal, Romania, Slovakia, Slovenia, Spain, Sweden, and the UK.

Article

Exploring loneliness in children, Great Britain: 2018

Analysis of children's (aged 10 to 15 years) reporting of loneliness and perception of their circumstances from The Children's Society Household Survey.

Contact:
Ellie Osborn
qualityoflife@ons.gov.uk
+44 (0)1633 651830

Release date:
3 April 2019

Next release:
To be announced

Table of contents

1 . Main points

The relationship between children's loneliness and their circumstances has been explored by seeing if each factor has a relationship when others are taken into account.

On average, the odds of children reporting loneliness are increased if:

- they have low happiness with their relationships with friends

- they have low happiness with the amount of choice they have

- their parent or guardian doesn't have very high life satisfaction

- they live in a city

- their household is in relative poverty

When taking other factors into account, the following are not significant in children's reporting of loneliness:

- age

- gender

- ethnicity

- number of children in the household

- living in a single parent household

- living away from parents (such as with another relative)

2 . Statistician's comment

"Loneliness is an issue of growing importance to many organisations and policy-makers. Our findings show that the type of area where a child lives and relative poverty are both important, but this research also highlights that the child's perspective of their situation is a significant contributing factor to loneliness."

Dawn Snape, Assistant Divisional Director, Sustainability and Inequalities, Office for National Statistics

3 . Background

In 2018, the Prime Minister announced the government's response to the Jo Cox Commission on Loneliness manifesto. As part of this, she requested that the Office for National Statistics (ONS) develops national measures of loneliness for all ages.

We worked with a cross-government group, charities, academics and other stakeholders, and in December 2018 published guidance and analysis on the National Measurement of Loneliness. As part of this work, it became clear that there is currently much more extensive and robust data available on loneliness in older people, but comparatively little data on how loneliness may affect children and young people.

We worked with The Children's Society to develop the guidance to comprehensively capture younger age groups to ensure the National Measures were suitable for children aged 10 years and over. We published an article in December 2018 using our proposed measures to look at loneliness in children (aged 10 to 15 years) and young people (aged 16 to 24 years), which included interviews with both age groups. The article reported the main findings from both our qualitative and quantitative research in relation to how common loneliness is in children and young people, what loneliness means to them, why they are feeling lonely and how they manage loneliness. The findings came from a sample of around 1,500 children aged 10- to 15-years, who completed The Children's Society Household Survey in 2018. The findings from the in-depth interviews came from a sample of 30 children aged 10- to 15-years.

4 . What does children's loneliness look like?

Loneliness can be normal and transient, but physical, mental and social problems can arise when it becomes chronic. It has been found to have a profoundly negative effect on health at all ages and can be considered to be the "social equivalent of physical pain" (Hawkley and Cacioppo, 2010). Loneliness is associated with poor health outcomes for younger ages as much as for adults (Harris, Robinson, and Qualter, 2013; Qualter and others, 2013).

In our previous analysis, we found that 11.3% of children in Great Britain aged 10 to 15 years answered "often" when asked how often they felt lonely. This answer was more common among younger children aged 10 to 12 years compared with those aged 13 to 15 years. As well as age, satisfaction with health and relationships, and the number of children in the household were also associated with the reporting of loneliness.

Our previous analysis also highlighted a relationship between deprivation and loneliness in children. However, it was unclear whether the association could be driven by other factors linked to both poverty and loneliness, such as family structure. In this article we use logistic regression to investigate if relative poverty is associated with loneliness even when accounting for these other elements.

5 . Things you need to know about this release

The data in this publication are from The Children's Society Household Survey and are not official government data. The survey covers Great Britain and asks questions to those aged 10 to 17 years; this analysis only includes children aged 10 to 15 years as per our definition of a child.

These data were collected in May to June 2018. Gender is self-identified with the response categories [male /female/trans/prefer not to say]; only male and female respondents are included, as is in line with The Children's Society's methods. For more information please see The Children Society's Good Childhood Report 2018 (PDF, 1.30MB).

Logistic regression has been used to analyse circumstances associated with loneliness while taking other factors into account. It allows us to provide a more accurate assessment of a child's reporting of loneliness and potential associated factors. In this article, we have analysed several variables taking a step-by-step approach to exclude and include them depending on their resulting statistical significance. More information on logistic regression can be found in the technical report accompanying our previous analysis on loneliness in those aged 16 years and over. The regression models are in the dataset.

In this publication loneliness is defined as children who answered either "often" or "some of the time" when asked, "How often do you feel lonely?" [Often/ Some of the time/ Hardly ever or never]. 45.4% of the children asked said they felt lonely "often" or "some of the time" compared with 54.6% who said that they felt lonely "hardly ever or never".

Our previous analysis showed that children who received free school meals reported higher levels of loneliness than those who did not; this article explores this relationship. Receipt of free school meals is commonly used as an indicator for childhood poverty. However, as a child may be eligible for free meals but not receive them it was appropriate to choose another measure to ensure accurate assessment of poverty in this analysis.

Relative poverty in this article is defined as those living below 60% of the average (median) equivalised income, a widely-used definition of relative poverty. This measure considers how many adults and children live in the household. The median income has been calculated from adult responses to the question "What is the usual [weekly/monthly/annual] income for your household, after any deductions such as Income Tax or National Insurance, and including any benefits or tax credits received?" within The Children's Society Household Survey. The median of the sample has been used rather than the national median to ensure that our analysis is representative of our respondents. More information on this can be found in the Quality and methodology section.

Income itself is not included in this analysis as it is a component of our poverty definition, and therefore could provide misleading results.

For a list of all variables included in the regression models please see the dataset.

6 . Children in relative poverty had almost twice the odds of reporting feeling lonely

The odds of a child reporting feeling lonely are nearly two times higher than them reporting "hardly ever or never" feeling lonely if they live in a household below the relative poverty threshold (model 1 in the dataset).

When interviewed, children highlighted that loneliness may arise:

"When [children] don't have the stuff that other kids may have. Like for example a new pair of trainers might come out, people might want to get it, they can't get it, they'll feel alone; like why can't I get this, why can't I get that?" (Female, 15 years).

Countries and English regions, being female rather than male, and living in cities compared with rural locations (village, hamlet or isolated rural location) also significantly contribute to loneliness (Figure 1; model 2 in the dataset).

Figure 1: Relative poverty, gender, countries and English regions, and area type independently influence children's loneliness

Significant odds ratios of reporting feeling lonely more often compared with the reference category, Great Britain, children aged 10 to 15 years

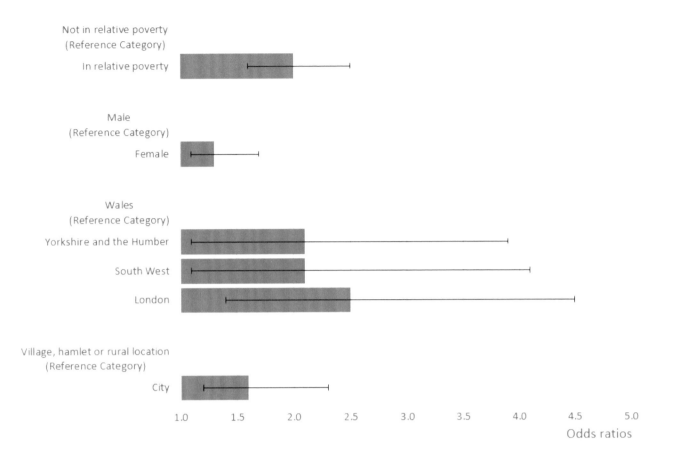

Source: The Children's Society Household Survey

Notes:

1. Odds ratios are reported from the logistic regression to show the odds of a child reporting feeling lonely "often" or "some of the time" in relation to reporting "hardly ever or never" feeling lonely when compared to the reference category within the group.

2. The reference category has been selected as being the category with the lowest proportion of children reporting feeling lonely.

3. 95% confidence intervals are displayed on the chart.

4. All variables on this chart are statistically significantly different to the reference category, which equates to a p value below 0.05. Variables tested at this stage are in model 3 in the dataset.

5. Statistically significant differences can only be reported in comparison with the reference category. For example, reported loneliness in London is statistically significantly higher than in Wales, but is not statistically significantly higher than those in the South West.

6. Definitions of the variables used in this analysis can be found in the dataset.

In our previous analysis, looking at the relationships between loneliness and other variables of interest one at a time, age group and the number of children in the household were significantly related to reported loneliness. In the current analysis, after holding relative poverty, gender, countries and English regions, and area type constant, age and number of children is no longer significantly related to loneliness.

Additionally, children in single parent households and children living away from their parents (for example, with another relative) are not significantly more likely to report loneliness than those who are not in single parent households or living with parents (respectively) when all the other factors are accounted for (model 2 in the dataset).

Having identified that relative poverty is a factor linked to children's reporting of loneliness, we now explore whether this could be related to the main adult's occupation. When at least one parent or guardian is in employment, as well as the type of this employment (such as managerial or routine occupations), are controlled for, the odds of children in relative poverty reporting feeling lonely are still around two times greater than those not in relative poverty (model 4 in the dataset).

7 . How children's happiness with the things they have influences the reporting of loneliness

Our previous research suggested that children may feel left out if they lack things that other children have:

"[They may feel lonely] if they feel they're in a different living situation, for example. If they feel like a friend's got more money than them or things like that. Or if someone's got the latest iPhone and you don't." (Female, 13 years)

To better understand the relationship between loneliness and relative poverty, we examine whether this relationship is affected by the child's perspective of their situation. We assess this by looking at the degree to which children said they were happy with what they have or with their home.

Adding children's happiness with the things they have and happiness with their home into the analysis only mitigated the effect of relative poverty on loneliness slightly, reducing the odds ratio from 1.9 to 1.8 (Figure 2; model 5 in the dataset). Notably, happiness with the things they have and happiness with home had a greater impact on reporting loneliness than being in relative poverty. This suggests relative poverty is more complicated than simply not having enough of something.

Figure 2: Having low happiness with the things they have and low happiness with their home has a greater impact on loneliness in children than relative poverty

Odds ratios of reporting feeling lonely more often compared with the reference category, Great Britain, children aged 10 to 15 years

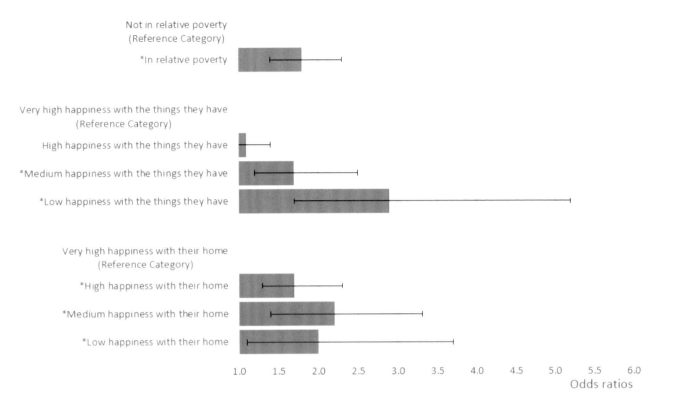

Source: The Children's Society Household Survey

Notes:

1. Odds ratios are reported from the logistic regression to show the odds of a child reporting feeling lonely "often" or "some of the time" in relation to reporting "hardly ever or never" feeling lonely when compared to the reference category within the group.

2. The reference category has been selected as being the category with the lowest proportion of children reporting feeling lonely.

3. 95% confidence intervals are displayed on the chart.

4. Statistically significantly different responses to the reference category, which equates to a p value below 0.05, are marked with an asterisk (*). Not all variables tested in this model are in the graph, please see model 5 in the dataset.

5. Statistically significant differences can only be reported in comparison with the reference category.

6. Definitions of the variables used in this analysis can be found in the dataset.

8 . Children's autonomy and happiness with relationships with friends are the largest significant contributors to loneliness

We next focus on understanding whether children's sense of autonomy is associated with reporting of loneliness. So far, relative poverty, gender, countries and English regions, area type and happiness with both the things they have and happiness with their home are associated with children's reporting of loneliness. When we also consider children's happiness with the amount of choice they have in life, happiness with the things they have no longer influences a child's reporting of loneliness (model 6 in the dataset). The odds of children reporting feeling lonely if they have low happiness with their amount of choice are nearly four times greater than children reporting very high happiness with their amount of choice.

The odds of children reporting loneliness when they are less happy with their home decreases when we include happiness with the amount of choice they feel they have. This suggests that children's autonomy is more important in relation to loneliness than how they feel about more material things.

Happiness with relationships with friends is the last aspect of children's perspectives we focus on. Interestingly, when happiness with relationships with friends is included in the analysis, gender is no longer significantly associated with loneliness (model 8 in the dataset).

As would be expected, children's happiness with their relationships with friends is an important contributor to loneliness even after taking other possible influences into account. The odds of loneliness are seven times greater in children who report low happiness with their relationships with friends compared with children who have very high happiness with their relationships. This factor has the strongest effect on loneliness identified in our analysis, indicating the importance of good relationships with friends (Figure 3).

These are not surprising findings because loneliness itself is defined as a mismatch between the perceived quantity and quality of social relationships a person wants compared with what they have. What is perhaps more interesting is that satisfaction with friendships only explains part of children's loneliness and many other objective circumstances and subjective perceptions also play an important role.

Figure 3: Happiness with relationships with friends has the greatest impact on reported loneliness in children

Odds ratios of reporting feeling lonely more often compared with the reference category, Great Britain, children aged 10 to 15 years

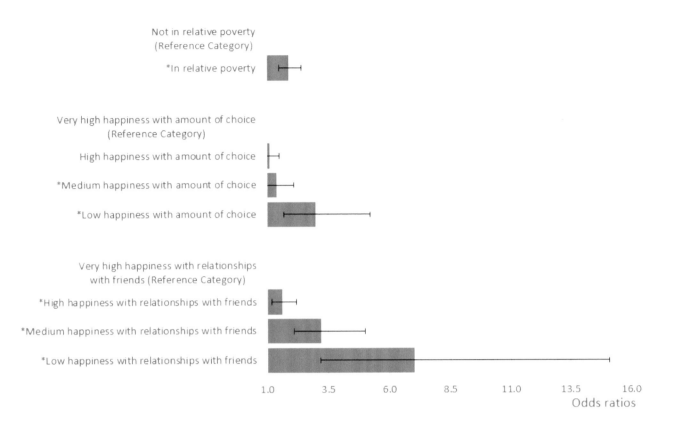

Source: The Children's Society Household Survey

Notes:

1. Odds ratios are reported from the logistic regression to show the odds of a child reporting feeling lonely "often" or "some of the time" in relation to reporting "hardly ever or never" feeling lonely when compared to the reference category within the group.

2. The reference category has been selected as being the category with the lowest proportion of children reporting feeling lonely.

3. Statistically significantly different responses to the reference category, which equates to a p value below 0.05, are marked with an asterisk (*). Not all variables tested in this model are in the graph, please see model 8 in the dataset.

4. Statistically significant differences can only be reported in comparison with the reference category.

5. 95% confidence intervals are displayed on the chart.

To explore why gender is no longer associated with loneliness, we look at the proportion reporting happiness with relationships with friends by gender and reporting of loneliness. In the sample, twice as many females than males report low happiness with relationships with friends. However, among those who report feeling lonely, females are four times more likely than males to report low happiness with relationships with friends. This could suggest that the commonly-noted association between gender and loneliness may be due to the differing expectations and quality of friendships of females and males (for example, Parker and Asher, 1993).

9 . How adults' life satisfaction levels contribute to children's loneliness

The final factor we focus on is whether adults' perspectives on their lives are associated with children's reporting of loneliness. In this survey, the main adult (whether a parent, guardian or other significant care giver) in the child's household was asked a series of questions about their life satisfaction (Student's Life Satisfaction Scale (SLSS); Huebner, 1991), which were used in this analysis. Please note that this is not the ONS question on life satisfaction.

When controlling for other circumstances found to be significantly related to children's loneliness (relative poverty, countries and English regions, area type, happiness with their home, happiness with amount of choice and happiness with relationships with friends), the main adult's life satisfaction score is also significantly associated with children's reporting of loneliness (model 9 in the dataset).

This showed that children living with a parent or guardian whose life satisfaction is very high are less likely to report loneliness than children whose parents or guardians rated their life satisfaction at lower levels.

10 . Conclusions

The findings from this article highlight certain risk factors associated with children's loneliness, with a focus on relative poverty and children's own perspectives on their lives. Our findings show that the type of area where a child lives and relative poverty are both important, but this research also highlights that the child's perspective of their situation is also an important contributing factor to loneliness. This is an area that can often be overlooked when studying loneliness in children (Asher and Paquette, 2003) and, indeed, across all ages (Qualter and others, 2015).

Our previous qualitative research provided suggestions from children and young people themselves, as to how loneliness could be improved including the desire for greater openness about discussing relationships at school and elsewhere. This research also highlights how the life satisfaction of significant adults in their lives can contribute to feelings of loneliness in children.

11 . Quality and methodology

Poverty and income

Poverty was previously reported by us using free school meals . However, this measure suffers from several shortcomings. Firstly, not all children who are eligible for free school meals have them. Second, the receipt of a free school meal was self-reported by the children and therefore may be subject to measurement error. Therefore, it was decided that a more precise measure was needed for the analysis in this article.

To create a more robust measure, we define individuals in poverty using a relative measure, such as that reported by the Department for Work and Pensions (DWP) in their Households below average income (HBAI) publication. This defines an individual, including children, as being in relative poverty if they live in a household with income less than 60% of the median. While we could have used the national median income as reported by HBAI to make this more consistent, due to the sampling of the survey (see the next section), the way the income information was collected and because our data only include households with children, we use the median income within the sample.

The income variable in this sample is "What is the usual [weekly/monthly/annual] income for your household, after any deductions such as Income Tax or National Insurance, and including any benefits or tax credits received?". Annual income was equivalised (using the Organisation for Economic Co-operation and Development (OECD) equivalisation scale (PDF, 165KB)), which accounts for the fact that households with many members are likely to need a higher income to meet their needs. It considers the number of people living in the household and their ages.

Statistical significance, odds ratios and sampling

Statistical significance is used in this article to communicate that a relationship between two variables is greater than would be expected by chance. When referring to proportions, the statistical significance of differences noted within the release are based on non-overlapping 95% confidence intervals (that is, the two bounds within which we are 95% sure the true figure lies, when taking into account sampling and variation). If it is part of the logistic regression analysis, a p-value of less than 0.05 was taken as significant.

Odds are the ratio of the probability that an event occurs to the probability that it does not. In our case:

$$\text{The odds of reporting loneliness} = \frac{\text{the probability of reporting loneliness "often" or "some of the time"}}{\text{the probability of reporting loneliness "hardly ever or never"}}$$

The odds ratio shows the relative difference in odds between two groups and is defined as the ratio of the odds of one group to another. For instance, if the odds of reporting feeling lonely are twice greater for females than males, then the odds ratio would be equal to two. An odds ratio of one tells us that the odds are the same in the two groups. The odds ratio can be easily computed based on the coefficients of a logistic regression and we use the odds ratio to present results from the regression models.

An odds ratio is said to be statistically significant (for example, significantly greater or lower than one) if the p-value of the log odds ratio (the coefficient of the logistic model) is lower than 0.05. It means that the odds ratio in the population has 95% chance to be greater than one. In other words, if we replicated our analysis 100 times, we would expect the odds ratio to be greater than 1 in 95 of the replications.

Please note that the results have been discussed on the basis of unrounded data.

Please note that because The Children's Society's Household Survey is based on quota sampling rather than probability sampling, the hypothesis testing methods used in this article should only be interpreted as indicative.

The survey: age, gender, and missing cases

Children were asked about loneliness as part of The Children's Society Household Survey, conducted in 2018, which covers Great Britain. The sample originally included young people aged 10 to 17 years, but we have only focused on those aged 10 to 15 years to correspond with our previous analysis. Children self-identified their gender, but the number of children who identified as transgender was too small for robust statistical analysis (for more information please see The Children Society's Good Childhood Report 2018 (PDF, 1.30MB)). The sample size included in the analysis was 1,540 children after removing those aged 16 to 17 years. This also excluded cases where children did not answer the loneliness question.

Statistical methods

We carried out a logistic regression to see if the factors we had identified previously as playing a part in children's loneliness were still significant when analysed together. This particular analysis took a step-by-step approach.

We first looked at objective measures to see which factors were significant (models 1 and 2 in the dataset), then worked through a number of subjective factors to explore the overall relationship between these and loneliness. Creating dichotomised loneliness in the logistic regression is in line with our previous analysis as it makes the distribution more even. Please see the technical report from the analysis for more information on logistic regression and how it is used. This logistic regression was carried out in the statistical package R v 3.4.0.

12 . References

Asher, S. R., and Paquette, J. A. (2003). Loneliness and peer relations in childhood. Current Directions in Psychological Science, volume 12(3), pages 75 to 78

Harris, R., Qualter, P. and Robinson, S.J. (2013). Loneliness trajectories from middle childhood to pre-adolescence: impact on perceived health and sleep disturbance. Journal of Adolescence, volume 36, pages 1295 to 1304

Hawkley, L. C. and Cacioppo, J. T. (2010). Loneliness matters: a theoretical and empirical review of consequences and mechanisms. Annals of Behavioral Medicine, volume 40(2), pages 218 to 227

Huebner, E. S. (1991). Initial development of the student's life satisfaction scale. School Psychology International, volume 12(3), pages 231 to 240

Parker, J. G. and Asher, S. R. (1993). Friendship and friendship quality in middle childhood: links with peer group acceptance and feelings of loneliness and social dissatisfaction. Developmental Psychology, volume 29, pages 611 to 621

Qualter, P., Brown, S.L., Rotenberg, K.J., Vanhalst, J, Harris, R.A., Goossens, L, Bangee, M. and Munn, P. (2013). Trajectories of loneliness during childhood and adolescence: predictors and health outcomes. Journal of Adolescence, volume 36, pages 1283 to 1293

Qualter, P., Vanhalst, J., Harris, R.A., Lodder, G., Bangee, M., Van Roekel, E., Verhagen, M. and Maes, M. (2015). Loneliness across the lifespan. Perspectives on Psychological Science, volume 10, pages 250 to 264

Article

Personal and economic well-being: what matters most to our life satisfaction?

Insights into socio-demographic and economic factors that matter to life satisfaction, such as an individual's characteristics or circumstances as well as household income and spending.

Contact:
Gueorguie Vassilev or Silvia Manclossi
PeopleAndProsperity@ons.gov. uk
+44 (0)1633 456265 or +44 (0) 1633 582486

Release date:
15 May 2019

Next release:
To be announced

Table of contents

1 . Main points

- Self-reported health, marital status and economic activity have the strongest associations with how positively we rate our life satisfaction.

- Comparing this with previous findings, marital status appears to matter more for people's life satisfaction in October 2017 to September 2018 than it did six years before, while economic activity contributed less.

- Age is the personal characteristic most strongly related to life satisfaction, with younger people reporting higher life satisfaction; this falls in middle age and rises again in later years.

- People who own their home outright or with a mortgage rate their life satisfaction more highly than those living in both private and social rented housing.

- In terms of household economic circumstances, higher household spending is more strongly related to how we rate our life satisfaction than higher household income, though both matter less than personal circumstances.

- How we spend our money also matters; comparing people with the same level of spending, those able to spend a higher share on experiences, such as hotels and restaurants, are more likely to be very satisfied with life than those spending more on food, insurance and mobile phone subscriptions.

2 . Introduction

In February 2019, we introduced a new series on "people and prosperity" as part of our "Beyond GDP" initiative, bringing together personal and economic well-being for the first time. The aim is to provide timely, quarterly indicators and analysis of household financial health as well as personal well-being. This release follows on from this in looking beyond gross domestic product (GDP) and investigating how a range of factors, including economic well-being indicators, may have a direct impact on people's personal well-being – as this is a clear area of interest identified by our users.

We have revisited the work carried out in relation to What matters most to Personal Well-being?, replicating analysis where possible, to enable comparisons from April 2011 to March 2012 to October 2017 to September 2018. We also built on other analysis, Income, Expenditure and Personal Well-being, to better examine the relationship between personal well-being and household income and spending.

Regression analysis is used to examine associations between personal well-being and individual characteristics and circumstances. This technique can identify the strength of these relationships but not cause and effect. Regression analysis can be used for prediction (how likely something is to occur given certain conditions); for example, how likely someone is to report higher life satisfaction given their age group or their marital status.

As was found in our What matters most to Personal Well-being? release, we can explain more of the variance in life satisfaction than the other three measures of personal well-being, so that is why we focus on it in this article, but we do discuss the other well-being measures where notable and provide the analysis in the accompanying datasets.

For further explanation of our approach and how to interpret our findings, see Section 9 and Section 10. For all the regression models reported in this article, see the datasets.

3 . Most important factors affecting life satisfaction

Figure 1: Reporting better general health increases the likelihood of higher life satisfaction more than any other factor

Odds ratios of factors affecting life satisfaction, UK, April 2016 to March 2017

Odds ratios of factors affecting life satisfaction, UK, April 2016 to March 2017

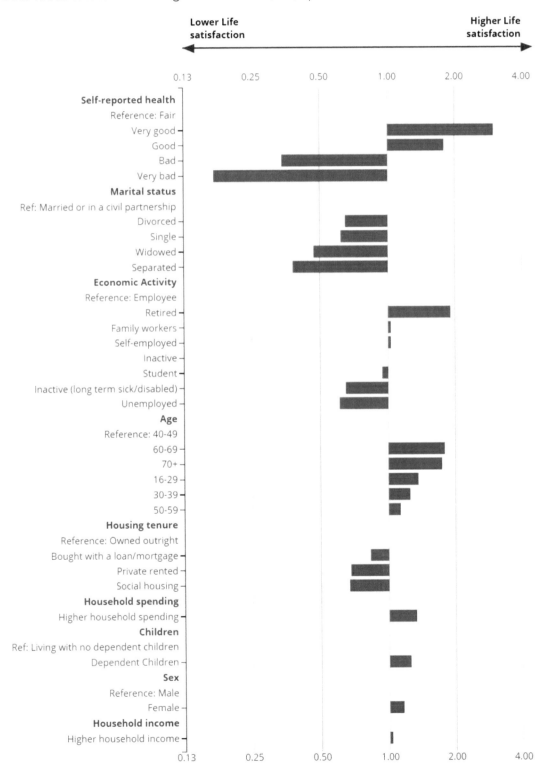

Source: Office for National Statistics - Effects of Taxes and Benefits (ETB)

Notes:

1. This chart reports findings from the ETB. Similar models using the bigger sample from the Annual Population Survey (APS) are broadly aligned and available in the datasets.

2. This chart includes a selection of factors having the highest impact on personal well-being. See the APS and ETB regression models for the full list.

3. Some of the reference categories presented in this chart differ from the reference categories used in the APS and ETB regression models for presentational purposes only.

4. The values reported in the chart are odds ratios and interpreted as highlighted in section 10.

Figure 1 shows the impact different factors have on reporting higher life satisfaction. We have considered both an individual's "characteristics" (such as sex and age) and "circumstances" (such as self-reported health, marital status, dependent children in the household, educational attainment, economic activity status, housing tenure, household income and spending), all of which could be associated with life satisfaction.

Self-reported health has a larger effect on reported life satisfaction than any other characteristic or circumstance considered in the analysis. The odds of reporting higher life satisfaction are 3.0 times greater for someone reporting very good health than for someone reporting fair health. In contrast, the odds of reporting higher life satisfaction are 5.7 times lower for someone reporting very bad health than for someone reporting fair health.

Marital status is a significant contributor to the odds of reporting high life satisfaction. People who are married or in a civil partnership are most likely to report higher life satisfaction than those in any other marital status. People who are separated from their partner or widowed are more likely to report lower life satisfaction, compared with people who are single.

Economic activity can also have a significant impact on life satisfaction ratings. Being retired has a positive impact, while being unemployed or economically inactive due to sickness or disability has a significant negative impact. Interestingly, both household spending and household income have less of an impact on life satisfaction than other personal and household circumstances.

Of the personal characteristics examined in the analysis, age is most strongly related to life satisfaction. Previous research has shown the relationship between age and life satisfaction to be S-shaped. That is, life satisfaction is higher on average for younger adults, dropping to its lowest point when people are in their 40s, rising again as people near retirement age, and falling again as we enter our 80s.

Figure 2: Retirees are most satisfied with their life

Percentage difference in average reported life satisfaction against reference categories, Great Britain, October 2017 to September 2018

Percentage difference in average reported life satisfaction against reference categories, Great Britain, October 2017 to September 2018

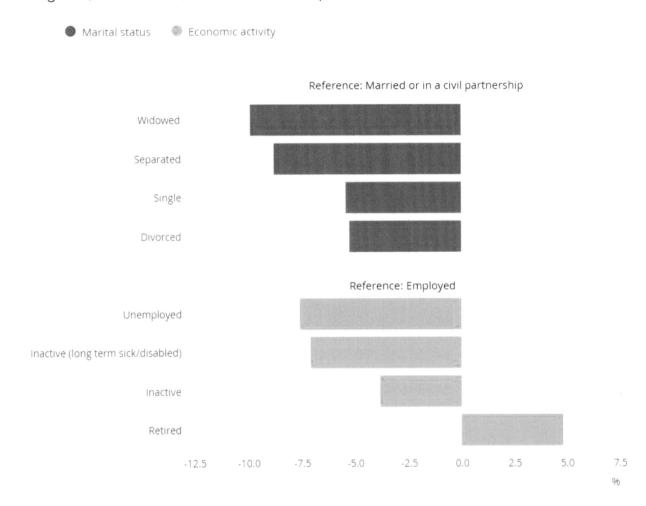

Source: Office for National Statistics - Annual Population Survey

Notes:

1. The reference category for marital status is 'married or in a civil partnership'; reference category for economic activity is 'employed'.

2. The values reported in the chart are all statistically significant compared to the reference categories.

3. Positive values denote greater average life satisfaction and negative values denote lower average life satisfaction, compared with the reference category.

People who are married or in a civil partnership rate their life satisfaction higher – in particular, 9.9% higher than those who are widowed, and 8.8% higher than those separated from a partner. Those who are unemployed report lower life satisfaction ratings than those in any other economic activity group. Those who are economically inactive due to sickness or disability report only slightly higher life satisfaction ratings than unemployed people. Compared with people who are employed, these groups rate their life satisfaction 7.6% and 7.1% lower, respectively.

4 . What has changed over time?

We have revisited the work carried out previously in relation to What matters most to Personal Well-being?, replicating analysis where possible, to enable comparisons from April 2011 to March 2012 to October 2017 to September 2018. Self-reported health is still the biggest contributor to life satisfaction of all the factors we considered (see the accompanying datasets for more information). It is also strongly associated with measures of happiness, anxiety and the feeling that the things we do in life are worthwhile.

For the latest period up to September 2018, economic activity overall showed less variance in life satisfaction than marital status, while it was the reverse in the April 2011 to March 2012 analysis. This may be influenced by historically low unemployment rates, which have fallen between the two periods considered.

5 . Associations with life satisfaction and household circumstances

Those living with dependent children report higher life satisfaction

As seen in Figure 1, those living with dependent children have 1.25 times greater odds of reporting higher life satisfaction. This is true once we control for the effect of income and spending of the household, which will likely be different for those with dependent children.

Those renting in social housing report worse life satisfaction than those who rent privately

Housing tenure has a strong association with life satisfaction. In comparison with those buying a property with a mortgage, the odds of reporting lower life satisfaction are 1.25 and 1.22 times greater for those in social housing and privately renting, respectively.

In Figure 3, we look at how people who own or rent their home compare in terms of the personal characteristics and circumstances with the greatest impact on life satisfaction.

Figure 3: There is a bigger share of people living in social housing who are either single, report bad health or are not employed, compared to those with a mortgage

Share of the population aged 16 years and over, UK, April 2016 to March 2017

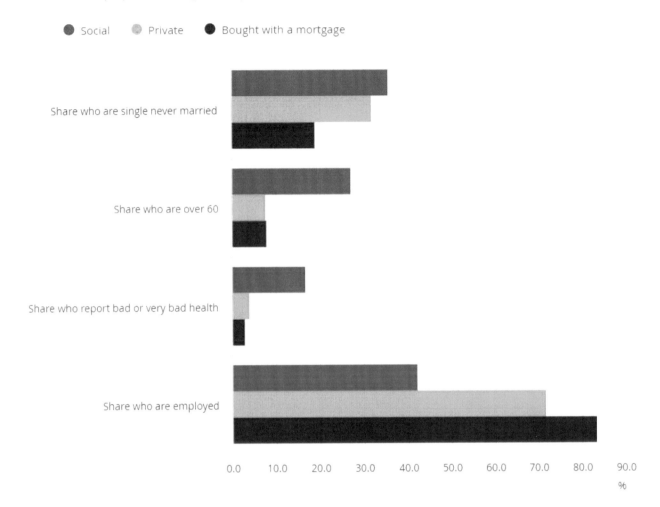

Share of the population aged 16 years and over, UK, April 2016 to March 2017

● Social   ● Private   ● Bought with a mortgage

Source: Office for National Statistics - Effects of Taxes and Benefits (ETB)

Notes:

1. "Share" refers to those in each tenure category aged 16 and over.

Those living in social housing tend to report worse employment situations and poorer health. Only 42.1% of those living in social housing report being employed, while 83.3% of those who bought with a mortgage or loan are in employment. Of those in social housing, 16.6% report bad or very bad health, compared with 4.0% of those privately renting and 3.0% of those buying with a mortgage.

Additionally, those who are renting privately are much more likely to be single rather than living with a partner or married, which is also associated with lower life satisfaction.

6 . Economic associations with life satisfaction

We have highlighted that being unemployed rather than employed is associated with lower life satisfaction. A job may impact people's personal well-being in multiple ways, from providing a sense of purpose and social interaction, through to providing financial security and more choices in the form of purchasing power. This section focuses more on the latter, while recognising the wider benefits employment may also contribute to well-being.

As reported in previous research, such as the Organisation for Economic Co-operation and Development's (OECD's) 2018 follow-up report to the Beyond GDP agenda, when considering economic measures of well-being, household income and household spending better take into account the full resources individuals have access to, rather than just earnings from their jobs.

Previous analysis considered wealth and income associations with personal well-being, while in this article we focus on spending, as it has been proposed as a better indicator of people's economic resources. This can be seen when looking at average life satisfaction across spending distribution (Figure 4).

Figure 4: Average life satisfaction is higher for those spending more

Quintiles of equivalised household spending, UK, April 2016 to March 2017

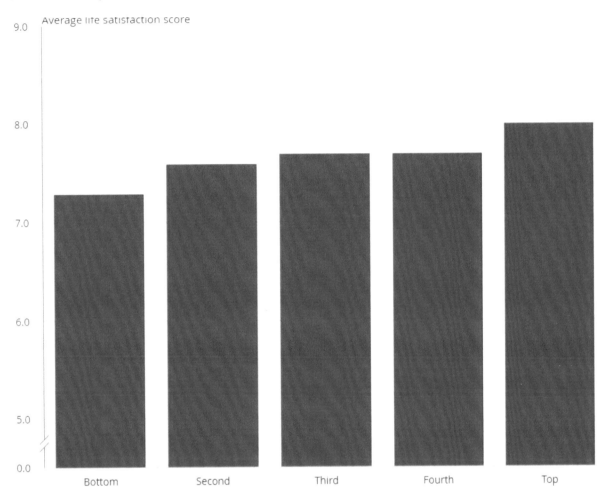

Quintiles of equivalised household spending, UK, April 2016 to March 2017

Source: Office for National Statistics - Effects of Taxes and Benefits (ETB)

Notes:

1. The average of every quintile shown, not controlling for any of the regression factors.

2. Spending values have been equivalised.

It may be that this pattern is simply explained by other characteristics such as self-reported health, age and employment status. To understand the role income and spending have on life satisfaction, it is therefore important to control for personal and household characteristics. The individual effects are shown in Figure 5.

Figure 5 shows that you are more likely to report higher life satisfaction if you have higher household spending, and spending appears to matter more than household income to people's life satisfaction. For someone with twice the level of household spending, their odds of reporting higher life satisfaction are 1.22 times greater. However, it is important to note that both impacts are smaller than most personal characteristics or circumstances shown previously.

Figure 5: Household spending has a larger positive association with life satisfaction than household income

Odds ratios of higher life satisfaction associated with a doubling of each monetary measure, UK, April 2016 to March 2017

Source: Office for National Statistics - Effects of Taxes and Benefits (ETB)

Notes:

1. Positive value means more likely to report higher life satisfaction for higher income/spending

2. The values reported in the chart are odds ratios and interpreted as highlighted in section 10.

3. Denotes statistical significance at 95% level, while income is only significant at the 90% level.

4. Data refers to equivalised household income and spending.

There is no evidence of a statistically significant association between household disposable income and life satisfaction overall after accounting for other characteristics. However, those whose household income is between £24,000 and £44,000 are significantly more likely to report higher life satisfaction with increasing income, as seen in Figure 6.

Figure 6: Higher disposable household income has a positive impact on the likelihood of reporting higher life satisfaction, if it is between £24,000 and £44,000

Odds ratios of higher life satisfaction associated with 10% higher household disposable income, UK, April 2016 to March 2017

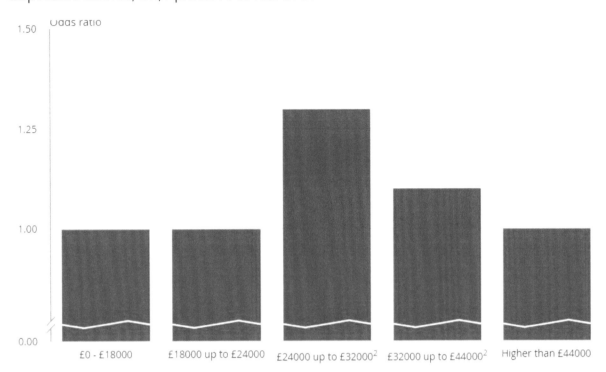

Source: Office for National Statistics - Effects of Taxes and Benefits (ETB)

Notes:

1. Quintiles used from Household Disposable Income and Inequality, financial year ending 2017.

2. Denotes values that are statistically significant at the 95% level.

3. The values reported in the chart are odds ratios and interpreted as highlighted in section 10.

4. Income values have been equivalised.

The impact from income for certain parts of the income distribution could be linked to the stronger effect from income associated with those in middle age, as well as evidence that higher income can impact people's life satisfaction through reduced worries regarding financial security.

There is a stronger relationship between spending and life satisfaction than between income and life satisfaction and this is consistent with the view that household spending is a better proxy for people's achieved living standards. This is in line with research showing spending better categorises the available resources to an individual (PDF, 286.6KB).

It may not be all forms of spending that have a positive association with personal well-being. For a given level of spending, different households may have higher or lower levels of essential costs on items such as food, accommodation and travel to work, which will in turn affect the amount they can spend on leisure and other more discretionary items. Figure 7 shows that, controlling for total household spending, what people spend their money on has a further impact on life satisfaction.

Figure 7: Of all categories of spending, a higher share of spending on hotels and restaurants is most positively associated with higher life satisfaction.

Marginal Effect on reporting very high life satisfaction from a doubling of the share of spending on a particular category, UK, April 2016 to March 2017

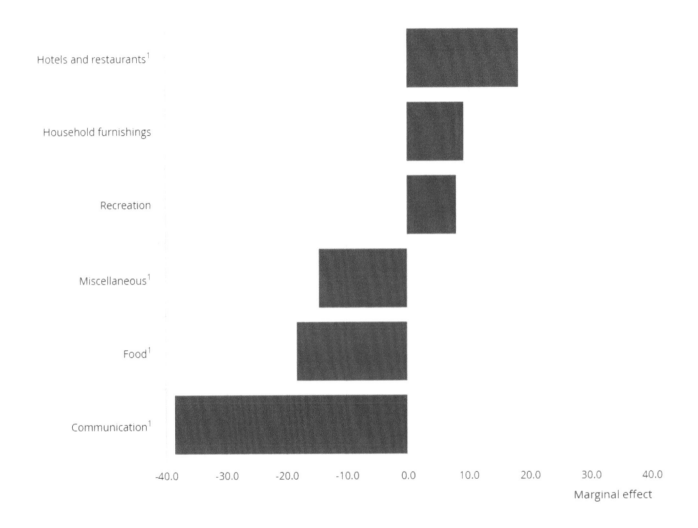

Marginal Effect on reporting very high life satisfaction from a doubling of the share of spending on a particular category, UK, April 2016 to March 2017

Source: Office for National Statistics - Effects of Taxes and Benefits (ETB)

Notes:

1. Denotes statistical significance at the 95% level, while other series are significant at the 90% level.

2. These are marginal effects, and are interpreted as outlined in section 10.

3. Other spending categories not shown (alcohol, clothing, housing and rental, health, transport, and education) are not significant even at the 90% level.

4. Miscellaneous spending is mostly captured by insurance such as car insurance, spending on personal care such as hairdressing, and hair products and other cosmetics.

5. Spending values have been equivalised.

Generally, a higher proportion of total spending on hotels and restaurants is positively associated with very high life satisfaction, as is spending on household furnishings and recreation.

In contrast, spending on goods and services – such as food, insurance and mobile phone subscriptions – tends to have a negative association, increasing the likelihood of reporting lower life satisfaction. Spending on categories like clothing, housing and transport were not found to have a statistically significant impact on reporting higher life satisfaction.

Looking at different age groups, different spending categories influence the retired and the working age populations.

Figure 8: Higher share of spending on transport for those of working age is associated with lower life satisfaction

Marginal Effect on reporting very high life satisfaction from a doubling of the share of spending on a particular category, UK, April 2016 to March 2017

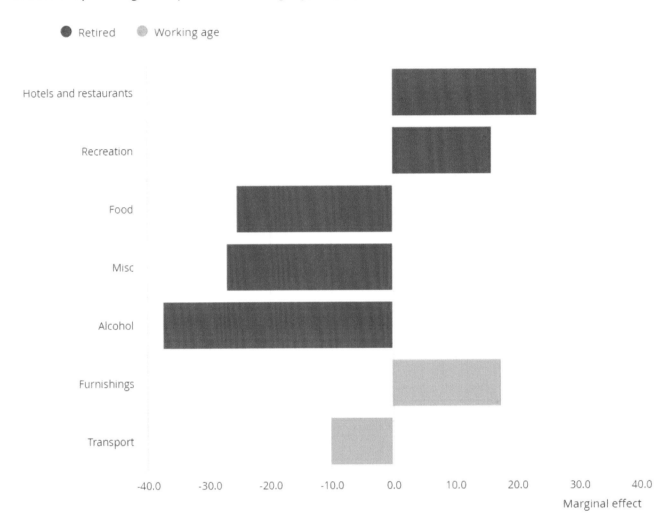

Marginal Effect on reporting very high life satisfaction from a doubling of the share of spending on a particular category, UK, April 2016 to March 2017

Source: Office for National Statistics - Effects of Taxes and Benefits (ETB)

Notes:

1. All factors significant at 90% level only, except furnishings for working age which is significant at the 95% level. Other categories not shown are not significant at the 90% level.

2. These are marginal effects and are interpreted as outlined in section 10.

3. 'Working age' is defined here as aged 16 – 65; 'retired' is defined as those over age 65.

4. Spending values have been equivalised.

Those who are retired are less likely to report very high life satisfaction if they have a higher share of spending on alcohol and tobacco, while those of working age are less likely to report high life satisfaction if they have a higher share of spending on transport. The latter may link to our previous analysis on commuting and personal well-being, which found longer commutes lasting between 61 and 90 minutes are associated with lower life satisfaction.

Finally, for those of working age, a higher share of total spending on furnishings and household improvements is associated with a rise in the likelihood of reporting very high life satisfaction. However, this is only among those households who own their property outright or with a mortgage.

7 . Your feedback: have your say

Your feedback will be very valuable in making our results useful and accessible. If you have any comments, please contact us via email at PeopleAndProsperity@ons.gov.uk.

8 . Authors

Gueorguie Vassilev, Silvia Manclossi, Ed Pyle, Meera Parmar, Jack Yull, Sunny Sidhu, Chris Payne and David Tabor from the Economic Well-being and Quality of Life Teams, Office for National Statistics.

9 . Quality and methodology

Why undertake a regression analysis?

To understand the relationship between personal well-being and economic or social factors, regression analysis has been used to measure the size and strength of the relationship between two variables, while holding all other variables in the model equal. While regression analysis can tell us the strength of the relationship between one variable and another, it cannot tell us about causality. Individuals will have many characteristics that could increase or decrease the chances of them reporting low personal well-being ratings that are not captured in our model and it can be difficult to identify the underlying causes of scoring their well-being this way.

It should be noted that our regression models explain between 9% and 21% of the differences in levels of personal well-being between people, suggesting that most of what influences a person's well-being is not explained by our data. This is to be expected, as many factors impact on well-being that are not quantified in our data sources or included in our regression models. These include genetic and personality factors, which have been claimed to account for about half of the variation in personal well-being.

Surveys used

The analysis presented in this publication is based on two different data sources, the Annual Population Survey (APS) and Effects of Taxes and Benefits (ETB).

Annual Population Survey (APS)

The APS has the largest coverage of any household survey in the UK. The topics covered include employment and unemployment, as well as housing, ethnicity, religion, health and education. For some of our well-being domains, such as "where we live", the APS has limited data available. To capture more of the differences between places, we included a place-related variable, which indicates urban and rural locations, as done in our previous analysis.

Due to Northern Ireland having a lower sample size than England, Wales and Scotland, these data could not be created. The regression analysis therefore does not include respondents from Northern Ireland and focuses on Great Britain rather than the UK.

The dataset used for this analysis covers October 2017 to September 2018 and has a total sample size of 286,059. Not all survey participants answer all the well-being questions; proxy responses, for example, are not valid. As a result, of the total sample size, we analysed data for around 145,000 for this period. We also analysed APS data for the period April 2011 to March 2012 to assess change from our previous analysis of What matters most to Personal Well-being?, as well as for the period October 2014 to September 2015 (as a mid-point period between the two reference periods considered).

Effects of Taxes and Benefits (ETB)

ETB data are from the Office for National Statistics' (ONS's) Living Costs and Food Survey (LCF), a voluntary sample survey of around 5,000 responding private households in the UK for the year. In addition, ETB uses several administrative sources to improve the quality of estimates, particularly to estimates of indirect taxes (for example, VAT) and benefits in kind (for example, education, NHS). The data cover the UK as a whole and are collected in the financial year from April 2016 to March 2017.

The main purpose of ETB is to provide quantitative analysis of the effects of government intervention (through taxes and benefits) on the income of private households in the UK. Further information on the ETB can be found in the ETB Quality and Methodology Information (QMI) report. Supporting information on the LCF can be found in the user guidance and technical information.

It is important to note that the data in this article were taken from household surveys to help understand well-being of those living in private residential households. People living in communal establishments (such as care homes) or other non-household situations are not represented in the APS or ETB. This may be important in interpreting the findings as we could possibly be excluding some of those more likely to have poor well-being.

These two data sources are used to complement each other. We used the APS for comparison with the previous What matters most to Personal Well-being? analysis and because the larger sample size allows for more sophisticated analysis and more granular estimates. However, the ETB provides better data on income and spending and so this is used where appropriate.

Personal well-being measures

The four personal well-being questions are:

- Overall, how satisfied are you with your life nowadays?

- Overall, to what extent do you feel the things you do in your life are worthwhile?

- Overall, how happy did you feel yesterday?

- Overall, how anxious did you feel yesterday?

People are asked to respond on a scale of 0 to 10, where 0 is "not at all" and 10 is "completely". We produce estimates of the mean ratings for all four personal well-being questions, as well as their distributions (as shown in Table 1).

Table 1: Labelling of thresholds for life satisfaction, worthwhile, happiness and anxiety scores

Life satisfaction, worthwhile and happiness scores		Anxiety scores	
Response on an 11-point scale	Label	Response on an 11-point scale	Label
0 to 4	Low	0 to 1	Very low
5 to 6	Medium	2 to 3	Low
7 to 8	High	4 to 5	Medium
9 to 10	Very high	6 to 10	High

Source: Office for National Statistics - Annual Population Survey

Approach used to develop models

The variables used in the APS and ETB regression models and their corresponding reference category were chosen to replicate previous analysis where possible.

The model presented in Figure 1 uses data from the ETB. This model controls for as many of the categories in the APS models as possible, alongside controlling for dependent children, log of household income, and log of household spending. However, for presentational purposes, different reference categories' odds ratio relationships were presented to more intuitively visualise the positive and negative associations between certain categories of individual and household circumstances and life satisfaction.

For example, for self-reported health, fair status is the baseline to represent good health as having a positive association with life satisfaction, rather than showing fair health as having a negative association (if the "good" category was used to represent the reference category). We used ETB data to produce a model capturing the full range of variables to show the relative impacts of different factors on life satisfaction using a single survey. Some of the estimates presented in Figure 1 were not statistically significant from this model, but have been shown to be significant within the APS models, which have a larger sample, to validate the statistical inferences made of associations between these factors, rather than the precise value of the magnitude of the effect.

Weighting

Datasets are weighted to reflect the size and composition of the general population, by using the most up-to-date official population data. Weighting factors take account of the design of the survey (which does not include communal establishments) and the composition of the local population by age and sex.

The APS datasets are reweighted historically to use more up-to-date mid-year population estimates and subnational projection estimates. Supporting information on methodological aspects on the APS can be found in Volume 6 of the APS user guide.

For more information on weighting in the LCF, see the Living Costs and Food Survey QMI.

Missing data

Missing data can produce biased estimates and invalid conclusions, particularly if data are not "missing at random" or, in other words, if there is some (unknown) patterning to that "missingness" (for more information, see <u>Missing data analysis: making it work in the real world</u>). Missing data in this analysis refers to incidences when respondents have either refused to answer questions or have answered "don't know". For the regression models, in instances of missing data for any of the variables included in the model, the entire case was excluded from analysis.

Goodness of fit

Goodness of fit describes how well a model fits the data from which it is generated. After the addition of each variable to the model, goodness of fit and change in the coefficients were assessed.

Regression techniques used

Ordinary Least Squares (OLS), Probit and Logit models were applied throughout the analysis. The main advantage of OLS is that the interpretation of the regression results is more straightforward than in alternative methods. Probit and Logit models were applied as important assumptions for the OLS regression may not hold for the ordered personal well-being data. Logit coefficients allow easier comparison through the derivation and use of odds ratios.

OLS

An important assumption in OLS regression is that the dependent variable is continuous. The personal well-being survey responses, however, are discrete. OLS regression also assumes that the values of the dependent variable (for example, personal well-being ratings) are cardinal (that is, the interval between any pair of categories such as between 2 and 3 is of the same magnitude as the interval between any other similar pair such as between 6 and 7). As the personal well-being responses are rankings we cannot know whether, for example, the distance between 2 and 3 is the same as the distance between 6 and 7.

However, OLS may still be implemented when there are more than five levels of the ordered categorical responses, particularly when there is a clear ordering of the categories, for example, levels of happiness, with 0 representing the lowest category and 10 representing the highest category (for an example see <u>Ordinary Least Squares Regression of Ordered Categorical Data: Inferential Implications for Practice</u>).

Probit

An alternative method is to treat the response variable as ordinal and use probit regression, which can deal with ordinal data. Ordinal data values can be ranked or ordered on a scale such as from 0 to 10 with each higher category representing a higher degree of personal well-being (or lower personal well-being in the case of anxiety).

Unlike the OLS method, probit regression does not assume that the differences between the ordinal categories in the personal well-being rankings are equal. It is important to note that probit performs several regressions simultaneously, assuming that the models are identical for all scores. The latter assumption can be relaxed but the interpretation of the results becomes more difficult.

The analysis was conducted in both OLS and probit regression methods. This also acts as a sensitivity check for the robustness of the OLS results as the main assumptions for the OLS regression may not hold for the ordered personal well-being data. Indeed, several studies applied both methods to personal well-being data and found that there is little difference between the OLS and the probit (for example, see How important is methodology for the estimates of the determinants of happiness?).

Logit

We also used an ordered logit model. The ordered logistic model (logit), like the probit, can account for variables that need to be considered as ordinal but treats them slightly differently to the probit model.

The main difference is that the logit makes use of the proportional odds assumption. This means the relationship between the independent variables and their effect on personal well-being is assumed to be the same for each level of personal well-being (the 0 to 10 ranking). For example, the effect of the independent economic and societal variables on the highest level of personal well-being will represent the same relationship for the lowest level of personal well-being.

Considerations for household income and expenditure analysis

The following information should be taken on when considering the analysis of income and expenditure (spending) to aid understanding of the complexities behind the findings, and of what has shaped the analysis that has been carried out.

Household income as opposed to individual or personal income

Income is analysed at household level, as the income of one household member is assumed to have an impact on all the members of the household.

Income relationships between household members

Different household members may feel differently about their life satisfaction depending on if they themselves are bringing in that particular type of income. For example, if other members of the same household are earning high wages and you are unemployed, you may feel particularly unsatisfied with your life. Alternatively, if you are in employment then increasing levels of household income acquired because of earnings from employment may be associated with higher levels of life satisfaction.

Omitted variables

Our survey data capture some individual and household characteristics, but of course there are other factors that are not captured in the data and, therefore, omitted from our models. For example, those in self-employment may have broadly different personalities to those in employment when considering them as large groups and this may have an impact on how they report their life satisfaction. Alternatively, those benefiting from different forms of income may lead very different lifestyles, which are not well captured in the survey data.

Direction of causality

It is also possible that some people are predisposed to report higher life satisfaction than others. This could be a personality trait or a socially learnt disposition. Either way, this possibility demonstrates that it is not possible in this analysis to infer causality.

Different types of income, the underlying activities associated with types of income, or even demographics associated with types of income, may lead to higher life satisfaction but it is also possible that the relationship might operate in part, or whole, in the opposite direction. Those with a predisposition to give higher self-reported life satisfaction may also be more likely to benefit from specific forms for household income. For example, those who report higher life satisfaction may be more likely to get a job with a higher income.

10 . Interpreting factors affecting life satisfaction

In this article, we have used different analytical approaches to answer the basic question of what contributes to higher or lower levels of life satisfaction. The two techniques used, logistic and linear regression, produce findings best expressed in different ways.

Logistic regression provides us with an "odds ratio". This tells us the odds of someone with a particular characteristic or circumstance reporting higher life satisfaction when compared with someone with another specified characteristic or circumstance, after taking other possible influences on life satisfaction into account. For example, the odds of reporting higher life satisfaction are 3.0 times greater for someone reporting very good health than for someone reporting fair health, after taking other possible influences on life satisfaction into account (see Section 3).

"Marginal effects" are an alternative way of expressing odds ratios. The marginal effect tells us how much life satisfaction changes with a change in individual characteristics or circumstances, after taking other possible influences on life satisfaction into account. For some numerical characteristics (for example, spending), it can be easier to explain effects in terms of marginal effects.

Take two people with the same level of household spending for example: one who spends double the share of their spending on hotels or restaurants is 18 percentage points more likely to report very high life satisfaction than another spending less in this way (see Section 6).

Linear regression results can be expressed in terms of differences in how people rated their life satisfaction when asked: "Overall, how satisfied are you with your life nowadays?". They respond on a scale from 0 to 10, with 0 being "not at all" and 10 being "completely". The findings can be expressed in terms of the percentage difference in average reported life satisfaction between someone with a particular characteristic or circumstance and someone else with a different characteristic or circumstance, after taking other possible influences on life satisfaction into account. For example, those who are economically inactive due to sickness or disability rate their life satisfaction 7.6% lower than people who are employed, after taking other possible influences on life satisfaction into account (see Section 3).

Office for
National Statistics

Statistical bulletin

Effects of taxes and benefits on UK household income: financial year ending 2018

The redistribution effects on individuals and households of direct and indirect taxation and benefits received in cash or kind analysed by household type, and the changing levels of income inequality over time.

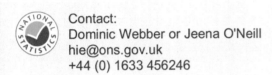

Contact:
Dominic Webber or Jeena O'Neill
hie@ons.gov.uk
+44 (0) 1633 456246

Release date:
30 May 2019

Next release:
To be announced

Notice

9 August 2019

An error has been identified in the Living Cost and Food (LCF) Survey which has been found to impact the Effects of taxes and benefits on UK household income: financial year ending 2018 release. This affects, to a small degree, most estimates of average VAT, and duties on alcohol, tobacco, and fuel that households pay. The overall impact is that average final income for all people is overestimated by 0.2%, while the interpretation of the statistics remains the same.

The error was due to the imputation of data collected through a diary being incorrect for three quarters of the financial year in the LCF. Users should note this issue if using these data. We will correct this error when the next release covering financial year ending 2019 is published in May 2020. We apologise for any inconvenience.

Please contact dominic.webber@ons.gov.uk for more information.

Table of contents

1 . Main points

- Before taxes and benefits, the richest one-fifth of people had an average household income of £88,200 in the financial year ending (FYE) 2018, based on estimates from the Living Costs and Food Survey.

- The ratio of average household income of the richest one-fifth of people (before taxes and benefits) compared with the poorest one-fifth (£7,900) was 11.2 in FYE 2018, continuing the downward trend from 15.5 in FYE 2008.

- Overall, taxes and benefits lead to income being shared more equally; after all taxes and benefits are taken into account, the ratio between the average household income of the richest and poorest fifth of people (£65,500 and £18,900 respectively) is reduced to less than 4.

- Cash benefits were most effective at reducing income inequality in FYE 2018, although their effect has diminished over the past seven years; this partly reflects the fall in their value relative to incomes before taxes and benefits.

- Direct taxes (such as income tax) are progressive in reducing income inequality; with the richest one-fifth paying 30.9% of their income in direct taxation, compared with 14.7% for the poorest one-fifth of people.

- However, indirect taxes (such as Value Added Tax (VAT) and alcohol duties) can be considered both regressive or broadly neutral; the poorest one-fifth of people paid the equivalent of 27.1% of their household disposable income in indirect taxation, compared with 14.3% for the richest one-fifth of people. However, the incidence of indirect taxes on expenditure – which they are levied on – is more evenly balanced; the poorest one-fifth of people paid 19.2% compared with 17.1% for the richest one-fifth.

- The proportion of people living in households receiving more in benefits than they paid in taxes fell from 49.6% to 47.9% in FYE 2018, continuing the downward trend since FYE 2010.

- This article introduces a number of improvements to how we measure and analyse the underlying data including: moving the analysis from a household to person level, presenting Experimental Statistics that adjust for under-reporting of the very rich, and the inclusion of estimates of adult social care; more details can be found in our accompanying blog.

2 . Overall taxes and benefits reduced inequality of household income between poorest and richest people in financial year ending 2018

Figure 1: Taxes and benefits lead to household income being shared more equally between people

Household original, gross, disposable, post-tax and final income, equivalised, by quintile group, and Q5 to Q1 ratio, all individuals, UK, 2017 to 2018

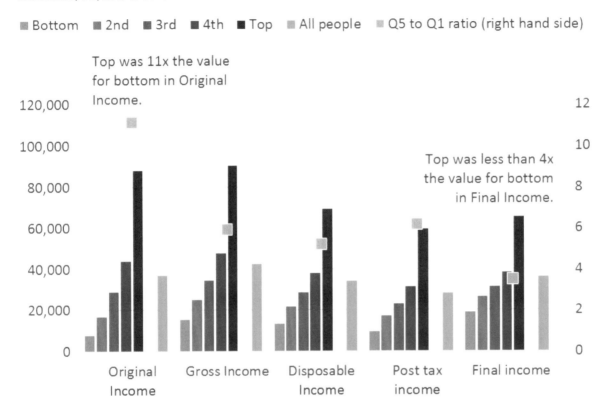

Source: Office for National Statistics - Living Costs and Food survey

Overall, taxes and benefits lead to household income being shared more equally between people. In the financial year ending (FYE) 2018, before taxes and benefits, the richest one-fifth of people had an average household original income 11.2 times larger than the income of the poorest one-fifth – £88,200 compared with £7,900, after adjusting for household size and composition.

This ratio has fallen in recent years, from a peak of 15.5 in FYE 2008, indicating that the inequality of original income has been falling. This is explored in more detail further in the bulletin. Original income includes income from employment, private pensions and investments.

The receipt of cash benefits and payment of direct taxes reduces income inequality between the poorest and richest 20% of people. The average household disposable income of the richest one-fifth of people was 5.2 times larger than the income of the poorest one-fifth – £69,400 compared with £13,300 (Figure 1). After indirect taxes (for example, Value Added Tax (VAT), alcohol duties and so on) and benefits-in-kind (for example, state education, National Health Service) are taken into account, the ratio further reduces to 3.5.

Figure 2: The richest one-fifth of people live in households that pay more in tax than they receive in benefits, while the poorest 20% receive more in benefits than they pay in taxes

Summary of the effects of taxes and benefits by quintile groups [1], UK, financial year ending 2018

Summary of the effects of taxes and benefits by quintile groups[1], UK, financial year ending 2018

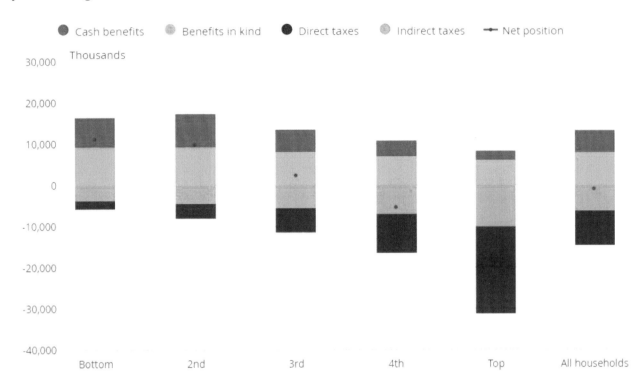

Source: Office for National Statistics - Living Costs and Food survey

Notes:

1. Individuals are ranked by their equivalised household disposable incomes, using the modified Organisation for Economic Co-operation and Development (OECD) scale.

To better understand how taxes and benefits reduce the income gap between the richest and poorest, Figure 2 summarises the net positions (in terms of benefits received and taxes paid by households) of each income quintile group. The poorest one-fifth of people live in households that received relatively large amounts of both cash benefits and benefits-in-kind and were net recipients in FYE 2018. Richer households, on the other hand, paid more in taxes – both direct and indirect – and received less in benefits, meaning the people in the top income quintile were net contributors.

As reported in the Average household income, UK: financial year ending 2018 bulletin, the average income of the poorest one-fifth of the population – when ranked by equivalised household disposable income – contracted by 1.6%. The average income of the richest one-fifth, on the other hand, increased by 4.7%.

Figure 3: Average household income of the poorest 20% of people fell in the financial year ending 2018, driven mainly by a fall in the value of cash benefits they received

Contribution to change in household disposable income by quintile groups [1], UK, financial year ending 2017 to financial year ending 2018

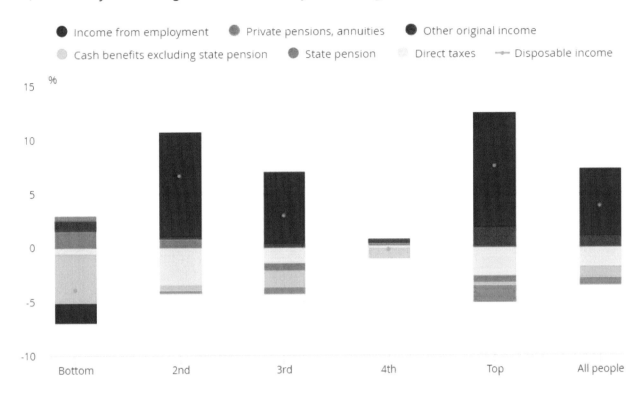

Contribution to change in household disposable income by quintile groups [1], UK, financial year ending 2017 to financial year ending 2018

Notes:

1. Income from employment is equal to the sum of wages and salaries, and self-employment income.

2. Individuals are ranked by their equivalised household disposable incomes, using the modified Organisation for Economic Co-operation and Development (OECD) scale.

3. Incomes are adjusted for inflation using the Consumer Prices Index including owner occupiers' housing costs (CPIH) excluding Council Tax.

Looking at this in more detail, Figure 3 examines the contribution to change in unequivalised household disposable income between FYE 2017 and FYE 2018. Overall, there was a 10.4% decline in the average real value of benefits (excluding state pensions) households received. As highlighted in Figure 2, the bottom income quintile has a greater reliance on cash benefits. The fall in the average real value of benefits (excluding state pensions) of the bottom income quintile contributed negative 4.6 percentage points to the 3.9% decline in average unequivalised household disposable income.

Many working-age benefits, such as Jobseeker's Allowance, Child Benefit and Housing Benefit, are held at FYE 2016 cash values from FYE 2017 to FYE 2020, meaning their value is falling in real terms. Pensioner, disability, sickness and carer benefits, including Personal Independence Payment, Carer's Allowance and the Employment and Support Allowance Support Group component are excluded from this freeze.

In addition, a benefit cap is in place in England, Scotland and Wales, which restricts the amount of certain benefits that most working-age households can receive. Any household receiving more than the cap has their Housing Benefit reduced to bring them back within the limit. This benefit cap was introduced in Northern Ireland from 31 May 2016 with a "Welfare Supplementary Payment" paid to any households with children in who have their Housing Benefit reduced due to the cap.

The basic State Pension increased in line with the "triple guarantee" (or "triple lock") that was introduced in FYE 2013. This ensures that it increases by the highest of the increase in earnings, price inflation (as measured by the Consumer Prices Index) or 2.5%. From April 2017, the basic State Pension increased by 2.5% (as neither inflation nor earnings growth was greater than 2.5%) from £119.30 to £122.30 per week.

Overall, income from employment (wages and salaries, and self-employment) increased by 6.7% in real terms, contributing to growth in disposable income for the second, third, and top income quintiles. This is likely to be due to increasing employment over this period.

Cash benefits were most effective at reducing income inequality in FYE 2018

There are various measures to assess how inequality of household income has changed over time. While one approach is to compare the ratio of income of the average household incomes of the richest and poorest one-fifth of people, as presented in the previous section, another widely used measure is the Gini coefficient.

Gini coefficients can vary between 0% and 100% and the lower the value, the more equally household income is distributed. One of the advantages of the Gini coefficient is that it considers the whole distribution, rather than just the top and bottom.

Figure 4: Cash benefits were most effective at reducing income inequality in the financial year ending 2018

Cash benefits had the largest effect on reducing income inequality in the financial year ending 2018, reducing the Gini coefficient from 46.3% for original income to 35.4% for gross income.

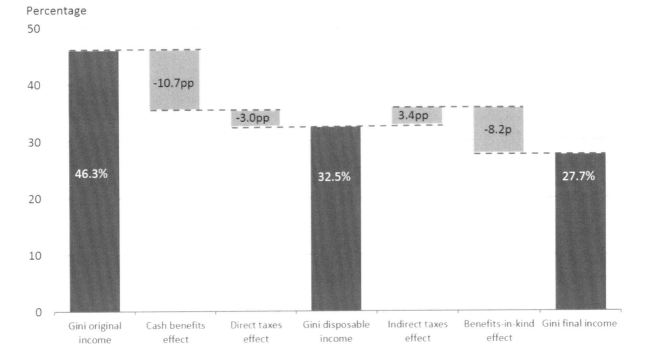

Source: Office for National Statistics - Living Costs and Food survey

Notes:

1. pp – percentage points.

2. Original income includes all sources of income from employment, private pensions, investments and other non-government sources. The receipt of cash benefits is then added to original income and direct taxes are subtracted to estimate disposable income. Indirect taxes (for example, VAT, alcohol duties and so on) are then subtracted and finally benefits-in-kind (for example, state education, National Health Service) are added to estimate final income.

3. Incomes are equivalised using the modified Organisation for Economic Co-operation and Development (OECD) equivalisation scale.

Figure 4 highlights how each stage of redistribution – from cash benefits, to direct and indirect taxes, and finally benefits-in-kind – work together to affect income inequality. Overall, the full effect of all taxes and benefits is to reduce income inequality in FYE 2018, with the Gini coefficient falling by 18.6 percentage points from 46.3% on an original income basis, to 27.7% on a final income basis.

Cash benefits have the largest effect on reducing income inequality, in FYE 2018, reducing the Gini coefficient by 10.7 percentage points from 46.3% for original income to 35.6% for gross income. Direct taxes act to further reduce it, by 3.0 percentage points to 32.5%. The addition of indirect taxes increases the Gini coefficient of income by 3.4 percentage points, which is more than offset by the addition of benefits-in-kind.

Table 1: Effect of taxes and benefits on Gini coefficient on different measures of income and expenditure, UK, financial year ending 2018

	Effect on Gini coefficient (pp)	
	Income	Expenditure*
Cash benefits	-10.7	
Direct taxes	-3.0	
Indirect taxes	3.4	0.8
Benefits-in-kind	-8.2	

Source: Office for National Statistics - Living costs and food survey

Notes

1. Incomes and expenditure are both equivalised using the modified Organisation for Economic Co-operation and Development (OECD) equivalisation scale.

2. Expenditure is calculated to be consistent with disposable income.

While it is important to consider the redistributive impact of indirect taxes on income, enabling a full judgement of the effectiveness of taxes and benefits system, there is a strong argument for also considering their impact on expenditure inequality.

Indirect taxes are directly levied on expenditure and, as previously explored in An expenditure-based approach to poverty in the UK (PDF, 824.3KB), some households can have temporarily low periods of income, which do not necessarily impact upon their consumption, and living standards. As a consequence, the indirect taxes that those households pay as a proportion of their income will be lower than as a proportion of their expenditure. This effect appears to be playing a role, as Table 1 highlights that the impact of indirect taxes on the Gini coefficient of expenditure is less pronounced on an expenditure basis compared with income (0.8 and 3.4 percentage points respectively).

Figure 5: Inequality of original income has fallen by 3.0 percentage points between financial year ending 2011 and financial year ending 2018

Gini coefficients for different income measures, UK, 1977 to financial year ending 2018

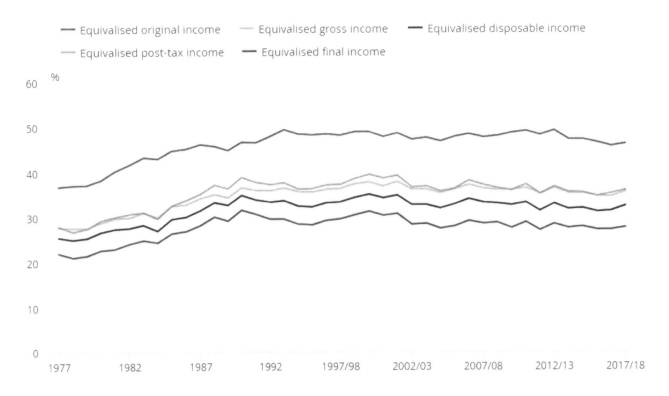

Gini coefficients for different income measures, UK, 1977 to financial year ending 2018

Source: Office for National Statistics - Living Costs and Food survey

Notes:

1. Original income includes all sources of income from employment, private pensions, investments and other non-government sources. The receipt of cash benefits is then added to original income to estimate gross income, and then direct taxes are subtracted to estimate disposable income. Indirect taxes (for example, VAT, alcohol duties and so on) are further subtracted to form post-tax income, and finally benefits-in-kind (for example, state education, National Health Service) are added to estimate final income.

2. Incomes are equivalised using the modified Organisation for Economic Co-operation and Development (OECD) equivalisation scale.

3. 2017 to 2018 represents the financial year ending 2018 (April to March), and this applies for all other years expressed in this format.

While The effects of taxes and benefits on income inequality: 1977 to financial year ending 2015 bulletin provides more detail on historical trends in income inequality, Figure 5 presents some important changes that have emerged over recent years. In particular, the inequality of original income has fallen by 3.0 percentage points between FYE 2011 and FYE 2018. This has not been matched by equivalent falls in the inequality of gross, or disposable income – falling by 0.9 and 0.7 percentage points respectively over this period.

The fall in original income for all households is observed for people living in both non-retired and retired households separately. For non-retired people, this likely reflects changes in the labour market over recent years, with rising employment driving an increase in the average number of working people in households towards the bottom of the distribution.

The smaller fall in inequality of gross income for those living in non-retired households is likely explained by an observed fall in the value of cash benefits received relative to households' original incomes. This is likely to be due partly to the rising employment levels mentioned previously but may also reflect the cash terms freeze since FYE 2017 (and 1% uprating for three financial years prior to this) in many working-age benefits (discussed in more detail earlier on).

The fall in inequality of original income for retired people coincides with a period in which the number of recipients of private pensions has increased, acting to reduce income disparities between richer and poorer retired people.

Figure 6: Effectiveness of cash benefits at reducing income inequality has diminished over the past seven years

Change in Gini coefficients due to cash benefits and taxes, UK, 1977 to financial year ending 2018

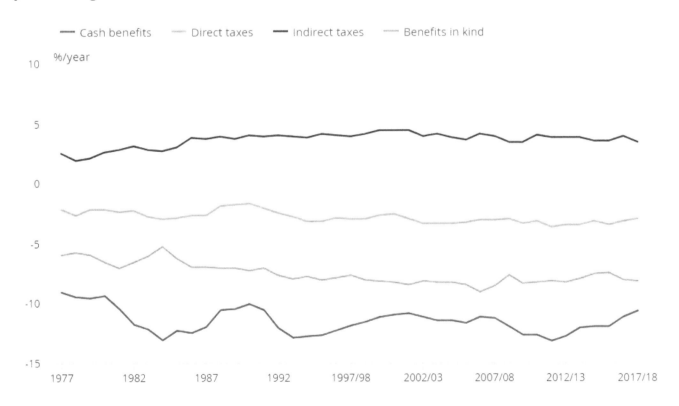

Change in Gini coefficients due to cash benefits and taxes, UK, 1977 to financial year ending 2018

Source: Office for National Statistics - Living Costs and Food survey

Notes:

1. 2017 to 2018 represents the financial year ending 2018 (April to March), and this applies for all other years expressed in this format.

Cash benefits and direct taxes remain progressive in financial year ending 2018

In FYE 2018, cash benefits composed a larger proportion of the poorest one-fifth of people's income – 52.5% of average household disposable income, falling to 2.9% for the richest one-fifth of people. This means that cash benefits continued to be progressive in FYE 2018.

Similarly, direct taxes were progressive, with the richest one-fifth paying 30.9% of their income, compared with 14.7% for the poorest one-fifth.

Figure 7: The incidence of indirect taxes varies across the income distribution depending on whether measured as a proportion of income or expenditure

Indirect taxes as a proportion of disposable income and expenditure, all people, UK, financial year ending 2018

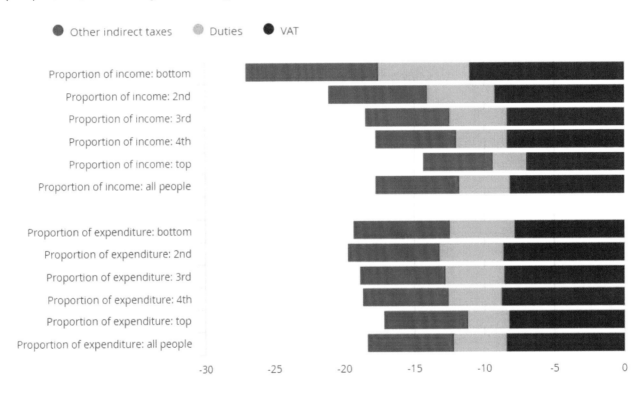

Indirect taxes as a proportion of disposable income and expenditure, all people, UK, financial year ending 2018

● Other indirect taxes   ○ Duties   ● VAT

Source: Office for National Statistics - Living Costs and Food survey

Notes:

1. Individuals are ranked by their equivalised household disposable incomes, using the modified Organisation for Economic Co-operation and Development (OECD) scale.

2. Duties include duty on tobacco, duty on beer and cider, duty on wines and spirits, duty on hydrocarbon oils, and Vehicle Excise Duty.

3. Expenditure is calculated to be consistent with disposable income.

The people in the richest income quintile paid an average of £12,300 in indirect tax in FYE 2018, 2.7 times that of the poorest group (£4,600). This reflects greater expenditure on goods and services subject to these taxes by higher income households. While the richest one-fifth of people paid more indirect taxes than the poorest one-fifth, they paid less as a proportion of their income. The poorest one-fifth paid the equivalent of 27.1% of their household disposable income in indirect tax on average, compared with 14.3% for the richest one-fifth of people, meaning that indirect taxes are regressive when considered on this basis.

To provide a complete picture of the effects of taxes and benefits, it is important to consider the redistributive effects of indirect taxes in terms of income, but it is also useful to analyse them in relation to expenditure. This reflects the fact that the amount of indirect taxes that households pay is determined by their expenditure rather than their income. Figure 5 shows that when expressed as a percentage of expenditure, the proportion paid in indirect taxes declines less sharply when moving up the distribution.

Benefits-in-kind are progressive and decrease income inequality. Benefits-in-kind are goods and services provided by the government to households that are either free at the time of use or at subsidised prices, such as education and health services. These goods and services can be assigned a monetary value based on the cost to the government, which is then allocated as a benefit to individual households.

Those in the poorest one-fifth of the income distribution received benefits-in-kind equivalent to £12,900 per household, driven largely by contributions from education services (49.5%) and the National Health Service (NHS) (42.9%). Those in the richest one-fifth of the income distribution, on the other hand, received benefits-in-kind equivalent to £7,700 per household, again with the NHS (60.9%) and education (30.4%) as the largest contributors.

The poorest one-fifth of people received more benefit-in-kind from education in total and, therefore, as a proportion of their income. This is largely because households towards the bottom of the income distribution have, on average, a larger number of children in state education. Our current methodology for allocating NHS spending to individuals is based on age and sex. Given that there are no substantial differences in the composition of households, in terms of age and sex, across the income distribution, NHS spending is allocated fairly evenly.

Households towards the bottom of the income distribution receive more in benefits-in-kind from adult social care

A new development in these statistics covering FYE 2018 is the introduction of new measures for the distribution of benefits-in-kind arising from publicly provided adult social care. Adult social care is the personal care and practical support provided to adults with physical or learning disabilities, or physical or mental illnesses, as well as support for their carers.

This could be for personal care (such as eating, washing, or getting dressed) or for domestic routines (such as cleaning or going to the shops). The forms of support we account for exclude residential care – about 37% of total adult social care in FYE 2018 – due to effects of taxes and benefits statistics covering only the private household population.

The methodology for measuring the distribution of adult social care benefit was developed with the National Institute for Economic and Social Research (NIESR) as part of the Economic Statistics Centre of Excellence. The effects of taxes and benefits on household income, financial year ending 2018: technical report provides more detail on the methodology used for measuring the distribution of adult social care.

Figure 8: The poorest 20% of people received the largest proportion of income from adult social care in the financial year ending 2018, with the richest 20% receiving the least

Average amount of adult social care per household, and as a proportion of disposable income by income quintile, UK, financial year ending 2018

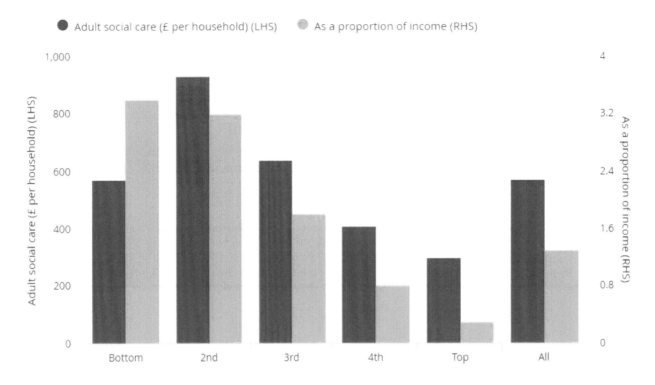

Source: Office for National Statistics - Living Costs and Food survey

Notes:

1. Individuals are ranked by their equivalised household disposable incomes, using the modified Organisation for Economic Co-operation and Development (OECD) scale.

Figure 8 highlights that the poorest 20% of people had the highest proportion of income from adult social care in the financial year ending 2018, with the richest 20% receiving the least. Households in the second income quintile received the most in total (£900), reflecting their increased likelihood to be in receipt of benefits related to disability, which we use to allocate this benefit-in-kind. The richest households received the least (£300) in FYE 2018 due to these households being least likely to receive disability-related benefits.

As the method to allocate adult social care across the income distribution is relatively new, we welcome feedback on the approach taken and results by email at hie@ons.gov.uk. Following feedback, we aim to update our historical datasets to include adult social care, enabling a better understanding of its distributional consequences over time.

Proportion of people living in households receiving more in benefits than they pay in tax has fallen over recent years

In FYE 2018, 47.9% of individuals lived in households receiving more in benefits (including in-kind benefits such as education) than they paid in taxes (direct and indirect) (Figure 9). This continues the decline from 53.1% since FYE 2011, but is still above levels recorded just before the economic downturn starting in FYE 2008.

Figure 9: In the financial year ending 2018, 47.9% of individuals lived in households receiving more in benefits than they paid in taxes

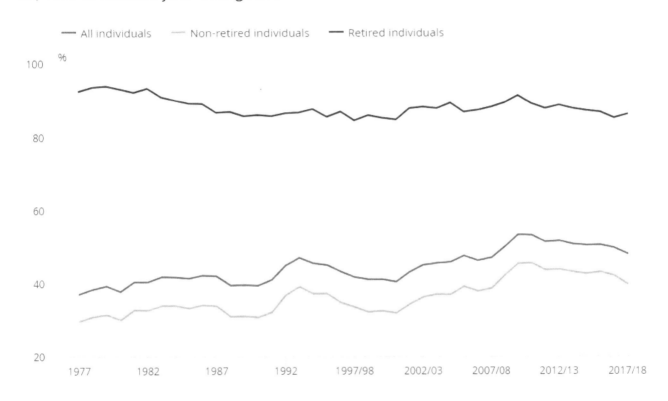

Proportion of individuals receiving more in benefits than they are paying in tax, UK, 1977 to financial year ending 2018

Source: Office for National Statistics - Living Costs and Food survey

Notes:

1. 2017 to 2018 represents the financial year ending 2018 (April to March), and this applies for all other years expressed in this format.

2. Incomes are adjusted for inflation using the Consumer Prices Index including owner occupiers' housing costs (CPIH) excluding Council Tax.

In FYE 2018, 39.6% of non-retired people received more in benefits than they paid in taxes, down from a peak of 45.4% in FYE 2011.

In contrast, there was a slight increase in FYE 2018 in the proportion of retired people living in households receiving more in benefits than they pay in taxes, up to 86.1% from 85.1% in FYE 2017. Retired people, on average, receive more benefits than they pay in tax due mainly to their reliance on the State Pension, which is classed as a cash benefit in this analysis.

Figure 10: Households whose head is aged 64 years and over received more in benefits than they paid in taxes on average in the financial year ending 2018

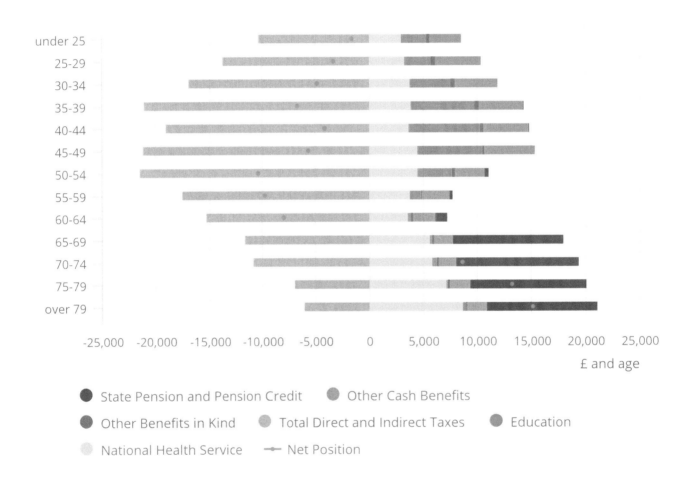

Figure 10: Households whose head is aged 64 years and over received more in benefits than they paid in taxes on average in the financial year ending 2018

Effects of taxes and benefits by age of head of household, UK, financial year ending 2018

Notes:

1. The household reference person is the householder who: owns the household accommodation; is legally responsible for the rent of the accommodation; has the household accommodation as an emolument or perquisite; or has the household accommodation by virtue of some relationship to the owner who is not a member of the household. If there are joint householders, the household reference person will be the one with the higher income. If the income is the same, then the eldest householder is taken.

2. A previous version of this chart included a series "All cash benefits". This has now been removed.

The fact that retired people are increasingly likely to receive more benefits than they pay in taxes is in Figure 10, showing how the effects of taxes and benefits change across the life course. On average in FYE 2018, households whose head is aged under 65 years paid more in taxes than they received in benefits (both cash and in-kind). Those aged between 50 and 54 years paid the most in taxes (£21,500), while those aged between 60 and 64 years received the least in benefits (£7,200). Households whose head is aged 79 years and over paid the least in taxes (£6,100) and received the most in benefits (£21,100).

For households with a head of household aged 65 years and over, State Pension and Pension Credit were the largest components of their cash benefits, followed by the benefits derived from the National Health Service, which tend to increase with age. The benefits derived from education peak with a household head aged between 40 and 44 years, because these households have the most children on average.

Experimental Statistics highlight that adjusting top incomes for under-reporting increases impact of taxes in reducing income inequality

As presented in the article, Using tax data to better capture top earners in household income inequality statistics , published in February 2019, we are developing a top income adjustment for effects of taxes and benefits (ETB) to address issues of under-reporting and under-coverage at the top of the income distribution. These adjustments tend to increase the amount of measured income for the very richest people and therefore increase levels of inequality.

Table 2: Comparing effectiveness of cash benefits and direct taxes before and after introduction of adjustment for top incomes, UK, financial year ending 2017 to financial year ending 2018

	Gini on original income (%)	Change in Gini due to cash benefits (pp)	Change in Gini due to direct taxes	Gini on disposable income (%)
Unadjusted ETB data	46.3	-10.7	-3.0	32.5
Adjusted ETB data	49.5	-10.5	-4.8	34.2
Impact of adjustment	3.3	0.2	-1.8	1.7

Source: Office for National Statistics - Living costs and food survey

Notes

1. Incomes are adjusted above the 97th percentile in 0.5% quantile bands. See Using tax data to better capture top earners in household income inequality statistics for more detailed information on adjustment methodologies.

Table 2 compares the impact on the Gini coefficient due to cash benefits, and direct taxes, in terms of the change in the Gini coefficient. It highlights that the adjustment increases the impact of direct taxes on reducing income inequality, but not enough to completely offset the increase in inequality of original income. The change in the impact on cash benefits is negligible as people who have had their incomes adjusted are not likely to be in receipt of benefits.

Figure 11: Impact of taxes in reducing income inequality increases when incomes are adjusted for under-reporting

Impact of top income adjustment on Gini coefficient of various measures of income, UK, financial year ending 2001 to financial year ending 2018

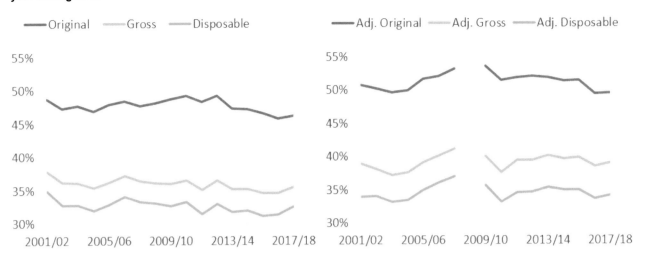

Source: Office for National Statistics - Living Costs and Food survey

Notes:

1. 2017 to 2018 represents the financial year ending 2018 (April to March) and this applies for all other years expressed in this format.

2. Incomes are adjusted for inflation using the Consumer Prices Index including owner occupiers' housing costs (CPIH) excluding Council Tax.

3. Adjusted incomes for financial year ending 2009 are missing as no Survey of Personal Incomes (SPI) dataset is available for that year.

While the introduction of a top income adjustment increases measured inequality on an original, gross and disposable basis, there is relatively little effect on trends over time (Figure 11). As discussed in the previous section, the introduction of a top income adjustment results in a larger fall in inequality when the effect of direct taxes is taken into account for all years.

In FYE 2011, the effect of direct taxes using adjusted data lowers the Gini on disposable income to a comparable level measured on the unadjusted data. As explored in the article Using tax data to better capture top earners in household income inequality statistics, published in February 2019, this is probably due to the introduction of a 50% top tax rate for FYE 2012, which resulted in people forestalling their income (see The Exchequer effect of the 50 per cent additional rate of income tax article).

These statistics, which present adjustments for top incomes to address under-reporting and under-coverage, are experimental and we welcome feedback by email at hie@ons.gov.uk. Following wider consultation, we aim to implement an adjustment in our headline statistics covering the reference period FYE 2019.

3 . Effects of taxes and benefits on household income data

Effects of taxes and benefits on household income
Dataset | Released on 30 May 2019
Tables 1 to 23 in the Effects of taxes and benefits on household income data provide more information on average values of main income components, taxes and benefits, and household characteristics of retired and non-retired households in the UK. Data are available for quintile and decile groups, country and region and tenure type.

4 . Glossary

Stages in the redistribution of income

The five stages are:

1. household members begin with income from employment, private pensions, investments and other non-government sources; this is referred to as "original income"

2. households then receive income from cash benefits; the sum of cash benefits and original income is referred to as "gross income"

3. households then pay direct taxes; direct taxes, when subtracted from gross income, is referred to as "disposable income"

4. indirect taxes are then paid via expenditure; disposable income minus indirect taxes is referred to as "post-tax income"

5. households finally receive a benefit from services (benefits-in-kind); benefits-in-kind plus post-tax income is referred to as "final income"

Note that at no stage are deductions made for housing costs.

Progressive and regressive taxes and benefits

A tax is progressive when high-income groups face a higher average tax rate than low-income groups. If those with higher incomes pay a higher amount but still face a lower average tax rate, then the tax is considered regressive; similarly, cash benefits are progressive where they account for a larger share of low-income groups' income.

Equivalisation

Comparisons across different types of individuals and households (such as retired and non-retired, or rich and poor) or over time are made after income has been equivalised. Equivalisation is the process of accounting for the fact that households with many members are likely to need a higher income to achieve the same standard of living as households with fewer members. Equivalisation considers the number of people living in the household and their ages, acknowledging that while a household with two people in it will need more money to sustain the same living standards as one with a single person, the two-person household is unlikely to need double the income.

This analysis uses the modified Organisation for Economic Co-operation and Development (OECD) equivalisation scale (PDF, 165KB).

5 . Measuring these data

This release provides estimates of the redistributive role of taxes and benefits on household income and inequality. These data are from our Living Costs and Food Survey (LCF), a voluntary sample survey of around 5,000 private households in the UK. These statistics are assessed fully compliant with the Code of Practice for Statistics and are therefore designated as National Statistics. The derivation of household income, and its components, is based on international best practice, following as close as possible guidelines laid out in The Canberra Group Handbook on Household Income Statistics (2011).

For the first time, these statistics are produced on an individual rather than a household level. This means that income quintiles, for example, are derived by ordering people, rather than households, on an equivalised household disposable income basis. This method is consistent with the statistics reported in Average household income, UK: financial year ending 2018 and Household income inequality, UK: financial year ending 2018, and ensures the variance in household size across the income distribution is better accounted for.

We are currently working on transforming our data on the distribution of household finances. The first part of this work has concentrated on combining the samples from the LCF and another of our household surveys, the Survey on Living Conditions (SLC), and harmonising the income collection in these questionnaires. This will result in a dataset formed of a sample of around 17,000 households. This first stage of work was carried out during financial year ending (FYE) 2018. Work is currently under way to quality assure these data before publishing initial results later this year.

In addition, the Office for National Statistics (ONS) is working towards linking data from administrative and other non-survey sources, including HM Revenue and Customs' (HMRC's) Real Time Information (RTI) and the Department for Work and Pensions' (DWP's) benefits data. Although these other sources also have their own limitations, by using them together with surveys we should be able to produce better data on household income. More information on our plans for transforming our household finance statistics is available in the article Transformation of ONS household financial statistics: ONS statistical outputs workplan, 2018 to 2019.

6 . Strengths and limitations

As with all survey-based sources, the data are subject to some limitations. The Living Costs and Food Survey (LCF) is known to suffer from under-reporting at the top and bottom of the income distribution as well as non-response error (see the Effects of taxes and benefits on household income Quality and Methodology Information (QMI) report for further details of the sources of error). We are exploring adjustments as presented in Using tax data to better capture top earners in household income inequality statistics for the under-reporting and under coverage of the richest people.

Further, as these data are based on a survey of the private household population, they do not include those living in communal establishments such as care homes and student halls of residence, as well as some core groups of the homeless populations.

The Department for Work and Pensions (DWP) also produces an analysis of the UK income distribution in its annual Households below average income (HBAI) publication, using data from its Family Resources Survey (FRS). While the FRS is subject to the same limitations as other survey sources, it benefits from a larger sample size (approximately 19,000 households) than the LCF and, as such, will have a higher level of precision than ETB estimates.

In addition, HBAI includes an adjustment for "very rich" households to correct for the under-reporting using data from HM Revenue and Customs' (HMRC's) Survey of Personal Incomes (SPI). As mentioned earlier, we are in the process of investigating top-income adjustment for these statistics. These differences make HBAI a better source for looking at income-based analysis that does not need a longer time series (the FRS data are available from financial year ending (FYE) 1995) and when looking at smaller subgroups of the population, particularly at the upper end of the income distribution.

7 . More about household income

The effects of taxes and benefits on household income, financial year ending 2018: technical report
Released 30 May 2019
Provides further detail on how the effects of taxes and benefits on household income estimates are produced. This report also provides further information on the measurement of income inequality.

Households below average income (HBAI)
Released 28 March 2019
The Department for Work and Pensions produces statistics on the number and percentage of people living in low-income households in the UK.

Average household income and Household income inequality
Bulletins | Released 26 February 2019
Two separate bulletins providing first survey-based estimates of average household income, and income inequality for financial year ending 2018.

Transformation of ONS household financial statistics: ONS statistical outputs workplan, 2018 to 2019
Article | Released 20 June 2018
Information on our plans for transforming ONS's Household Finance Statistics, including combining the samples from the Living Costs and Food Survey and the Survey on Living Conditions. It also looks at how we are working towards using administrative data from HM Revenue and Customs and the Department for Work and Pensions.

Using tax data to better capture top earners in household income inequality statistics
Article | Released 26 February 2019
Experimental Statistics examining the impact of replacing incomes at the very top of the distribution with tax records information contained within HMRC's Survey on Personal Incomes (SPI).

8 . You may also be interested in

A guide to sources of data on earnings and income
Article | Updated 4 February 2019
Further information on other sources of income and earnings data, including the appropriate uses of and limitations of each data source.

Employee earnings in the UK
Statistical bulletin | Updated 25 October 2018
Important measures of employee earnings, using data from the Annual Survey of Hours and Earnings (ASHE). Figures are presented mainly for full-time employees, although some detail for part-time workers is also included.

Centre for Equalities and Inclusion
Article | Updated April 2019
The Centre for Equalities and Inclusion aims to improve the evidence base for understanding equity and fairness in the UK today, enabling new insights into important policy questions. We are a multi-disciplinary convening centre based at the Office for National Statistics, bringing together people interested in equalities data and analysis from across central and local government, academia, business and the third sector.

Personal and economic well-being in the UK: April 2019
Statistical bulletin | Updated 11 April 2019
Estimates looking across both personal well-being (January to December 2018) and economic well-being (October to December 2018) in the UK. This bulletin is part of a new series on "people and prosperity" introduced in February 2019.

Wealth in Great Britain Wave 5: 2014 to 2016
Statistical bulletin | Updated 1 February 2018
Main results from the fifth wave of the Wealth and Assets Survey covering the period July 2014 to June 2016.

Family spending in the UK: April 2017 to March 2018
Statistical bulletin | Updated 24 January 2019
Average weekly household expenditure on goods and services in the UK, by region, age, income, economic status, socio-economic class and household composition.

Article

Persistent poverty in the UK and EU: 2017

Comparisons of persistent poverty between UK and other EU countries.

Contact:	Release date:	Next release:
Dominic Webber / Oliver Mann	6 June 2019	To be announced
hie@ons.gov.uk		
+44 (0) 1633 456246		

Table of contents

1 . Main points

- In the UK, 7.8% of the population were in persistent poverty, equivalent to roughly 4.7 million people; persistent poverty is defined as experiencing relative low income both in the current year and at least two out of the three preceding years.

- Persistent poverty rates in the UK in 2017 are comparable with levels in 2008, while Eurostat reported an estimated increase of 2.6 percentage points for the European Union (EU) over this period to 11.3%.

- Out of the 28 EU member states, the UK had the 12th highest poverty rate in 2017, but only the 20th highest persistent poverty rate; this reflects that in the UK, for those experiencing relative low income, it is more likely to be for a shorter period of time.

- An estimated 2.4 million working people were in poverty in 2017, of which 31% also experienced in-work poverty in 2016

- The most frequent reason for leaving in-work poverty was for employees to keep the same job and number of hours, but to increase their hourly pay, accounting for 44% of those who exited.

- Persistent material deprivation – which provides an estimate of the proportion of people whose living conditions are severely affected by a lack of resources – fell to 2.1% in 2017, continuing the decline over the past four years.

- People who were in persistent poverty were over four and a half times and five times more likely to be material deprived and persistently material deprived respectively than the average individual.

2 . Persistent poverty in the UK is lower than the average for the rest of Europe

Figure 1: Persistent poverty in the UK is lower than the average for the rest of Europe

Persistent at risk of poverty rates and at risk of poverty rates, EU28 and other select countries, 2017

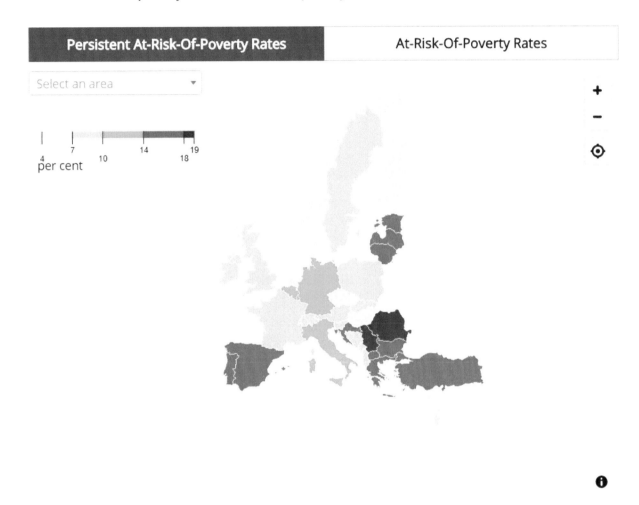

Source: Office for National Statistics, Eurostat

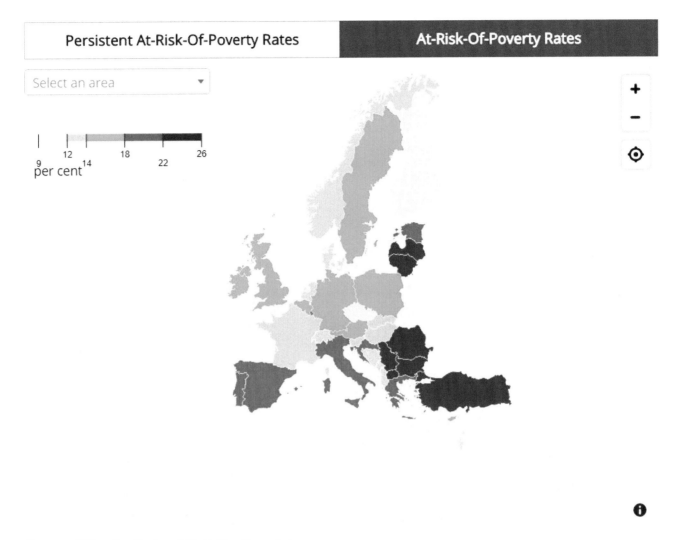

Select an area ▾

per cent
9 12 14 18 22 26

+
−
⊙

ⓘ

Source: Office for National Statistics, Eurostat

Notes:

1. Includes data from EU28 and for other select countries, Norway, Turkey, Serbia and North Macedonia who are not members of the EU. Slovakia's data for persistent poverty is unavailable.

This release presents estimates of poverty, and persistent poverty in the UK, and Europe.

The definition of poverty used is at-risk-of-poverty, and people are defined as such if they live in a household with an equivalised disposable income that falls below 60% of the national median in the current year.

Persistent poverty is defined as being in poverty in the current year and at least two of the three preceding years. This type of relative indicator does not measure absolute wealth or poverty, but low income in comparison with others living in the same country, which in itself does not necessarily imply a low standard of living. More information about the definitions of poverty, and the sources used is contained within the Measuring the data section.

In 2017, the persistent poverty rate for the UK was 7.8% – the eighth lowest in the European Union and 3.5 percentage points lower than the EU28 average rate of 11.3%. Among EU member states, Czechia has the lowest persistent poverty rate, while Romania has the highest – 4.4% and 19.1%. France and Slovenia have similar persistent poverty rates to the UK – 8.0% and 8.2% respectively.

In contrast to persistent poverty, the UK's and EU's poverty rates rate were similar – 17.0% and 16.9% respectively. The UK's poverty rate is similar to Malta (16.7%) and Portugal (18.3%).

Countries have, for the most part, similar poverty and persistent poverty rates as their neighbours. For example, the Nordic countries (Sweden, Norway, Denmark, and Finland) all have lower than average poverty and persistent poverty rates. The Baltic states (Latvia, Lithuania, and Estonia) and countries in the Balkans (Romania, Bulgaria, North Macedonia and Serbia) all have higher than average poverty and persistent poverty rates. One exception is Czechia, which has lower poverty and persistent poverty compared with neighbouring countries.

Figure 2: UK's persistent poverty rates are relatively stable between 2008 to 2017, while the EU average has increased

Poverty and persistent at risk of poverty from 2008 to 2017 in the UK and EU28

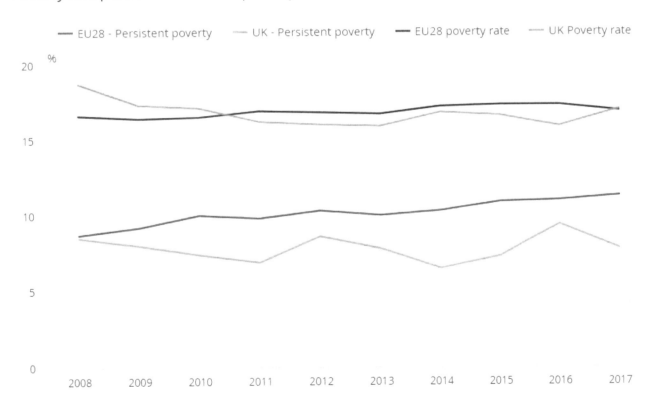

Poverty and persistent at risk of poverty from 2008 to 2017 in the UK and EU28

Source: Eurostat, Office for National Statistics

Between 2009 and 2017, the UK's overall poverty rate is broadly comparable with the average of EU member states, both fluctuating between 15.9% and 17.3%. In contrast, the UK persistent poverty rate was lower than the EU average over the same period. While the UK has remained at a broadly similar level (8.5% in 2008 and 7.8% in 2017), the EU average has been slowly rising over the decade. This has led to a widening gap over the long-term, so that in 2017 the EU persistent poverty rate was 3.5 percentage points higher than the UK's (Figure 2).

This relationship between rates of persistent poverty and overall poverty can be most clearly seen when considering the ratio between the two rates expressed as a percentage (Figure 3). A ratio of 50% would suggest that half of those currently in poverty were also poor in at least two out of the last three years.

Figure 3: Poverty in the UK tends to be more temporary compared with other European countries.

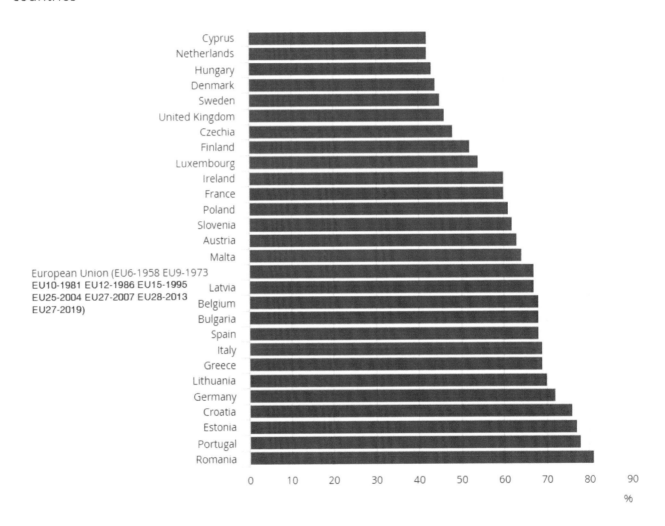

Proportion of those in poverty who are persistently in poverty, UK and EU28 countries

Source: Eurostat, Office for National Statistics

Notes:

1. Excludes Slovakia as their persistent poverty rates are unavailable.

In 2017, 46% of the people in the UK who were in poverty were also in persistent poverty. This is the sixth lowest of EU member states and 21 percentage points below the EU28 average (67%). This indicates that people in poverty in the UK are relatively more likely to exit poverty quickly, rather than it being a longer-term phenomenon. In this regard, the UK is similar to Sweden and Czechia, although in Czechia individuals are overall less likely to enter poverty. Cyprus has the lowest proportion of individuals in poverty and persistent poverty (42%), while Romania has the highest (81%).

Poverty entry and exit rates provide useful insight into transitions in and out of poverty, and can reflect the changes those with low incomes can experience. Poverty entry rates are defined as the proportion of population that enter poverty each year, while the exit rates show the proportion of those in poverty who exit poverty each year.

Figure 4: Poverty entry rates in the UK have been broadly stable over recent years, while the exit rates have declined

Poverty entry and exit rates for the UK, 2008 to 2017, percentage of individuals

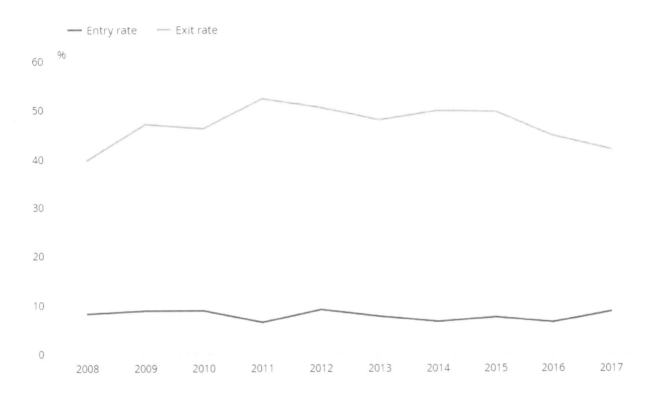

In 2017, the UK's poverty entry rate was 8.6%, while the exit rate was 41.8%. Entry rates have been steady between 2008 and 2017. Typically, the poverty exit rate has been above 40% since 2008 and was closer to 50% between 2011 and 2014. Since 2014, the exit rate has declined and is at its lowest point since 2008 in 2017, indicating that people experiencing relative low incomes are less likely to exit poverty than they were for most of the previous decade.

As there are fewer people in poverty than not in poverty, it is expected that exit rates expressed as a percentage of those in poverty would be higher than entry rates as a percentage of those not in poverty. Small changes in the number of people in each case would equate to a much larger percentage change for those in poverty.

Figure 5: Most individuals remain in the same work and poverty status in 2017

Transitions between work status and poverty status, 2016 to 2017, UK, percentage

Select a variable: [All transitions ▾]

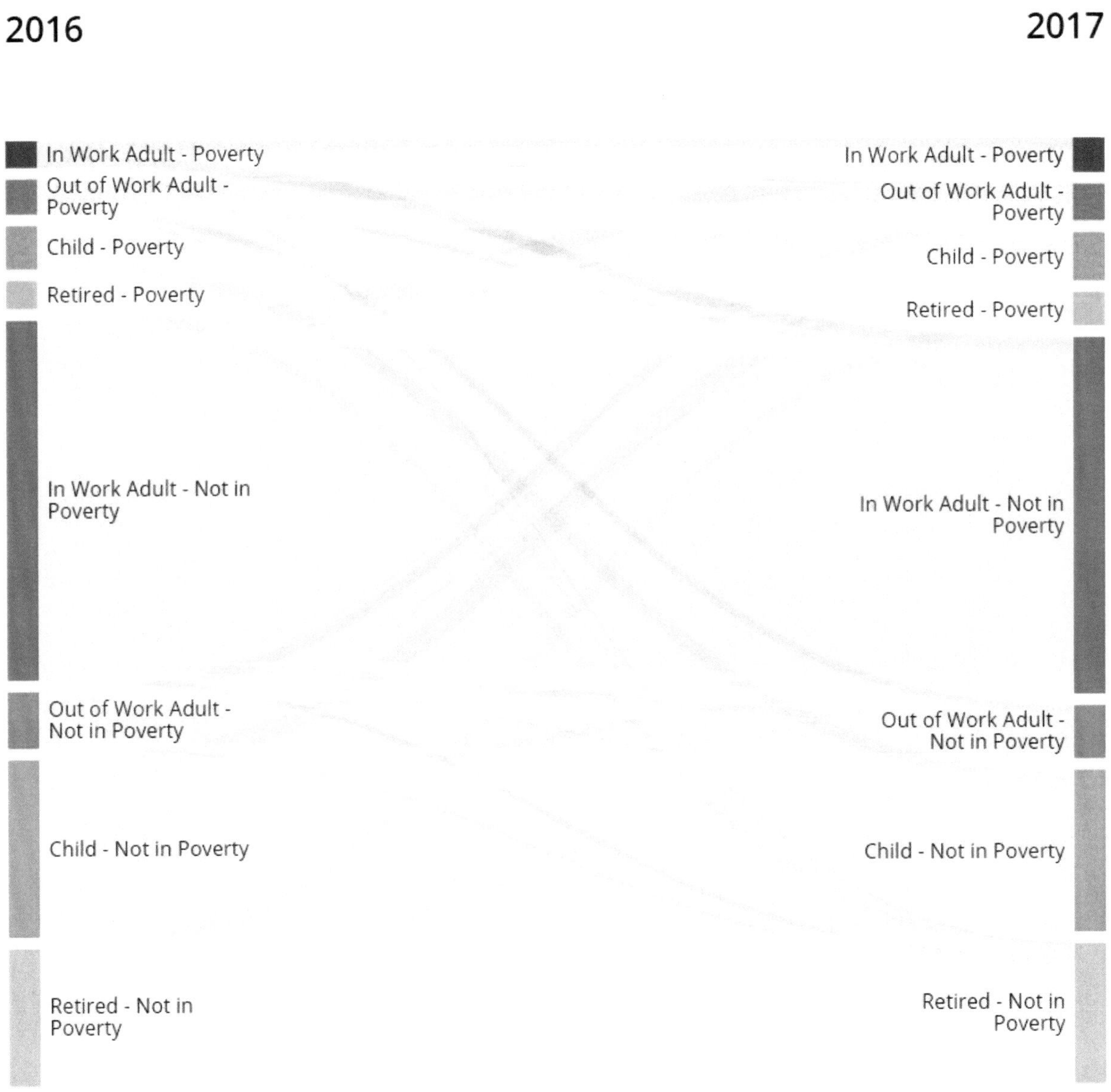

2016   2017

2016	2017
In Work Adult - Poverty	In Work Adult - Poverty
Out of Work Adult - Poverty	Out of Work Adult - Poverty
Child - Poverty	Child - Poverty
Retired - Poverty	Retired - Poverty
In Work Adult - Not in Poverty	In Work Adult - Not in Poverty
Out of Work Adult - Not in Poverty	Out of Work Adult - Not in Poverty
Child - Not in Poverty	Child - Not in Poverty
Retired - Not in Poverty	Retired - Not in Poverty

Notes:

1. Number of people in each transition available via csv and xls download (Rounded to nearest 100,0000).

Figure 5 highlights the proportion of people in each type of work and poverty status in 2016 and 2017, as well as the transitions between them (see glossary for definition of work status). In 2016, 42% of the population were both in-work and not in poverty, falling by 1 percentage point to 41% in 2017.

Overall, 79% of individuals remained in the same work and poverty statuses in 2017, mainly driven by the 37% of people who stayed in work and out of poverty for both years.

Looking in more detail, the majority (62%) of those who were in child poverty in 2016 were also in poverty the following year, while 38% left poverty in 2017. Conversely, 13.1% of those children who were not in poverty in 2016 were in a household with relative low income the following year.

Of those who were in in-work poverty in 2016, around half – equivalent to 1 million people – left in-work poverty the following year, while the rest remained in in-work poverty in 2017.

Exploring further those who enter poverty, the largest amount (29.8%) are dependent children (in both years), closely followed by in-work adults (26.2%). While the majority of transitions (89%) were people who stayed within their original work status, 4.2% moved from in-work to out-of-work, and 1.8% from retired to being in-work.

Similarly, the largest amount of those exiting poverty (26.5%) were dependent children, followed by those who remained in-work (26.3%). Fourteen per cent of people who exited poverty, entered work from being out-of-work – the largest proportion out of those who exited poverty, and changed their work status.

There are multiple ways in which a person can exit in-work poverty, and often these factors can occur simultaneously. Figure 6 examines different circumstances such as people increasing their hours or pay or both, either in their current job or in a new job. The "Other" category denotes circumstances not captured, such as changes to the composition of the household, changes in the income from sources other than employment, or increased earnings from another household member.

Figure 6: Employees keeping the same job and number of hours, but increasing their hourly pay is most frequent reason for exiting in-work poverty

Proportion of people exiting in work poverty by reason, 2016 to 2017, UK

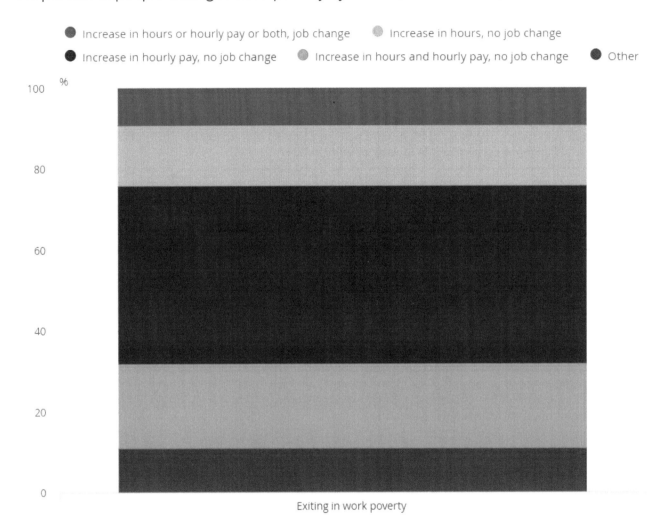

Proportion of people exiting in work poverty by reason, 2016 to 2017, UK

- ● Increase in hours or hourly pay or both, job change
- ● Increase in hours, no job change
- ● Increase in hourly pay, no job change
- ● Increase in hours and hourly pay, no job change
- ● Other

Exiting in work poverty

Source: Office for National Statistics

Notes:

1. An increase in hourly earnings refers to a nominal increase of 5% or more.

2. An increase in hours worked refers to an increase of 5% or more.

Figure 6 shows that 44% of people exited in-work poverty due in increases in their hourly pay, without a significant change in the hours they worked, while remaining in the same job. The majority of people who exited in-work poverty were those who stayed within the same job – 81%.

While assessing living standards in terms of looking at households with relative low income, it is also useful to expand the focus on other measures. For example, income tends to be volatile and, as such, it may not adequately reflect an individual's well-being. For example, short-term unemployment or sickness may cause a temporary reduction in income, which will not necessarily be matched by a corresponding drop in consumption or well-being. Similarly, more systematic lifetime fluctuations that lead to a reduction in income may not adversely affect their consumption, as people might be spending their wealth, for example.

Severe material deprivation describes the proportion of individuals in the population who are unable to afford four or more items considered by most people to be desirable or even necessary for everyday life. More information on these items are contained within the Glossary. Similar to poverty and persistent poverty, if someone is in severe material deprivation for the current and two of the three previous years, then they are in persistent severe material deprivation.

The severe material deprivation and persistent severe material deprivation rates were 4.1%, and 2.1% respectively in 2017. This suggests that just over half of those who are in material deprivation are in persistent material deprivation. For those in poverty, as a comparison, under half of them were also in persistent poverty.

Figure 7: Severe material deprivation and persistent severe material deprivation have fallen in recent years

Severe material deprivation and persistent severe material deprivation rates, 2008 to 2017, UK

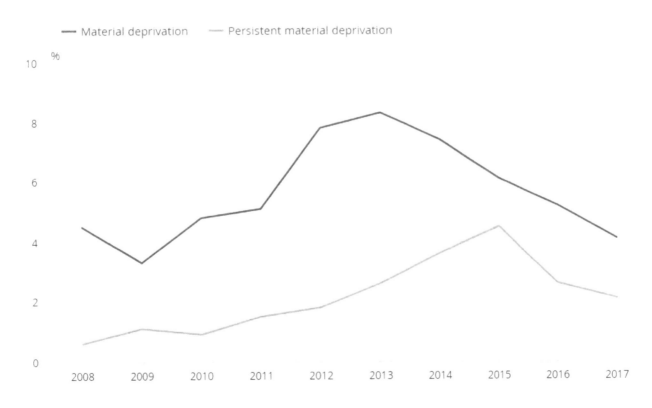

Severe material deprivation and persistent severe material deprivation rates, 2008 to 2017, UK

Source: Eurostat, Office for National Statistics

Material deprivation has decreased by nearly 1 percentage point each year in the last four years, falling 4.2 percentage points from 8.3% to 4.1% in-between 2013 and 2017. Persistent material deprivation has been on a downward trend since 2015, after increasing from 2008 although at a slower rate, falling 1.5 percentage points from 3.6% to 2.1%.

Figure 8: People who are in persistent poverty are more likely to be materially deprived and persistently material deprived

Material deprivation and persistent material deprivation by poverty status of individual, 2017

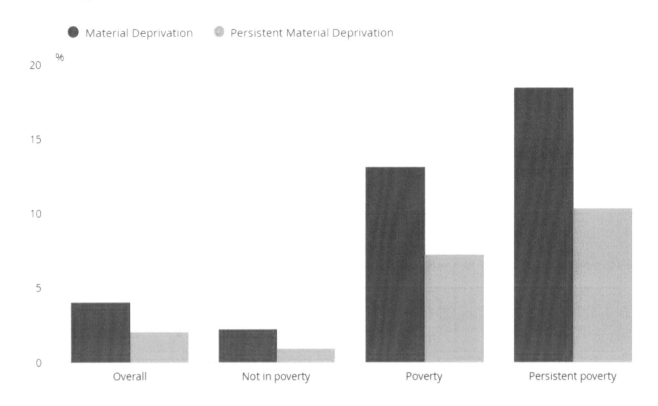

Source: Office for National Statistics

Poverty and persistent poverty rates are positively associated with severe material deprivation. In 2017, of those who were in poverty, 13.2% of individuals were severally materially deprived, while 7.3% were in persistent material deprivation. While, out of those who were persistently in poverty 18.5% of them were also in material deprivation and 10.4% were in persistent material deprivation. Those who were not in poverty had a lower material deprivation with 2.3% of individuals being in material deprivation, while 1% were in persistent material deprivation.

Figure 9: 33% of population can't afford an unexpected expense

Proportion of individuals who meet a material deprivation condition,
percentage UK 2017

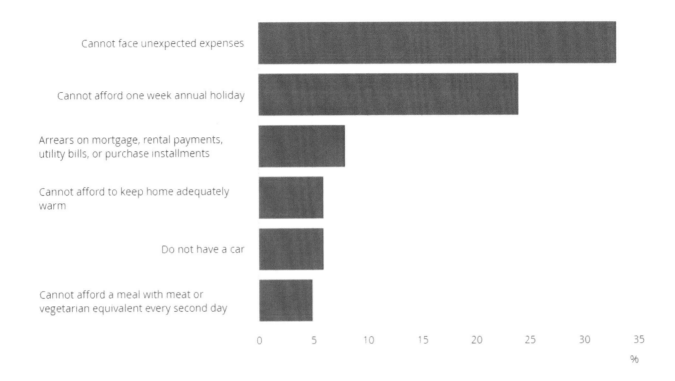

Source: Source: Office for National Statistics

Figure 9 highlights the proportion of individuals who have an enforced lack of each material deprivation item defined in the Glossary. A third of people cannot face unexpected expenses, while 23.7% cannot afford a one-week annual holiday.

3 . Related statistics and analysis

The Department for Work and Pensions publish experimental data on Income Dynamics, using data from the Understanding Society survey. This release included estimates of "persistent low income", a similar measure to the persistent poverty rate considered in this release. For comparison, experiencing persistent poverty is defined as being in poverty in the current year and at least two of the three preceding years, whereas experiencing persistent low income is defined as being in low income for any three of the last four survey periods. As the definition of persistent low income does not require the individual to be in low income in the current year, the proportion of people experiencing persistent low income higher compared with on a persistent poverty measure (Figure 10).

Comparisons of persistent relative low income using different data sources

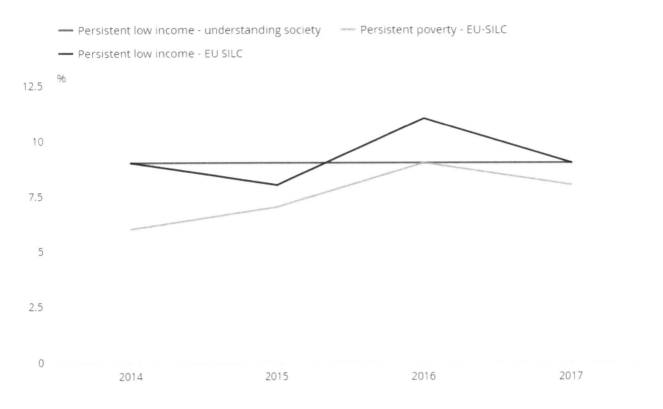

Source: Department for Work and Pensions, Office for National Statistics

4 . Background information

This article uses the latest longitudinal data from the European Union Statistics on Income and Living Conditions (EU-SILC), which covers the years 2014-2017. EU-SILC is coordinated by Eurostat (the European Commission's statistical agency) under EU regulation and provides cross sectional and longitudinal data on income, poverty and living conditions across Europe. Alongside the 28 EU countries, other countries including Norway, North Macedonia, Serbia and Turkey submit data. These four countries identified here are included with in the article.

5 . Measuring this data

What is persistent poverty?

In this release, individuals are experiencing relative poverty if they live in a household with an equivalised disposable income that falls below 60% of the national median in the current year. This is a relative low-income measure also referred to as the "at risk of poverty" rate, which measures income compared with other people. As such, being at risk of poverty does not necessarily imply a low standard of living.

Experiencing persistent poverty is defined as being in relative income poverty in the current year and at least two of the three preceding years.

Results are based on the European Union Statistics on Income and Living Conditions (EU-SILC), a household survey conducted since 2005 in EU member states and other select countries.

It is generally agreed that the effects of experiencing relative low income for long periods of time are more detrimental than experiencing low income for short periods. These measures are used by the European Commission as part of their indicators to monitor poverty and social exclusion across the EU.

A household's disposable income is the money available for spending after Income Tax, National Insurance and Council Tax are subtracted. It consists of wages and salaries from employment and self-employment, investment income, private and state pensions, and other benefits.

Equivalisation adjusts the income to consider the size and composition of the household. Income in this analysis is equivalised using the modified Organisation for Economic Co-operation and Development (OECD) (PDF, 165KB) scale.

While the focus in this release is on relative low income, in terms of measuring poverty, there are alternative approaches, some of which take into account a wider measure of the resources available to people. For example, the Social Metrics Commission's A new measure of poverty for the UK report (PDF, 1MB) details how a poverty measure was developed which takes into account not just incomes but liquid assets such as savings, as well as certain inescapable costs, such as rent or mortgage payments and childcare. The Department for Work and Pensions will publish experimental statistics in the second half of 2020 that will take the current Social Metrics Commission measure as a starting point and assess whether and how this can be developed and improved further to increase the value of these statistics to the public.

6 . Glossary

Disposable income

Disposable income is the amount of money that households have available for spending and saving after direct taxes (such as Income Tax and Council Tax) have been accounted for. It includes earnings from employment, private pensions and investments as well as cash benefits provided by the state.

Equivalisation

Equivalisation is the process of accounting for the fact that households with many members are likely to need a higher income to achieve the same standard of living as households with fewer members. Equivalisation takes into account the number of people living in the household and their ages, acknowledging that whilst a household with two people in it will need more money to sustain the same living standards as one with a single person, the two-person household is unlikely to need double the income.

Poverty

This release uses at-risk-of-poverty to define poverty. An individual is deemed to be at-risk-of-poverty if they live in a household with an equivalised disposable income below the poverty threshold. This threshold is set at 60% of national median equivalised disposable income.

Persistent poverty

An individual is in persistent poverty if they are in poverty for the current year as well as two of the past three years.

Entry and exit rates

The poverty entry rate is the percentage of people not in poverty in one year who transition into poverty in the following year. The poverty exit rate is the percentage of people in poverty in one year who transition out of poverty in the following year.

In-work poverty

An individual who identifies as being in work and whose equivalised household income is below 60% of the median equivalised household income across the UK. In-work includes being employed or self-employment and full-time and part-time employment.

Dependent children

A dependent child is defined as an individual who is below 18-years-old or is below 25-years-old, out of work, and is living with at least one parent.

Material deprivation

An individual is in severe material deprivation if they do not have the ability to afford four or more of the following conditions:

- to not have arrears on your mortgage or rent payments, hire purchase instalments or other loan payments

- to afford a one-week annual holiday away from home

- to afford a meal with meat, chicken, fish or a vegetarian equivalent every other day

- to be able to face unexpected financial expenses

- to afford a telephone or mobile phone

- to afford a colour television

- to afford a washing machine

- to afford a car

- to afford to keep the home adequately warm

Persistent material deprivation

An individual is in persistent material deprivation if they are in material deprivation for the current year and two of the previous three years.

7 . More about household income

<u>Households below average income (HBAI)</u>

Released 28 March 2019

The Department for Work and Pensions produce statistics on the number and percentage of people living in low-income households in the UK.

<u>Average household income</u> and <u>Household income inequality</u>

Bulletins | Released on 26 February 2019

Two separate bulletins providing first survey-based statistics on average household income, and income inequality for financial year ending 2018.

<u>Effects of taxes and benefits on UK household income: financial year ending 2018</u>

Released 30 May 2019

The redistribution effects on individuals and households of direct and indirect taxation and benefits received in cash or kind analysed by household type, and the changing levels of income inequality over time.

<u>EU-SILC</u>

European Union member states produce statistics on income and living conditions. These include social indicators at risk of poverty, persistent at risk of poverty and material deprivation.

8 . You may also be interested in

<u>A guide to sources of data on earnings and income</u>

Article | Updated 4 February 2019

For further information on other sources of income and earnings data, including the appropriate uses of and limitations of each data source see Contact name.

<u>Employee earnings in the UK</u>

Statistical bulletins | Updated 25 October 2018

Important measures of employee earnings, using data from the Annual Survey of Hours and Earnings (ASHE). Figures are presented mainly for full-time employees, although some detail for part-time workers is also included.

Centre for Equalities and Inclusion

Article | Released on 12 December 2018

The Centre for Equalities and Inclusion aims to improve the evidence base for understanding equity and fairness in the UK today, enabling new insights into key policy questions. We are a multi-disciplinary convening centre based at Office for National Statistics, bringing together people interested in equalities data and analysis from across central and local government, academia, business and the third sector.

Personal and economic well-being in the UK: April 2019

Statistical bulletins | Updated 4 April 2019

Estimates of the combined findings for personal well-being (January 2018 to December 2018) and economic well-being (October to December 2018) in the UK. This is part of a new series on people and prosperity.

Wealth in Great Britain Wave 5: 2014 to 2016

Statistical bulletins | Updated 1 February 2018

Main results from the fifth wave of the Wealth and Assets Survey covering the period July 2014 to June 2016.

Family spending in the UK: April 2017 to March 2018

Statistical bulletins | Updated 24 January 2019

Average weekly household expenditure on goods and services in the UK, by region, age, income, economic status, socio-economic class and household composition.

Are young people detached from their neighbourhoods?

Born in the digital age, young people are thought to be disconnected from their local area.

24 July 2019

How close do you feel to your neighbourhood? With much of our lives having moved online, there is a perception that people have become detached from their local community.

Young people – as the biggest users of the internet and social media – are thought to be most likely to forego conversation in person for their phone or device.

But last year's Ofcom communications report (PDF, 12,21MB) showed that most people of all ages see the internet as important for maintaining personal relationships, while recognising that it hampers face-to-face communications.

So, is it fair to single young people out, or are we all losing touch with our community?

We have analysed data from the Community Life Survey[1] to understand how young people engage with their local area, compared with the rest of the adult population.

What percentage of young people say they belong to their neighbourhood?

% who feel 'very' or 'fairly' strongly that they belong to their neighbourhood

Young people are less likely to say they belong to their neighbourhood than the rest of the population, but the gap has closed over time.

Nearly 55% of 16- to 24-year-olds felt they belonged to their neighbourhood in 2017 to 2018, compared with 64% of 25 and overs. Back in 2013 to 2014, just 42% of young people reported a sense of belonging, versus 61% of older adults.

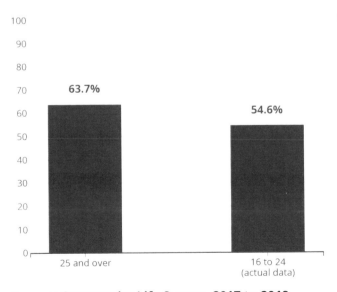

Source: Community Life Survey, 2017 to 2018

What percentage of young people trust people in their neighbourhood?

% who feel they can trust 'some' or 'many' people living in their neighbourhood

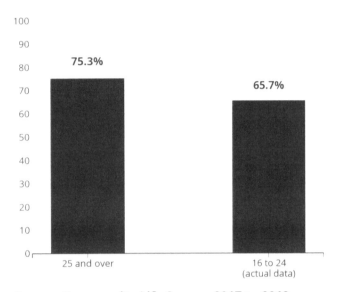

75.3%

65.7%

25 and over	16 to 24 (actual data)

Source: Community Life Survey, 2017 to 2018

What percentage of young people are satisfied with their local area as a place to live?

% who feel 'very' or 'fairly' satisfied with their area as a place to live

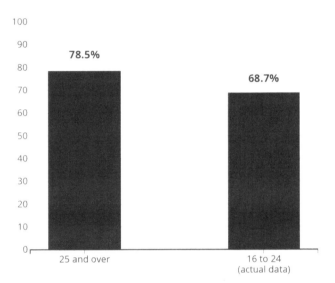

78.5%

68.7%

25 and over	16 to 24 (actual data)

Source: Community Life Survey, 2017 to 2018

Almost two-thirds (66%) of 16- to 24-year-olds say at least some of their neighbours can be trusted, compared with 75% of those aged 25 and over.

Young people remain as likely to trust their neighbours as in 2013 to 2014, while levels of trust among older adults have fallen slightly.

Around 69% of 16- to 24-year-olds think their area is a satisfactory place to live, compared with 79% of 25 and overs.

Local area satisfaction is little-changed since 2013 to 2014 for both age groups.

By any of these measures, young people feel less connected to their neighbourhood than older adults.

This is despite many young people having lived locally for all or most of their life. More than half (55%) of 16- to 24-year-olds have lived in their neighbourhood for at least 10 years, compared with 57% of those aged 25 and over.

But it is wrong to say that young people are losing touch with their community. In fact, they feel a greater sense of belonging now compared with a few years ago, while levels of trust and local area satisfaction remain unchanged.

The next part looks at how people engage with their community.

What percentage of young people do civic activities in their community, such as contacting a local official, signing a petition or attending a rally?

% who have taken part in civic activities in the last year

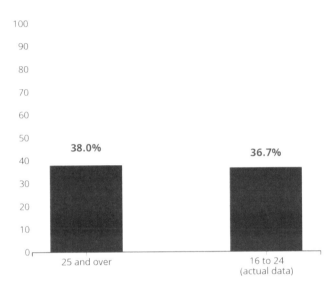

Source: Community Life Survey, 2017 to 2018

Around 37% of 16- to 24-year-olds have contacted a local official, signed a petition or attended a rally in the last 12 months, up from 32% in 2013 to 2014.

This compares with 38% of people aged 25 and older, which is down slightly from 40% in 2013 to 2014.

What percentage of young people say they can influence decisions affecting their local area?

% who agree they can influence decisions affecting their local area

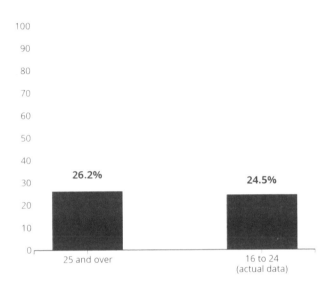

Source: Community Life Survey, 2017 to 2018

Most people don't feel they can influence local decisions – 25% of 16- to 24-year-olds say they can influence decisions affecting their area, compared with 26% of those aged 25 and over.

Both of these are unchanged since 2013 to 2014.

What percentage of young people participate in formal volunteering?

% who have participated in formal volunteering in last 12 months

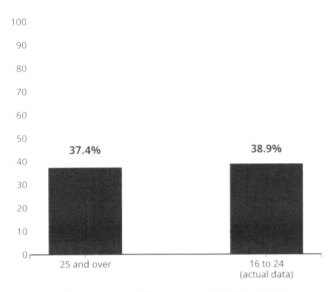

37.4%	38.9%
25 and over	16 to 24 (actual data)

Source: Community Life Survey, 2017 to 2018

Using these measures, it's clear that young people are as likely to participate in their local community as the rest of the population.

But, despite seeing an improvement since 2013 to 2014, young people are less likely to say they belong to their neighbourhood than older adults.

This could be linked to the fact that young people are more likely to report feelings of loneliness. According to the most recent Community Life Survey (PDF, 725KB), 8% of 16- to 24-year-olds living in England felt lonely "often" or "always" in 2017 to 2018, compared with 5% of those aged 25 and over[2].

Research by King's College London has investigated the possible link between young people's loneliness and neighbourhood belonging. Their study – based on a sample of 18-year-olds living in the UK – found that "feeling lonely could put a negative bias on people's subjective perceptions of their local area", leading them to "miss out on opportunities to connect with people around them".

Nearly 39% of young people said they had done formal volunteering in the last 12 months, compared with 37% of older adults. Both are down since 2013 to 2014, from 48% and 45% respectively.

Formal volunteering is defined as providing unpaid help to groups, clubs and organisations.

Footnotes

1. Findings from the Community Life Survey refer to England only in 2017 to 2018. For the purposes of this analysis, "young people" are those aged 16 to 24, while the rest of the population are aged 25 and over.

2. The rate of loneliness was 8% among 25- to 34-year-olds in 2017 to 2018, the same as 16- to 24-year-olds. Those age groups were most likely to feel lonely often or always.

Contact

policy.evidence.analysis@ons.gov.uk

Statistical bulletin

Personal well-being in the UK: April 2018 to March 2019

Estimates of life satisfaction, feeling that the things done in life are worthwhile, happiness and anxiety at the UK, country, regional, county and local authority level.

Contact:
Laurence Day and Liam Clements
qualityoflife@ons.gov.uk
+44 (0)1633 456300

Release date:
23 October 2019

Next release:
14 November 2019

Table of contents

1 . Main points

- In the year ending March 2019, there was little change in personal well-being measures in the UK, apart from a slight improvement in average happiness ratings which increased from 7.52 to 7.56.

- Over this period, the only significant change at country level was in Northern Ireland, where anxiety ratings increased from 2.53 to 2.83 (out of 10). This brought Northern Ireland back into line with the other UK countries on this measure.

- The first year from which we have a full UK baseline at local level is the year ending March 2013. Since then, average life satisfaction improved by 3.4% in the UK, with the largest improvement recorded in London (4.6%) at regional level.

- Over the same long-term period, average anxiety ratings in the UK improved by 5.3%, with the North West seeing the largest improvement (by 9.7%) at regional level.

- Across the UK, areas with persistently higher average well-being ratings, between the years ending March 2012 and March 2019, included the Orkney Islands, Na h-Eileanan Siar, and Shetland Islands in Scotland, and Fermanagh and Omagh in Northern Ireland.

- Over the same period, areas with persistently lower average well-being ratings included the London boroughs of Lambeth, Hackney, Islington and Camden.

2 . UK and country-level personal well-being

Between the years ending March 2018 and March 2019, there was very little change in the ratings of personal well-being measures. The only slight improvement was in the average rating of happiness, which increased slightly across the UK from 7.52 to 7.56, measured on a scale from 0 to 10. For the other measures of personal well-being – life satisfaction, feeling that the things done in life are worthwhile, and anxiety – average scores remained level with no significant changes over this period. For further details about UK-wide headlines, please see Personal and economic well-being in the UK: August 2019.

At country level (Figure 1), there was an 11.9% increase in anxiety ratings in Northern Ireland, from 2.53 to 2.83 (out of 10), between the years ending March 2018 and March 2019. This was driven by a substantial decrease in people reporting very low ratings of anxiety from 47.0% to 41.1%. Looking at the long term, the anxiety scores in Northern Ireland continuously improved over the last seven years. The year ending March 2018 marked the end of a generally downward trend in anxiety in Northern Ireland since we began measuring in the year ending March 2012, with anxiety increasing markedly between 2018 and 2019.

As has been the case in previous years, people in Northern Ireland gave better average ratings for life satisfaction, feelings that things done in life are worthwhile and happiness than people in England, Scotland or Wales. The increase in average anxiety score seen in 2018 to 2019 brought the average for Northern Ireland closer in line with the rest of the UK. For more information on headlines 2018 to 2019 personal well-being data for Northern Ireland, please see Personal Well-being in Northern Ireland: 2018/19.

Figure 1: The average rating of anxiety has increased by 11.9% in Northern Ireland, bringing Northern Ireland into line with the other UK countries on this measure

Average ratings of anxiety, UK countries, years ending March 2012 to March 2019

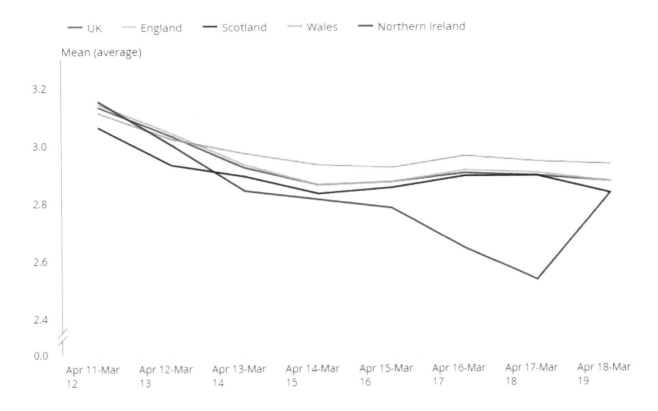

Source: Office for National Statistics - Annual Population Survey

3 . Main changes over time: life satisfaction and anxiety

We selected life satisfaction and anxiety as aspects of personal well-being to focus on as they capture both how we feel about our lives overall, and an important aspect of our day-to-day emotional state. For further analysis of the other well-being measures (happiness and feeling the things done in life are worthwhile), please see our accompanying dataset.

Average life satisfaction ratings in the UK improved by 3.4% between the years ending March 2013 and March 2019. Among the constituent countries of the UK, they improved by 3.6% in England, 3.2% in Wales, 2.5% in Northern Ireland and 2.1% in Scotland.

Figure 2: Average life satisfaction has improved most in London over the last six years

Improvement in life satisfaction (% change), UK countries and regions,
from the year ending March 2013 to the year ending March 2019

Source: Office for National Statistics - Annual Population Survey

Notes:

1. The personal well-being measures were first collected in England, Scotland and Wales at local level in April 2011 while in Northern Ireland in April 2012. The first year from which we have a full UK baseline at local level is therefore the year ending March 2013.

2. Data are weighted mean averages.

3. Changes in life satisfaction are positive, showing an improvement in average ratings over time.

4. The percentage changes over time for life satisfaction are significant for all the UK countries and regions.

We have seen the greatest improvements over time in areas that had some of the lowest average well-being ratings when we began measuring (Figure 2). For example, London continued to report some of the lowest average life satisfaction in the UK in the year ending March 2019 (7.58 compared to the UK average of 7.71), but also saw the largest improvements in well-being since the year ending March 2013 (4.6% compared to the UK percentage change of 3.4%).

By contrast, Northern Ireland, which consistently had the highest well-being ratings in the UK since we began measurement, saw the least improvement (2.5%). Although Northern Ireland still had the highest reported life satisfaction in the UK on average in the year ending March 2019 (7.89, compared to 7.71 in England, 7.68 in Wales and 7.69 in Scotland), the gap narrowed somewhat with other areas of the UK. For example, the average life satisfaction in Northern Ireland (7.70) was 3.5% higher than in England (7.44) in the year ending March 2013, while it was only 2.3% higher in the year ending March 2019.

Also at the local authority level, areas making the biggest improvements in life satisfaction were those that typically reported some of the lowest well-being. Between the years ending March 2013 and March 2019, Harlow had the greatest average increase in life satisfaction at 14.4%, followed closely by Fylde, Lancashire at 14.2%, and North Warwickshire at 14.1% (compared with the 3.6% average increase in England).

Welsh local authorities displaying a significant improvement in life satisfaction over this period peaked with Blaenau Gwent at 6.6%, followed by Merthyr Tydfil at 5.6%, Bridgend at 5.5%, Powys at 5.2%, and Torfaen 5.0%. These compared with an overall 3.2% for Wales.

In the case of the Scottish council areas, Midlothian at 6.9% recorded the greatest average increase in life satisfaction, followed by East Ayrshire at 6.6% – each approximately three times the average increase for Scotland (2.1%). Derry City and Strabane demonstrated a distinct increase in life satisfaction across this period at 8.0%, more than three times the Northern Ireland average of 2.5%. No other Northern Irish local areas showed a significant increase in life satisfaction during this time.

Looking at another measure of well-being (Figure 3), average anxiety ratings in the UK improved by 5.3% between the years ending March 2013 and March 2019. Within the UK, England is the only country to have seen a statistically significant improvement in anxiety ratings (5.6%) over this period, with the North West seeing the largest improvement (by 9.7%) at regional level. Overall, average anxiety levels in the UK showed a greater percentage decrease across the period from the years ending March 2013 to March 2019 than the percentage increase shown in average life satisfaction. Average anxiety at the UK level improved by 5.3%, whereas life satisfaction improved by 3.4%.

Figure 3: Average anxiety has improved most in North West England over the last six years

Improvement in anxiety (% change), UK countries and regions, from the year ending March 2013 to the year ending March 2019

Improvement in anxiety (% change), UK countries and regions, from the year ending March 2013 to the year ending March 2019

Source: Office for National Statistics - Annual Population Survey

Notes:

1. The personal well-being measures were first collected in England, Scotland and Wales at local level in April 2011 while in Northern Ireland in April 2012. The first year from which we have a full UK baseline at local level is therefore the year ending March 2013.

2. Data are weighted mean averages.

3. Changes in anxiety are negative, showing an improvement in average ratings over time.

4. The percentage changes over time are significant for England and the North East, North West, East, London and South East regions.

5. The percentage changes over time are not significant for Wales, Scotland, Northern Ireland and the regions of Yorkshire and the Humber, East Midlands and West Midlands and South West.

At a regional level, the most significant improvements in average anxiety levels were in areas where anxiety levels were consistently higher than the national average. Several regions in England, such as the North West, the North East, and the East of England reported relatively high average anxiety levels in the year ending March 2013 and subsequently showed greater improvements of 9.7%, 6.6% and 8.1% respectively by the year ending March 2019.

At the local authority level, the most significant improvement includes Horsham in West Sussex, showing a 46.4% decrease in average anxiety levels during this period, followed by Wellingborough, Northamptonshire at 39.4%, Eden, Cumbria at 37.3%, and South Derbyshire at 36.1%.

Lesser pronounced improvements, though still significantly above the England average, were recorded in the London boroughs of Brent and Harrow at 27.1% and 25.5% respectively as well as Wolverhampton, West Midlands at 26.0%.

In Wales, the local authorities of Wrexham and Denbighshire recorded significant improvements in average anxiety levels across this period at 16.5% and 14.9%, far above the Welsh average of 3.0%. In Scotland, North Ayrshire had the only significant improvement in average anxiety levels, with anxiety improving by 17.2%, over five times the Scottish average of 3.4%. There were no significant improvements in average anxiety levels in Northern Ireland at country and local level.

4 . Personal well-being by local area

Our personal well-being explorer tools shown in Figure 4 and 5, allow everyone to observe well-being in their local area and compare it with other areas. Some of the most insightful comparisons may relate to how specific areas have progressed over time.

It is possible to rank local authorities based on their average scores alone, however this may be misleading for various reasons such as different sample sizes, different confidence intervals and mode effects, as well as not comparing like with like (for example, we know that people in rural areas tend to rate their well-being more highly than people in urban areas). Comparisons between areas should be made with caution, and confidence intervals should be taken into account when assessing differences.

Figure 4: Personal well-being interactive maps

Average ratings, UK, years ending March 2012 to March 2019

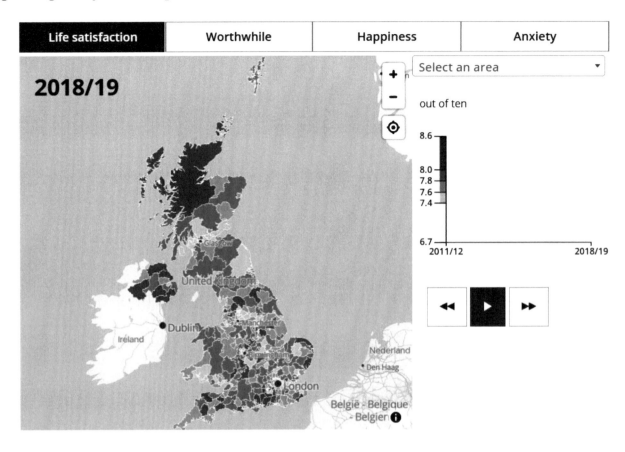

Average ratings, UK, years ending March 2012 to March 2019

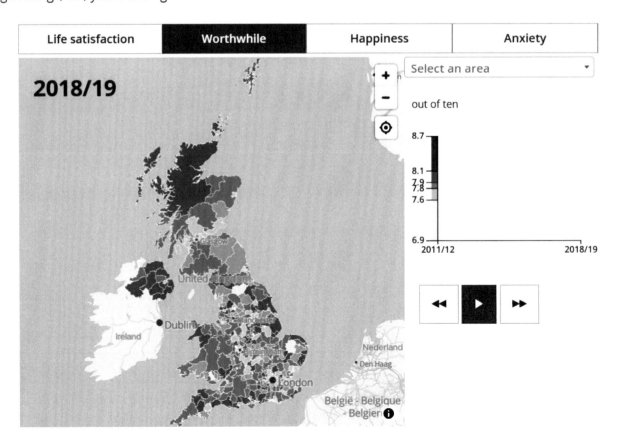

Average ratings, UK, years ending March 2012 to March 2019

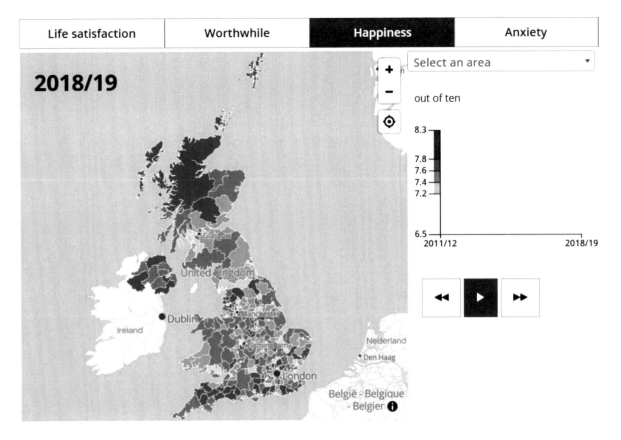

Average ratings, UK, years ending March 2012 to March 2019

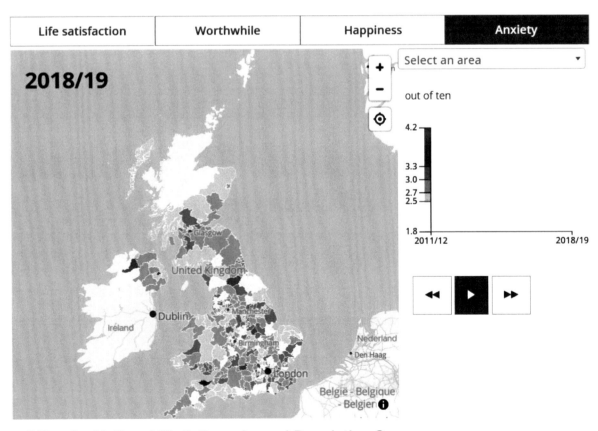

Source: Office for National Statistics - Annual Population Survey

Notes:

1. Data are weighted mean averages.

2. The personal well-being measures were first collected in England, Scotland and Wales at local level in April 2011 while in Northern Ireland in April 2012. The first year from which we have a full UK baseline at local level is therefore the year ending March 2013.

Figure 5: Personal well-being explorer

Average ratings, UK, years ending March 2012 to March 2019

Average ratings, UK, years ending March 2012 to March 2019

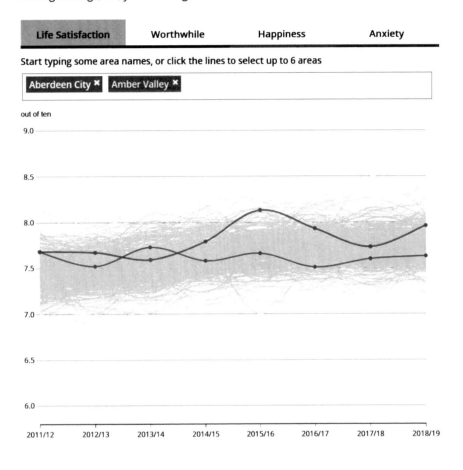

Average ratings, UK, years ending March 2012 to March 2019

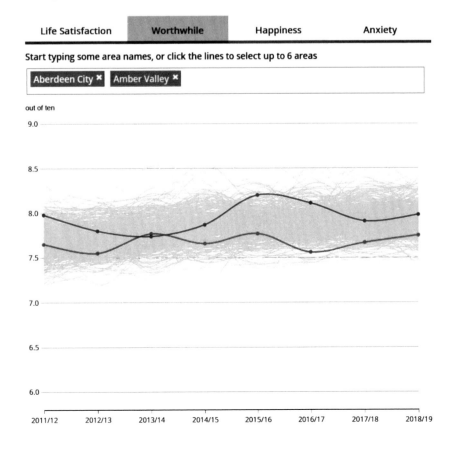

Average ratings, UK, years ending March 2012 to March 2019

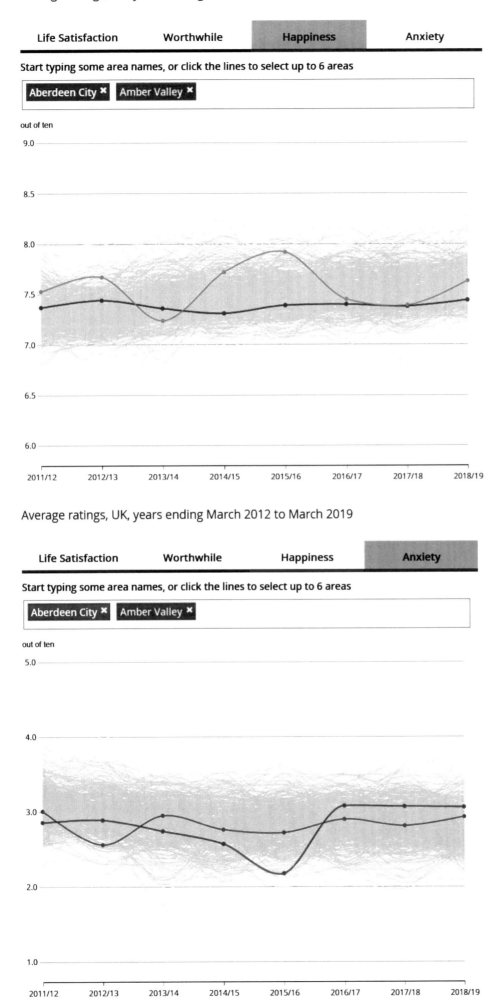

| Life Satisfaction | Worthwhile | **Happiness** | Anxiety |

Start typing some area names, or click the lines to select up to 6 areas

Aberdeen City ✖ Amber Valley ✖

out of ten

9.0

8.5

8.0

7.5

7.0

6.5

6.0

2011/12 2012/13 2013/14 2014/15 2015/16 2016/17 2017/18 2018/19

Average ratings, UK, years ending March 2012 to March 2019

| Life Satisfaction | Worthwhile | Happiness | **Anxiety** |

Start typing some area names, or click the lines to select up to 6 areas

Aberdeen City ✖ Amber Valley ✖

out of ten

5.0

4.0

3.0

2.0

1.0

2011/12 2012/13 2013/14 2014/15 2015/16 2016/17 2017/18 2018/19

Source: Office for National Statistics - Annual Population Survey

Notes:

1. Data are weighted mean averages

2. The personal well-being measures were first collected in England, Scotland and Wales at local level in April 2011 while in Northern Ireland in April 2012. The first year from which we have a full UK baseline at local level is therefore the year ending March 2013.

5 . Areas of persistently high and low well-being

In this section, we explore whether some areas of the UK persistently had high or low ratings of personal well-being. For this analysis, we considered local authorities to have persistently high or low well-being if their average personal well-being ratings were in the top or bottom 10% for the UK in at least five years since the year ending March 2012 (year ending March 2013 for Northern Ireland) and for at least two of the four well-being measures.

Figure 6: Several London boroughs persistently report low well-being across all measures of personal well-being

Local authorities consistently reporting low average personal well-being ratings, UK, between the years ending March 2012 to March 2019

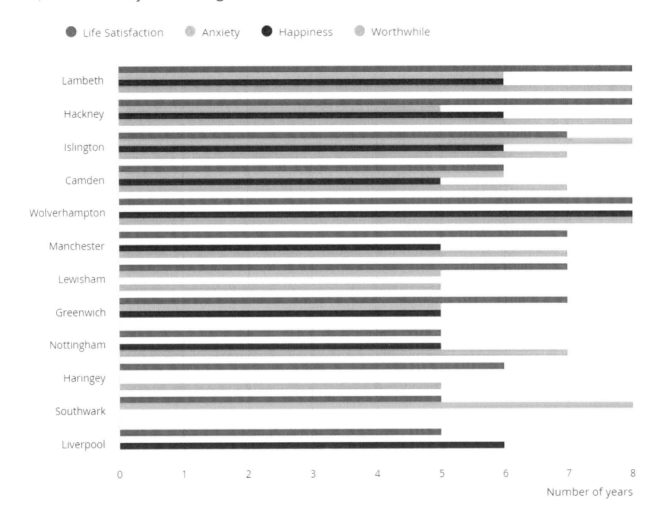

Local authorities consistently reporting low average personal well-being ratings,
UK, between the years ending March 2012 to March 2019

Source: Office for National Statistics - Annual Population Survey

Notes:

1. The chart shows the local authorities consistently in the bottom 10% for average personal well-being in at least five of eight years (seven years for Northern Ireland) and for at least two out of four well-being measures, where one of those was either life satisfaction or anxiety.

Looking across the whole UK, several London boroughs (Lambeth, Hackney, Islington and Camden) persistently had some of the lowest personal well-being ratings reported across all measures since the year ending March 2012 (Figure 6). They were followed by Wolverhampton, Manchester, Lewisham, Greenwich and Nottingham which reported poor well-being scores for three measures. Although Wolverhampton scored poorly in most measures, it scored very well where anxiety is concerned, reporting consistently lower levels of anxiety compared to the UK average for five of the last eight years.

Figure 7: Areas of Scotland and Northern Ireland persistently report high well-being across all measures of personal well-being

Local authorities consistently reporting high average personal well-being ratings, UK, between the years ending March 2012 to March 2019

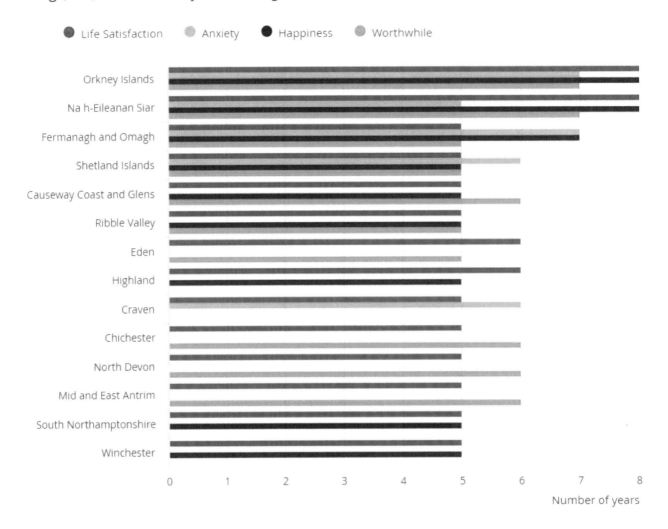

Local authorities consistently reporting high average personal well-being ratings, UK, between the years ending March 2012 to March 2019

Source: Office for National Statistics - Annual Population Survey

Notes:

1. The chart shows the local authorities consistently in the top 10% for average personal well-being in at least five out of eight years (seven years for Northern Ireland) and for at least half of the well-being measures, where one of those was either life satisfaction or anxiety.

In the UK, the Scottish council areas of Orkney Islands, Na h-Eileanan Siar and Shetland Islands, and Fermanagh and Omagh in Northern Ireland consistently reported high ratings for all the four measures of personal well-being since the year ending March 2012 (Figure 7). They were followed by Causeway Coast and Glens in Northern Ireland, and the English local authorities of Ribble Valley and Eden, which reported high well-being scores for three measures. Additionally, as shown in previous research, people's well-being seemed to be highest in relatively rural areas across England, such as Chichester and North Devon.

Use caution when interpreting the results from Orkney Islands, Na h-Eileanan Siar and Shetland Islands. These areas are subject to mode effects as because of their remoteness, interviews took place only by telephone. All other areas used both telephone and face-to-face interviews.

Wales, as a whole, generally reported personal well-being average ratings similar to the UK, with fewer variations across local authorities compared with the other UK countries. This could explain why there are no areas in Wales standing out as scoring consistently high or low in well-being when compared with the UK average.

6 . Differences in personal well-being at local levels: case studies

What might help to shed light on why people persistently report higher or lower well-being in some areas more than others? We used the Happy City Thriving Places Index (TPI) to consider a wide range of local circumstances and how this might help us understand differences in personal well-being at local level. The TPI uses local-level indicators focused on local conditions, sustainability and equality to measure and inform progress towards well-being. The indicators from the latest 2019 TPI were used which are currently available for England and Wales only. It should be noted that the local authority personal well-being estimates included in this release are based on the most recent available data (April 2018 to March 2019), while the data for the local context indicators are often from different sources with varying timeliness. All TPI data used in these case studies is from 2016 or later.

In this section, two areas that reported low well-being (Lambeth and Wolverhampton) and two that reported high well-being (North Devon and Chichester) are presented as case studies to explore how well-being differs in each area and how this may be related to the range of local circumstances considered by the TPI. These areas were chosen as they have been identified as having particularly high or low average well-being ratings based on the analysis in Section 5. As the TPI indicators are currently available for England and Wales only, the case studies focused on local authorities with persistently high or low average well-being from these areas.

The case studies help illustrate that each local authority may face very different challenges in creating the conditions in which local people can thrive.

Lambeth: Low well-being case study

Lambeth was chosen as a case study because of its consistently poor average well-being levels for all four personal well-being measures. "Place and environment" is one of the 2019 TPI domains for which Lambeth reported a low score. In this area, the Housing, Safety and Local environment subdomains received a particularly low score. Another domain in which Lambeth had a low score is "Work and local economy". Lambeth scored particularly low in relation to children in low income families (aged under 16 years).

Local environment

Lambeth received a low score of 2.55 out of 10 for the Local environment subdomain. This relates to the level of air pollution (fine particulate matter) in the area. According to data from Public Health England (2017), residents of Lambeth experienced a higher than average level of exposure to air pollution (fine particulate matter) at 12.0 micrograms per cubic metre in 2017, compared to 8.9 micrograms per cubic metre for England overall. Air pollution for Lambeth was also slightly higher than its surrounding areas in London – Wandsworth (11.6 micrograms per cubic metre), Merton (11.4 micrograms per cubic metre) and Richmond upon Thames (11.0 micrograms per cubic metre). As shown by previous studies, living in an area of high air pollution can pose a health risk to residents and negatively influence personal well-being.

Crime

Lambeth received a low score of 2.34 out of 10 for the "Safety" category in the 2019 TPI, specifically relating to crime rates. It displayed an offence rate of 109 per 1,000 population for the year ending March 2019. This was a higher rate than some surrounding boroughs such as Wandsworth (80 per 1,000 population), Merton (68 per 1,000 population) and Richmond Upon Thames (66 per 1,000 population).

Additionally, Lambeth received a crime severity score[1] of 19.9 for the same period. The crime severity score gives more severe crimes a higher weight, to better reflect the level of harm to society and demand on the police caused by crime. The score for Lambeth was again higher than the surrounding boroughs of Wandsworth (13.7), Merton (11.5) and Richmond Upon Thames (10.8). It should be noted that research has found that fear or worry about crime happening to someone can have a real impact on personal well-being. If higher levels of actual crime also contribute to higher levels of fear of crime, then both of these factors may be a source of lower average well-being for residents of Lambeth.

Housing

Lambeth received a low score of 3.28 out of 10 for the "Housing" category in the 2019 TPI. This looks at issues such as housing affordability and quality of housing. House-purchase costs may be a particular challenge for many people living in areas of London, as indicated by the House price to residence-based earnings ratio data. This provides a measure of average house prices relative to average earnings for full-time employees in 2018. In Lambeth, a house-buyer could expect to pay around 13.9 times their average earnings to own a home. This is compared to a ratio of 8.0 for England overall, suggesting that residents of Lambeth may find housing less affordable than people living elsewhere in England. However, the ratio for Lambeth was only slightly higher than the one for London overall (13.1).

Income deprivation

For the "Basic needs" domain, Lambeth received a medium-low score of 3.85 out of 10. This was mostly because of a high number of children under 16 years living in low-income families, defined as those in receipt of Child Tax Credit whose reported income is less than 60% of the median income or are in receipt of Income Support or Income-Based Jobseekers Allowance. According to figures from Public Health England, 23.4% of children under 16 years in Lambeth were living in a low-income family in 2016. This is higher than the percentage for England overall (17.0%). The percentage for Lambeth was also higher than some of the surrounding areas, such as Wandsworth (17.2%) and Merton (13.1%).

Wolverhampton: low well-being case study

Wolverhampton was chosen as a case study as it had persistently low average scores for life satisfaction but, more unusually, also had low average anxiety ratings. Overall, average life satisfaction, happiness, and worthwhile scores in Wolverhampton were all lower than the UK average. Wolverhampton is also one of 100 places recently invited to develop proposals for investment from the Towns Fund aimed at helping areas of industrial and economic heritage to benefit more from future economic growth. Wolverhampton presented a low 2019 TPI score for "Mental and physical health", "Work and local economy" and "Education and learning" domains.

Health

Research shows that many factors influence our quality of life and well-being. Our previous analysis highlighted that, at national level, how people view their health is the most important factor related to personal well-being. Other studies (PDF, 826.18KB) have provided evidence which indicates that the things that matter most to personal well-being are people's social relationships and their mental and physical health.

Wolverhampton scored low in the TPI "Mental and physical health" domain; especially in the mortality and life expectancy category (2.82 out of 10). According to the City of Wolverhampton Public Health Annual Report 2017, men and women in Wolverhampton live 7.0 and 4.6 years respectively in poorer health than the average in England. The difference between total life expectancy and healthy life expectancy for men in Wolverhampton was 21 years, compared to an average of 16.1 years for men in England. Meanwhile, the difference between total life expectancy and healthy life expectancy for women in Wolverhampton was 21.9 years, compared to an average of 19 years for women in England.

Wolverhampton also had a low score in the "Healthy and risky behaviours" category (2.15 out of 10). This category includes levels of physical activity in the population. According to Public Health England, only 52.1% of adults in Wolverhampton reported being physically active in the year ending March 2018, meeting recommended levels of physical activity. This is much lower than both the national average (66.3%) and the average for the West Midlands region (63.2%).

Education

Wolverhampton received a low score for the "Education and learning" domain. In particular, it received a score of 3.09 out of 10 for children's education. According to ONS figures, 58.0% of GCSE students achieved a standard 9 to 4 pass including Maths and English in the academic year 2016 to 2017. This is lower than the figure for the West Midlands as a whole (61.2%) and some surrounding areas such as Solihull (65.6%) and Birmingham (60.1%). This was also slightly less than the average for England (59.1%).

Employment

Wolverhampton received a low score for the "Unemployment" category (2.64 out of 10). According to ONS figures, the unemployment rate in the year ending March 2019 for Wolverhampton was 6.5%. This was higher than some surrounding areas such as Solihull (3.7%), Coventry (4.6%) and Walsall (4.9%), and additionally higher than the national unemployment rate (3.9%). In this respect, it should be noted that a large body of evidence shows that unemployment has a particularly large, negative and long-lasting effect on subjective well-being, particularly life satisfaction.

Chichester: high well-being case study

Chichester recorded consistently high levels of personal well-being, specifically for average life satisfaction and residents feeling as though the things they do in life are worthwhile in at least five of the last eight years. The Thriving Place Index (TPI) indicated four domains in which Chichester scored particularly highly: "Place and environment", "Mental and physical health", "Work and local economy" and "People and community" domains. This is linked to its lower than average crime levels, high levels of physical activity, high employment rate and high voter turnout. Each of these are discussed in more detail below.

Crime

Chichester scored 5.82 out of 10 for the TPI domain of "Place and environment", recording a score of 6.89 out of 10 for the safety subdomain. Lower than average crime severity scores[1] for year ending March 2019 in Chichester (8.0) as opposed to the average for England and Wales (14.1) may further the average life satisfaction of residents. A number of studies have found fear or worry about crime can have a real impact on personal well-being, regardless of whether the individual actually experiences crime themselves. A lower level of local crime and lower crime severity is likely to enhance the well-being of residents.

Health

Chichester scored 6.93 out of 10 for the "Mental and physical health" domain, scoring highly across all three subdomains of healthy and risky behaviours at 7.31 out of 10, overall health status at 6.91 out of 10, and mortality and life expectancy at 6.56 out of 10. According to the National Child Measurement Programme (NCMP), Chichester presented a lower than average prevalence of obesity among children aged 10 to 11 years (school year 6) with 13.6% of children within this age group meeting this criterion for the 2017 to 2018 academic year compared to the England average of 20.1% for the same period.

Chichester also had a larger average percentage of physically active adults, where physical activity is defined as consistently meeting the Chief Medical Officer (CMO) recommendations for physical activity (150 plus moderate intensity equivalent minutes per week). According to the NCMP, in the year ending March 2018, an average of 71.4% of adults in Chichester were regularly engaging in physical activity, significantly higher than the average for England of 66.3%.

These examples of above average physical health and healthy lifestyles in Chichester may contribute to greater life satisfaction, as previous analysis has indicated poor health has among the most detrimental impacts on personal well-being, and better health is related to higher well-being.

Employment

Chichester recorded a score of 6.33 out of 10 for the TPI "Work and local economy" domain. The area also scored 5.12 out of 10 in the employment subdomain. Data from the Annual Population Survey (APS) showed that the employment rate in Chichester for the period between April 2018 and March 2019 was at 85.2%, significantly higher than the same measure across the same period for Great Britain, at 75.4%. This comparatively high employment status could be linked to its high scores for life satisfaction and feeling that the things done in life are worthwhile.

Community

Chichester recorded a score of 5.38 out of 10 in the TPI "People and community" domain, scoring highly in the participation subset of this domain (7.14 out of 10), which is exemplified by its high turnout at the 2017 general election. This local authority recorded a voter turnout of 70.5% compared with the UK figure of 68.8% at the most recent general election, potentially indicating a higher than average political engagement among residents.

North Devon: high well-being case study

North Devon recorded consistently high average levels of well-being, specifically for average life satisfaction and residents' feeling as though the things they do in life are worthwhile in at least five of the last eight years.

The TPI indicates four domains in which North Devon scores particularly highly, offering potential insights into the this local authority scores in the life satisfaction and feeling that the things done in life are worthwhile measures. It scored highly in the "Place and environment" domain, particularly with the local environment and safety subdomains. This is mainly linked to low air pollution and crime levels.

North Devon also reported a high score for the "People and community" domain. Indicators that can influence this score include community participation, volunteering, clubs and societies, voter turnout and social fragmentation. North Devon had a high voter turnout which contributed to this high score. The area also scored highly in health and education domains, which are also investigated below.

Air pollution

North Devon recorded a moderate score of 5.48 out of 10 in the "Place and environment" domain of the TPI, scoring particularly highly in the subdomain of local environment at 6.86 out of 10. According to data from Public Health England, North Devon presented a "lower annual concentration of human-made fine particulate matter at an area level in 2017, adjusted to account for population exposure". Residents of this local authority experience a lower than average level of exposure to air pollution (fine particulate matter) at 6.2 micrograms per cubic metre, compared to 8.9 micrograms per cubic metre for England. This can contribute to heightened levels of life satisfaction through a lowered health risk posed to residents, possibly providing assurance that their local environment is not damaging to their physical well-being. As shown by a study by the University of York (PDF, 1MB), living in an area of high air pollution can pose a health risk to residents and negatively influence personal well-being.

Crime

North Devon scored high in the 2019 TPI "Place and environment" domain; especially in the safety category (6.81 out of 10). According to the ONS Crime Severity Index[1], North Devon had a lower than average crime severity score (8.0 compared to the average for England and Wales of 14.1) which may further the average life satisfaction of residents. It should be noted that research has found that fear or worry about crime happening to someone can have a real impact on personal well-being. If lower levels of actual crime also contribute to lower levels of fear of crime, then both of these factors may be a source of higher average well-being for residents of North Devon.

Participation

North Devon scored highly in civic participation with a higher than average recorded voter turnout of 73.5% at the 2017 general election compared with the UK figure of 68.8%.

Unemployment

North Devon recorded a score of 5.07 out of 10 on the "Work and local economy" domain, scoring highest in the unemployment subdomain at 6.58. According to ONS figures, the unemployment rate in the year ending March 2019 for North Devon was 2.1%, which was lower than the average for England (3.9%). This may contribute to a heightened degree of both life satisfaction and individuals feeling as though the things they do in their lives are worthwhile. In this respect, it should be noted that research shows that being employed has a particularly positive and long-lasting effect on subjective well-being, particularly life satisfaction.

Health

North Devon recorded a score of 5.98 out of 10 for the "Mental and physical health domain" of the TPI. The highest scoring subdomain was healthy and risky behaviours at 6.96 out of 10, which describes the respondent's engagement in activities beneficial or detrimental to their overall mental or physical health. North Devon reported a significantly lower average rate of "excess weight" among children aged 10 or 11 years, that is those classified as overweight or very overweight. In North Devon, 26.1% of children met these criteria for the 2017 to 2018 academic year, falling below the English average for the same period of 34.3%.

In this section, we have highlighted that there are some aspects of life that have a significant impact on well-being, such as good health, positive relationships, and employment. Job quality is also important to well-being and this specific aspect will be explored in the upcoming release on Job quality in city regions across the UK: 2018, including experimental analysis on the percentage of good jobs in city regions across the UK, broken down by demographic indicators, occupation and industry.

1. The crime severity score has been designated as Experimental Statistics and developed as an additional measure to supplement existing Office for National Statistics (ONS) statistics on crime. This new measure weights different types of crime according to severity, with more serious crimes carrying a higher weight to better reflect the level of harm to society and demand on the police caused by crime.

7 . Personal well-being data

Personal well-being estimates

Dataset | Released on 23 October 2019
Estimates of life satisfaction, feeling that the things done in life are worthwhile, happiness and anxiety in the UK at country, regional and local authority level.

Quality information for personal well-being estimates

Dataset | Released on 23 October 2019
Confidence intervals and sample sizes for estimates of life satisfaction, feeling that the things done in life are worthwhile, happiness and anxiety in the UK at country, regional and local authority level.

8 . Glossary

Personal well-being

Our personal well-being measures ask people to evaluate, on a scale of 0 to 10, how satisfied they are with their life overall, whether they feel they have meaning and purpose in their life, and about their emotions (happiness and anxiety) during a particular period.

Thresholds

Thresholds are used to present dispersion in the data. For the life satisfaction, worthwhile and happiness questions, ratings are grouped in the following way:

- 0 to 4 (low)

- 5 to 6 (medium)

- 7 to 8 (high)

- 9 to 10 (very high)

For the anxiety question, ratings are grouped differently to reflect the fact that higher anxiety is associated with lower personal well-being. The ratings for anxiety are grouped as follows:

- 0 to 1 (very low)

- 2 to 3 (low)

- 4 to 5 (medium)

- 6 to 10 (high)

Mode effects

A mode effect occurs when a different way of administering a survey affects the data collected. Testing has shown that people respond more positively to the personal well-being questions when interviewed by telephone rather than face-to-face.

9 . Measuring the data

Since 2011, we have asked personal well-being questions to adults aged 16 years and over in the UK to better understand how they feel about their lives. This release presents headline results for the year ending March 2019, along with changes over time since we started collecting well-being data in 2011. It provides data at a national level, country and local authority level. The four personal well-being questions are:

- Overall, how satisfied are you with your life nowadays?

- Overall, to what extent do you feel the things you do in your life are worthwhile?

- Overall, how happy did you feel yesterday?

- Overall, how anxious did you feel yesterday?

People are asked to respond on a scale of 0 to 10, where 0 is "not at all" and 10 is "completely". We produce estimates of the mean ratings for all four personal well-being questions, as well as their distributions.

Measuring National Well-being programme

The four personal well-being questions are included as measures for the wider Measuring National Well-being (MNW) programme. The programme began in November 2010 with the aim of developing and publishing an accepted and trusted set of National Statistics, which help people understand and monitor well-being. The statistics in this bulletin are displayed through our well-being dashboard, which reports how the UK is doing for the different areas of life that people in the UK said matter most to their well-being.

Quality and methodology information

The Personal well-being in the UK Quality and Methodology Information report contains important information on:

- the strengths and limitations of the data and how it compares with related data

- uses and users of the data

- how the output was created

- APS data reweighting

- the quality of the output including the accuracy of the data

For more information on personal well-being, please see:

- Personal well-being user guide

- Harmonised principles of personal-well-being

Feedback and future publications

Our users expressed a need for more information on lower geographies and more analysis on factors associated with personal well-being. Our release today aims to provide further analysis in this respect and we are planning to carry out more work on this for our next releases. If you would like to provide additional feedback about this specific work at local level or any opinions you might have about our well-being outputs, please contact us at QualityOfLife@ons.gov.uk.

10 . Strengths and limitations

Accuracy of the statistics: estimating and reporting uncertainty

The personal well-being estimates are from the Annual Population Survey (APS), which provides a representative sample of those living in private residential households in the UK. People living in communal establishments (such as care homes) or other non-household situations are not represented in this survey. This may be important in interpreting the findings in relation to those people reporting lower personal well-being.

The sample is designed to be as accurate as possible given practical limitations such as time and cost constraints. Results from sample surveys are always estimates, not precise figures. This can have an impact on how changes in the estimates should be interpreted, especially for short-term comparisons.

As the number of people available in the sample gets smaller, the variability of the estimates that can be made from that sample size gets larger. Estimates for small groups – for example, respondents from a single local authority – which are based on quite small subsets of the APS, are less reliable and tend to be more volatile than for larger aggregated groups.

From year ending March 2018, the sample for Northern Ireland received a boost, resulting in greater accuracy in a set of local authorities that had had relatively small sample sizes compared to others in the UK.

If the sample size of an estimate is less than 50 or if a corresponding threshold has a sample size less than five, then the estimate is suppressed. Additionally, we assess each estimate's critical value (or coefficient of variance) and colour code the estimates in the Headline Estimates download. If the critical value exceeds a score of 20, indicating that there is too much variance in the data to constitute a reliable estimate, then this estimate is suppressed. For more information on suppression, see the personal well-being in the UK QMI.

Annual Population Survey data reweighting

Weighting answers to survey questions ensures that estimates are representative of the target population. Each person in the survey data has a "weight", the number of people that person represents in the population, which is used to produce estimates for the population.

More accurate weighting is based on the latest available population estimates for that time period. When new population estimates become available, data can be reweighted to ensure better representation and so precision of estimates. For greater accuracy, it is common practice to revise previously published estimates when new weights become available.

Based on new population estimates, new well-being weights have been available for the APS data since March 2019. We have used this reweighted data to produce annual personal well-being estimates for the years ending March 2012 to 2019 at the UK country, regional and local authority level estimates, as we did for our previous publication for the years ending December 2012 to 2018. The reweighted data for the years ending June 2012 to 2019 and September 2012 to 2019 will be available in our upcoming publications early next year.

Statistical significance

Please note that:

- any changes mentioned in this publication are "statistically significant"

- the statistical significance of differences noted within the release are determined based on non-overlapping confidence intervals

11 . Related links

Measures of National Well-being Dashboard

Dashboard | Released on 23 October 2019
Latest data, times series data and detailed information for the measures of national well-being.

Personal and economic well-being in the UK: August 2019

Bulletin | Released on 12 August 2019
Estimates looking across both personal well-being (April 2018 to March 2019) and economic well-being (January to March 2019) in the UK. This bulletin is part of a new series on "people and prosperity" introduced in February 2019.

Personal and economic well-being: what matters most to our life satisfaction?

Article | Released on 15 May 2019
Examines how socio-demographic and economic factors are associated with life satisfaction. These factors include sex, age, health, marital and economic status as well as household income and expenditure.

Measuring national well-being in the UK: international comparisons, 2019

Article | Released on 6 March 2019
How the UK is faring in important areas of well-being compared with the member states of the EU and the member countries of the OECD.

Understanding well-being inequalities: Who has the poorest personal well-being?

Article | Released on 11 July 2018
Analysis of the characteristics and circumstances associated with the poorest life satisfaction, feeling the things done in life are worthwhile, happiness and anxiety in the UK, from 2014 to 2016

Article

Human capital estimates in the UK: 2004 to 2018

National estimates of human capital and lifetime earnings for the economically active population in the UK.

Contact:
Sunny Sidhu, Chris Payne
economic.wellbeing@ons.gov.uk
+44 (0)1633 65 1701

Release date:
28 October 2019

Next release:
To be announced

Table of contents

1 . What is human capital?

This release presents the latest results on the UK's human capital.

According to The Well-being of Nations: The Role of Human and Social Capital, human capital is a measure of the "knowledge, skills, competencies and attributes embodied in individuals that facilitate the creation of personal, social and economic well-being". It plays an important role in productivity and sustainability, and it is one of the main resources that may affect individual well-being. In this release, we measure human capital through people's expected lifetime earnings, one of the recommended international methods.

2 . Main points

- The UK's human capital stock was £21.4 trillion in 2018, equivalent to around 10 times the size of UK gross domestic product (GDP).

- There was an annual increase of 0.2% in 2018 in real terms, using the new indexing methodology; this was the result of an increase in the educational attainment of those who were economically active and an increase in their population size, though these increases were partially offset by the effects of an ageing population.

- Men's average lifetime earnings fell by 0.1% in 2018, while women's average lifetime earnings increased 0.2% compared with 2017.

- The average lifetime earnings of women grew more rapidly than those of men between 2004 and 2018 but remain 41% lower than those of men.

- Those with a Master's degree or PhD qualification have an average £65,000 extra in future lifetime earnings – a 10% premium – compared with those with an undergraduate or equivalent degree in 2018; this premium has been consistent since 2004.

- There are now more economically active people with a Master's or PhD degree, at 4.5 million, than those without any formal academic qualifications, at 3.4 million.

3 . Information about this release

There has been increased interest in measuring and understanding human capital recently, both in the UK and internationally, to better understand the skills of national workforces and the drivers of growth. We have therefore published a workplan outlining the developments we are considering to meet user needs.

We have a public consultation open until 18 November on measuring human capital through an indicator-based approach. The proposal considers the impacts on people's development across their lifetime; this involves aspects of health, the family, home, education and work, among other themes. We encourage interested individuals and organisations to respond so their views can be taken into account.

In this release, we estimate human capital by looking at what qualifications people have and what they earn as well as how much longer they will continue to work, in line with international recommendations from the United Nations Economic Commission for Europe (UNECE) Guide on Measuring Human Capital. As such, an individual's human capital, referred to as their lifetime earnings, tends to be higher for younger workers, as they have more years in the labour market ahead of them.

When interpreting differences between groups or over time in these statistics, it is necessary to consider a range of potential factors. If one group has higher human capital than another, this may be because they have, on average, more qualifications, better education progression rates, higher salaries for any given level of qualifications, or because they are younger. Two people with identical characteristics (for example, sex and qualifications) will have different levels of human capital if one is younger. This is because the younger person has more years' earning potential, or because they can work and therefore earn for longer.

Further information on how human capital is calculated and the methodology for this can be found at the end of the release and in more technical detail in Measuring the UK's Human Capital Stock (PDF, 208KB).

In summary, estimates are constructed by adding together the labour income people would receive over the rest of their working life, for every combination of age, sex and highest qualification obtained. For every "age–sex–highest qualification" combination, next year's lifetime earnings are assumed to be the average discounted value of people a year older with the same sex and highest qualification who are currently in the labour market. This is adjusted by calculating the probability of someone obtaining a further formal qualification and hence increasing their earnings trajectory to that of someone with a higher qualification. It also accounts for the mortality rate of an individual, to consider if they would still be in the workforce. Full information on data sources and methodology can be found in Measuring the UK's Human Capital Stock (PDF, 208KB).

It is important to note that within this release, there has been a change in calculating the headline changes in human capital.

Internationally, the Törnqvist index is one of the most widely used approaches to measure changes in human capital, and the UNECE Guide on Measuring Human Capital recommends it as a way to measure change over time. We have developed a new measure based on the Törnqvist index that takes into account the differing lifetime earnings of people with varying ages, qualifications and sex and how the demography of the population changes over time. This effectively provides a different deflator to each sub-population and so provides a more comprehensive view of how human capital has changed over time.

In previous releases, the real changes for all estimates have been measured by deflating by the Consumer Prices Index (CPI), which is a measure of the change in prices for a basket of goods and services that people buy.

4 . Human capital in 2018

Figure 1: Human capital continued to rise in 2018 but at a slower pace since 2016

Human capital stock in the UK, full, in nominal and real terms, 2004 to 2018

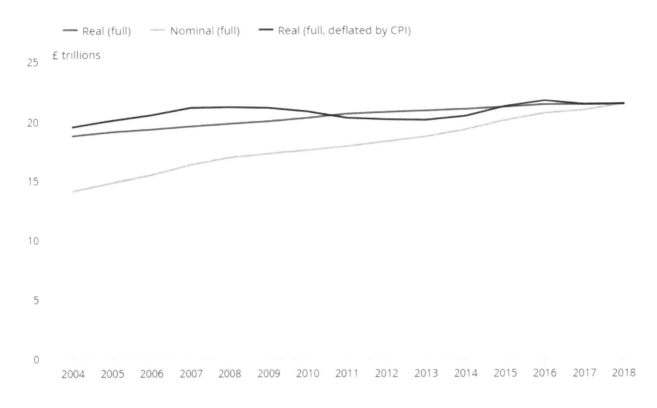

Human capital stock in the UK, full, in nominal and real terms, 2004 to 2018

— Real (full)   — Nominal (full)   — Real (full, deflated by CPI)

Source: Office for National Statistics – Annual Population Survey and Labour Force Survey

Notes:

1. Real figures with 2018 as the base year, derived using new methodology outlined in the Methodology developments section. This is based on the Törnqvist index, which is the internationally recommended approach of measuring Human Capital over time.

2. Full human capital captures the human capital of the employed and the unemployed.

The value of the UK's real full human capital stock, or the human capital of the employed and the unemployed, was £21.4 trillion in 2018. This relates to people between 16 and 65 years who were working or looking for work. This was a 0.2% increase compared with 2017, when derived using the Törnqvist volume methodology. This continues the slower rate of growth seen since 2016, compared with the rest of the period since 2004. Using the previous Consumer Prices Index (CPI) deflated method, the UK's real full human capital also increased by 0.2% between 2017 and 2018. This follows a fall of 1.4% the previous year.

The Törnqvist method is the preferred method of measuring real human capital as it directly measures volume estimates, taking account of differences in lifetime earnings across the population, while deflating by the CPI does not.

Since 2004, the real measure derived using the Törnqvist index shows human capital steadily increasing each year. On the other hand, human capital as deflated through CPI has varied more over time, rising more rapidly in the years until 2008 but then falling between 2009 and 2013. This difference arises from a difference in what the measures include.

Within the rest of the analysis, the Törnqvist index will be used. Further information about this method including why and how it is used can be found at the end of the report.

The UK's real employed human capital increased by 0.2% between 2017 and 2018. This occurred during a period when the employment rate grew at 0.6%. The increase in human capital mainly occurred in Northern Ireland and London, which saw an increase in their human capital stock by 3.4% and 1.9% respectively. The South West and the North East saw their human capital stock reduced by 0.5% in 2018. More regional data can be found in the accompanying reference tables, and we will be looking to publish more regional analysis in the future.

Figure 2: Real human capital increased in 2018 while average human capital per person remained unchanged

Growth rates of real human capital stock and real lifetime earnings per person, UK, 2004 to 2018

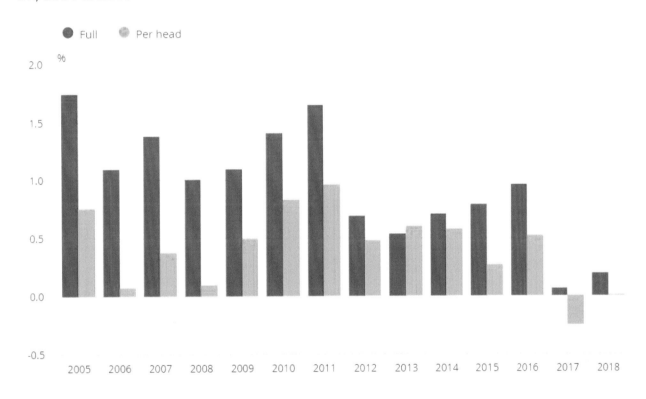

Source: Office for National Statistics – Annual Population Survey and Labour Force Survey

Notes:

1. Real figures are in 2018 values.

2. Per head figures are divided by the economically active population.

The increases in real full human capital over the last two years are slower than the longer-term average annual increase of 0.9% from 2011 to 2016. This suggests there has been a slowdown of growth in human capital since 2016. This is also seen in the average human capital per person or average lifetime earnings of individuals, which grew at the second-slowest rate over the period since 2004. The reduction and slowdown of growth of human capital per head in the last two years has meant that human capital per head has a lower value in 2018 than it did in 2016.

Figure 3: An increase in people's educational attainment and the growth of the working population are the main causes of human capital increases

Contributions to annual growth in real human capital stock, UK, 2004 to 2018

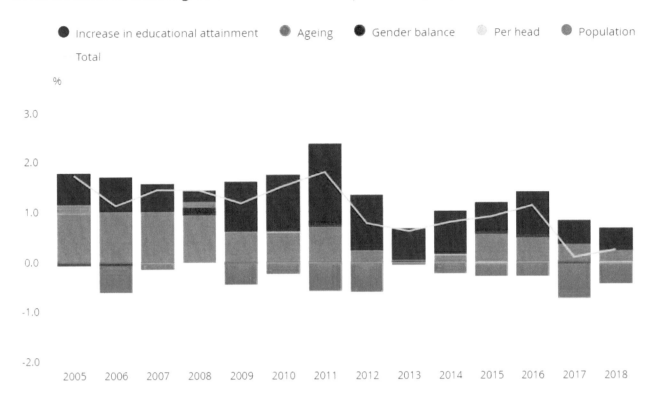

Source: Office for National Statistics – Annual Population Survey and Labour Force Survey

Notes:

1. May not sum because of the rounding and chain-linking methodology, which is not additive.

2. Population changes are calculated by applying the average increase in the economically active population only, for the year, compared with the year before, while keeping average lifetime earnings fixed to the previous year.

3. Increase in educational attainment or formal qualifications is calculated by applying the qualification distribution only, for that year compared with the year before, while keeping average lifetime earnings fixed to the previous year.

4. Ageing is calculated by applying the age distribution of the population only, compared with the year before, while keeping average lifetime earnings fixed to the previous year.

5. Gender balance is calculated by applying the balance of both sexes for each age and qualification category for each year measured and the year before, while keeping average lifetime earnings fixed to the previous year.

The increase in people's educational attainment in 2018 had the largest positive effect on real growth, followed by the effect of the increased working population, contributing 0.46 and 0.20 percentage points respectively towards the 0.2% increase in real human capital. These were similar contributions to those in 2017.

Looking across the past 15 years, the increase in educational attainment or formal qualifications of the economically active population and the increase in the size of that population have made the biggest contributions to the growth in total human capital. They have contributed 10.8% and 7.8% respectively since 2004. At the same time, an ageing population has had a negative effect on human capital levels, as an older workforce has less time available to participate in the labour market. Since 2011, this ageing effect has more than offset the rise in human capital from a larger active population and particularly in the last two years, it has brought down growth of human capital.

The increase in educational attainment or formal qualifications has mainly been driven by more individuals obtaining degree or equivalent-level qualifications and there being fewer people without any qualifications.

Figure 4: The number of people with a degree or equivalent increased the most between 2004 and 2018

Economically active population, highest educational attainment, UK, 2004 to 2018

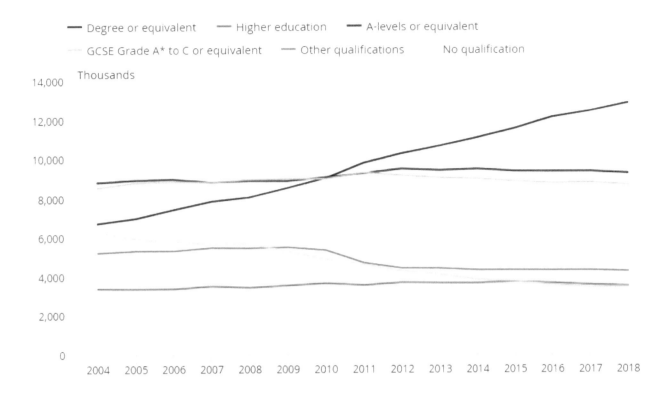

Source: Office for National Statistics – Annual Population Survey and Labour Force Survey

Notes:

1. "Degree or equivalent" includes undergraduate degrees and Master's and PhD degrees.

2. "Higher education" includes Diploma in Higher Education, Teaching Diplomas and National Vocation Qualification Level 4 .

3. "A levels or equivalent" includes A levels, AS levels and International Baccalaureates.

4. "GCSE grades A* to C or equivalent" includes GCSE A* to C and BTEC first diploma.

5. "Other qualifications" includes GCSE below grade C and BTEC first certificate.

6. "No qualifications" includes individuals who have no formal qualifications.

Since 2004, the number of economically active individuals with a degree (or equivalent) or higher qualification has increased by 91.3%, rising from 6.7 million to 12.8 million people. At the same time, the number of economically active people with no qualifications has nearly halved, from 6.3 million to 3.4 million in the same period.

The share of the active population with a degree has increased the most, which would suggest that this is the cause of the increases in attainment that led to higher human capital. It is worth noting that someone with a higher educational attainment will have, on average, higher lifetime earnings than the same individual with a lower attainment. For example, those aged 26 to 35 years who have a degree will have a 19% higher average human capital than those whose highest level of qualification is higher education, which are qualifications that are higher than A levels but lower than an undergraduate degree.

Notes for: Human capital in 2018

1. We refer to those people with no qualifications as having no formal academic qualifications.

5 . Human capital of people with a Master's or PhD degree

In this section, we have expanded the methodology to consider those with a Master's or PhD degree separately to people with an undergraduate degree or equivalent. Further detail on our approach can be found in the Methodology developments section.

Figure 5: Individuals with a Master's or PhD degree had a higher human capital in 2018 than those with an undergraduate degree or equivalent

Average premium in lifetime earnings for those with a Master's or PhD degree and those with an undergraduate degree or equivalent, compared with people with A levels, UK, 2004 to 2018

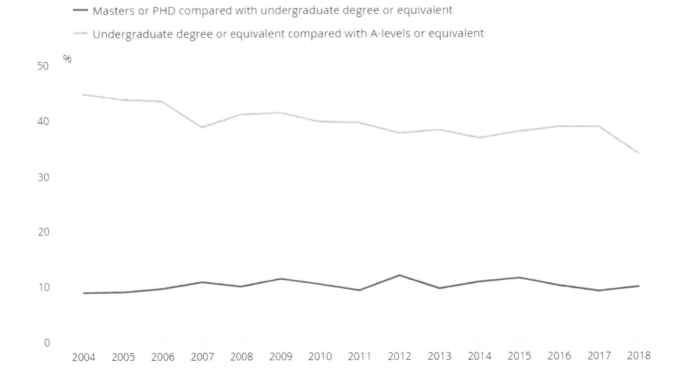

Average premium in lifetime earnings for those with a Master's or PhD degree and those with an undergraduate degree or equivalent, compared with people with A levels, UK, 2004 to 2018

Source: Office for National Statistics – Annual Population Survey and Labour Force Survey

As shown in Figure 5, the lifetime earnings premium for someone with a Master's or PhD degree over and above an undergraduate or equivalent degree has remained fairly stable, at between 9% and 11%. There is also a significant premium for those with an undergraduate degree compared with people who have obtained A levels as their highest qualifications. However, it has fallen from 45% higher average lifetime earnings in 2004 to 34% higher average lifetime earnings in 2018.

Figure 6: The greatest difference in lifetime earnings between people with a Master's or PhD degree and between those with an undergraduate or equivalent degree occurred for the 36 to 45 years age group

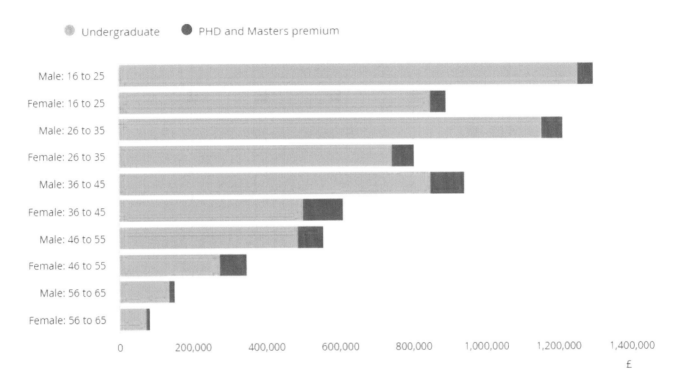

Difference between lifetime earnings for those with a Master's or PhD degree and those with an undergraduate degree or equivalent, by age group and by sex, UK, 2018

Source: Office for National Statistics – Annual Population Survey and Labour Force Survey

Notes:

1. Positive figures show that lifetime earnings for those with a Master's or PhD degree are larger than for those with an undergraduate degree or equivalent.

Figure 6 shows average future lifetime earnings for those with an undergraduate degree or equivalent for men and women across different age groups. It also shows the additional lifetime earnings premium associated with having a Master's or PhD degree. For those aged between 26 and 55 years, the premium associated with having a higher degree is greater for women than for men. For example, among those aged 36 to 45 years, women with a Master's or PhD degree will earn, on average, £108,000 more over the rest of their working life than those with an undergraduate degree, compared with a premium of £92,000 for men. This suggests that, in terms of future earnings, it is more beneficial for women to obtain higher degrees than for men.

However, despite this higher premium, women with a Master's or PhD degree have around 33% lower lifetime earnings than men, on average, with the same level of qualifications, depending on their age. Across every age group, the average future lifetime earnings of women with Master's or PhD degrees is substantially lower than that for men with undergraduate degrees. For example, women aged 26 to 35 years with higher degrees have average lifetime earnings of £803,000, whereas men of the same age with undergraduate level qualifications have average lifetime earnings of around £1,160,000.

The population of those with a Master's or PhD degree who are either working or looking for work has increased from 1.9 million in 2004 to 4.5 million in 2018. This equates to a 130% increase throughout this time period, while those with an undergraduate degree or equivalent have increased by 75%. This increase in Master's and PhD degree qualifications shows that there has been a continued increase in advanced qualifications in the UK's workforce.

There are now more people with a Master's or PhD degree, at 10.7% of the population, than people with no qualifications.

We recognise people can take other training at work that does not lead to a recognised formal qualification, so we would like to measure this effect and incorporate it into future releases.

6 . Human capital by sex

Figure 7: Women's average lifetime earnings has grown more since 2004 than those of men, but remain 41% lower than those of men in 2018

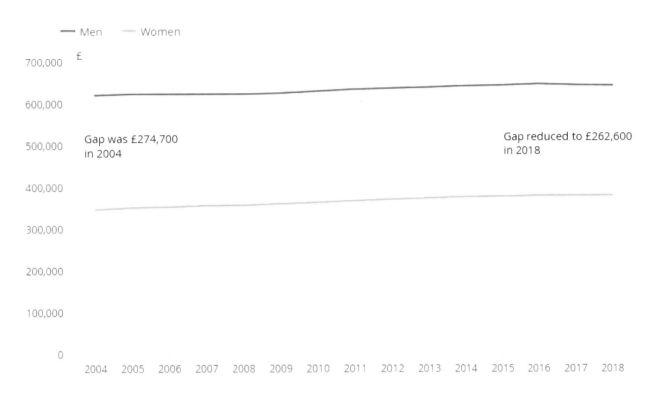

Men's and women's real lifetime earnings, UK, 2004 to 2018

Source: Office for National Statistics – Human capital estimates

Notes:

1. Real figures are in 2018 values.

2. This shows human capital per head of the population for each sex.

Men have a higher average human capital than women, when measured in terms of lifetime earnings. In 2018, the average lifetime earnings of men were £643,000 while those of women were £380,000. Taking account the effect of weekly hours worked for men and women, women's human capital is 22.7% lower than men's. Despite this, women's average lifetime earnings have grown at a faster rate since 2004. The average rate of increase has been 0.7% annually, while for men it has grown by an average of 0.3% a year during this period. Most recently, men's human capital per head has fallen by a cumulative 0.6% in 2016 and 2018, owing to a bigger negative effect from an ageing workforce than positive effects from improved educational attainment.

This means that the gap in average lifetime earnings for men and women has narrowed, with women now receiving, on average, equal to 59% of men's average lifetime earnings; this is up from 56% in 2004.

Figure 8: Women's human capital has increased more than men's owing to a greater increase in educational attainment than among men

Decomposition in cumulative changes of human capital stock, men and women, UK, 2018 compared with 2004

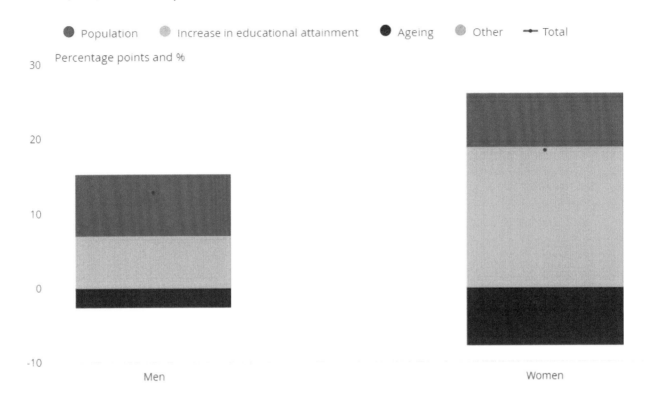

Source: Office for National Statistics – Human capital estimates

Notes:

1. Real changes in 2018 values, as measured through the Törnqvist index.

2. Population changes are calculated by applying the average increase in the economically active population only, for the year, compared with the year before, while keeping average lifetime earnings fixed to the previous year.

3. Increase in educational attainment or formal qualifications is calculated by applying the qualification distribution only, for that year compared with the year before, while keeping average lifetime earnings fixed to the previous year.

4. Ageing is calculated by applying the age distribution of the population only, compared with the year before, while keeping average lifetime earnings fixed to the previous year.

5. Measuring total human capital stock for men and women.

6. "Other" includes the effect of the relative change in average lifetime earnings across age, sex and qualification categories.

Figure 8 shows the contribution of different factors to changes in human capital for men and women. The biggest contributor to women's rising human capital has been an increase in average levels of educational attainment or formal qualifications. This has led to an 18.8 percentage point contribution to their human capital increase between 2004 and 2018, compared with only 7 percentage points for men. This indicates that women have become more formally and academically qualified, comparatively, than men. For every additional formal qualification, women also gain more in average lifetime earnings than men. Additionally, increases in the population had a significant impact on the rise in human capital for both men and women.

Earnings differences between men and women throughout working life

Figure 9: Men reach their peak in earnings in their late 40s, while women level off after their 30s

Annual average earnings for men and women with their highest qualification as A levels or equivalent, UK, 2018

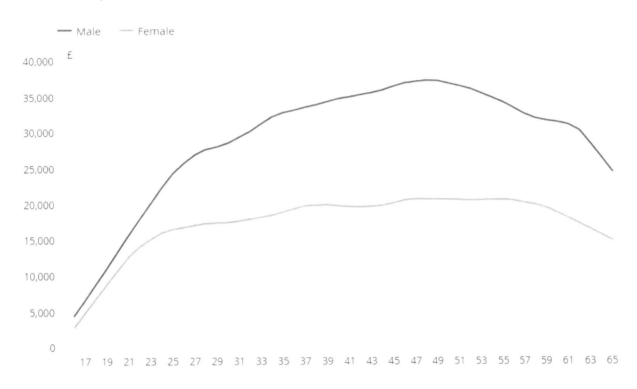

Annual average earnings for men and women with their highest qualification as A levels or equivalent, UK, 2018

Source: Office for National Statistics – Annual Population Survey and Labour Force Survey

The differences in average lifetime earnings between men and women, as shown in Figure 9, reflect the fact that men, on average, earn more annually throughout their lifetime than women. Figure 9 looks at the average annual earnings for each age group from 16 to 65 years by sex for those who have A levels or equivalents. Both men and women have similar annual employee earnings early on in their lives. However, after they reach their 20s, they diverge and men begin to have much higher total average annual earnings. Men, on average, peak at 48 years old, at which point there is a £16,600 difference between men and women's average earnings.

It is important to note annual earnings are shown here, which also reflect differences in working patterns. Further analysis can be found in Gender pay gap in the UK: 2018 as well as in an interactive tool to see the differences in hourly pay for different occupations.

Notes for: Human capital by sex

1. We refer to those people with no qualifications as having no formal academic qualifications.

7 . Human capital across age groups

Figure 10: The average lifetime earnings of people aged between 16 and 25 years has only increased by 2.8% compared with those of the same age 15 years ago, the lowest amount of any age group

Lifetime earnings per head, different age groups, UK, 2004 to 2018

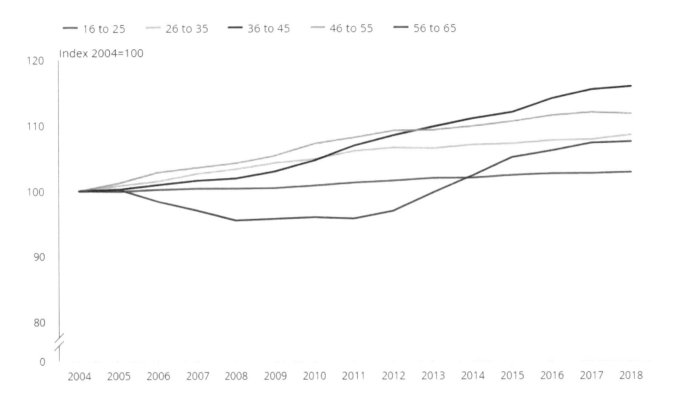

Source: Office for National Statistics – Human capital estimates

Notes:

1. Index is set at 2004 = 100.

2. Age groups constant over time, meaning as people age, different populations are in each category, which may have different sex and highest qualification compositions within them over time.

Each age group in 2018 had higher lifetime earnings, compared with their 2004 counterparts. Those aged 36 to 45 years in 2018 had an estimated 15.9% higher average lifetime earnings than they would have 15 years ago, the largest increase of any age group. This in part reflects higher average levels of educational attainment among this group. For example, there are now 1.6 million more people aged between 36 and 45 years with a degree or equivalent than there were 15 years ago. This in turn reflects long-term trends in the number of people attending university after leaving school and an increased share of people obtaining further qualifications during their working life.

56- to 65-year-olds in 2018 had, on average, a 7.5% higher human capital compared with this age group in 2004. However, 56- to 65-year-olds in 2011 had, on average, lower human capital than those in 2004 by 4.2 percentage points. Since 2011, on average, the age group's human capital is 1.6% higher than the equivalent group a year before.

The ageing of the 56 to 65 years age group impacted average human capital between 2004 and 2018.

Figure 11: Ageing had a bigger negative impact for 56- to 65-year-olds up to 2011, after which it has had a positive impact

Decomposition of changes in average human capital for 56- to 65-year-olds, UK, 2004 to 2011 and 2012 to 2018

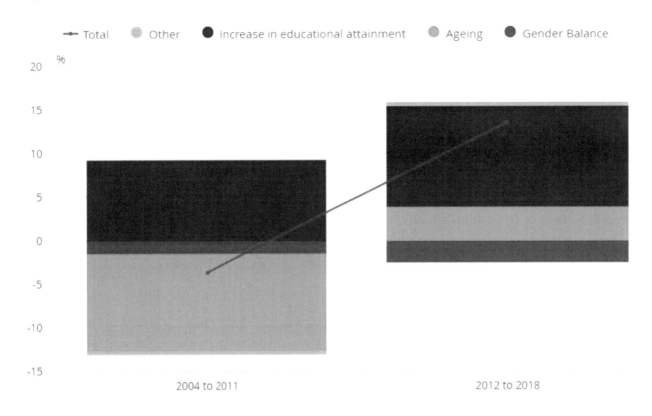

Source: Office for National Statistics – Human capital estimates

Notes:

1. In real 2018 values.

2. Increase in educational attainment or formal qualifications is calculated by applying the qualification distribution only, for that year compared with the year before, while keeping average lifetime earnings fixed to the previous year.

3. Ageing is calculated by applying the age distribution of the population only, compared with the year before, while keeping average lifetime earnings fixed to the previous year.

4. Measuring total human capital stock for men and women.

5. "Other" includes the effect of the relative change in average lifetime earnings across age, sex and qualification categories.

6. Measured as a full human capital stock.

Figure 11 shows the contribution to the changes in the average human capital of 56 to 65 year olds during these time frames.

From 2004 to 2011, on average, the lifetime earnings of 56- to 65-year-olds fell because of ageing. This meant that within the 56 to 65 years age group, the average age increased and the average human capital for this age group fell. This was despite the fact that those aged 56 to 65 years in 2011 had, on average, higher qualifications than those aged 56 to 65 years in 2004. This change resulted from the fact that between 2012 and 2018, the average age of the 56 to 65 years age group reduced and so there was an increase in human capital. At the same time, 56- to 65-year-olds in 2018 also had, on average, higher qualifications than 56- to 65-year-olds in 2011.

An individual's occupation also impacts their human capital. There are breakdowns of human capital by occupation within the reference tables, and we will be looking to publish more analysis on this in the future.

Human capital per productive hour

When we look at the overall average human capital of different ages groups, individuals have lower human capital on this measure the more they age. This is because their working life becomes shorter and their potential future earnings reduce. However, we can remove the effect of age to see when in an individual's career their productivity peaks. This gives a more nuanced understanding of how human capital develops throughout an individual's working life, without it simply decreasing as they age.

Figure 12: The 26 to 35 years age group had the highest average productivity of human capital

Employed human capital per productive hour, broken down by age group, UK, 2018

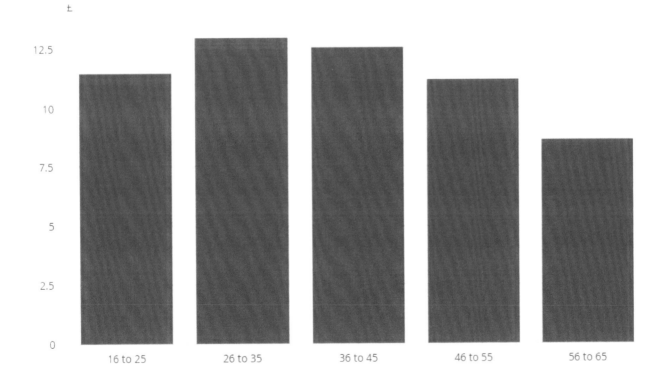

Employed human capital per productive hour, broken down by age group, UK, 2018

Source: Office for National Statistics – Human capital estimates

323

Removing the impact of age provides a different picture of the changes within human capital. In 2018, those who are employed and aged 26 to 35 years had, on average, the highest human capital per hour. This means for each hour left in their working life, they would be earning an average of £13.30. After this age group, this hourly measure decreases, with those aged 56 to 65 years earning an average of £8.90 per working hour for the remainder of their working life.

Notes for: Human capital across age groups

1. We refer to people's productivity as their lifetime earnings per hour left in the workforce.

8 . Methodology developments

Measuring Human Capital with the Törnqvist index

We have developed a new index, which we believe to be a more accurate measure of how real human capital changes over time. This is using the Törnqvist method of indexing the "quantity"" of UK stock explicitly. The main advantage of this method is it considers the changes within the number of people within each of the population categories by age, sex, and highest qualification attainment and the changes in the shares of them. This allows for an indication of how human capital changes over time, as it specifically looks at these age, sex and qualification groups.

We considered several other methods, including other chain-linked indexes such as the Laspeyres, Paasche and Fisher indexes. The Fisher price index is generally seen as optimal of the three, as it allows the estimate to capture changes in the shares of different components' quantities and prices simultaneously. The Törnqvist index approximates the Fisher index well and requires less data to be calculated. Note, we could have derived a price or quantity index, but we chose to derive a quantity index as this automatically gives real volume estimates rather than deflating the price index.

We also considered finding another "price" of human capital that could be relevant. As documented in our previous release, we considered whether a minimum-wage-type index could capture a price measure that does not take into account any of the improvements in quality of people's skills and knowledge. However, minimum-wage jobs generally still require some form of formal schooling, which can change in quality over time. Further, the upbringing of children through their schooling can change, which might impact their skills development (see our current consultation for an elaboration on this point). This means that using some kind of average earnings measure would not capture a general increase in quality of the population, which would be the main purpose of measuring real volumes of human capital.

We believe that using the Törnqvist index presents a few important advantages, including:

- different populations have different effective "prices" of their human capital, rather than deflating by the same number for everyone

- at an aggregated level (for example, nationally), changes in the composition of the population are taken into account in considering the change in the UK as a whole; this allows changes in the age, sex and highest qualification shares of the population to explicitly impact on the measure

- decomposition of the drivers of changes in human capital stock can be tailored to user needs, decomposing into the types of population change and into differing contributions from age groups, sexes and highest qualifications to varying detail

At the same time, we recognise two main downsides to such an index, including:

- as the measure takes account of the change in distribution of age, sex and highest qualification of the population in each year (termed "weights" in index methodologies), the measures are not additive when deriving indexes of the sub-populations; this effect, called chain-linking, means users cannot simply add up components of the population or add numbers across years, as the results would not match the index-derived equivalent measure

- an increase in the lifetime earnings of a specific age–sex–highest qualification category in the population (for example, 29-year-old females with a degree) is assumed to not impact on volumes, by definition; it is assumed to be a pure "price effect" rather than a "quality effect", meaning an increase in average earnings is assumed to not be a result of an increase in people's skills and knowledge; to improve this, we can consider a separate source to remove the effect from quality that would feed into earnings, using hedonic regression techniques

Measuring Master's and PhD degrees separately from other degrees

In previous releases, the methodology of human capital groups individuals' qualification attainments into six categories, with the highest being degree or above. This has limitations as it does not provide a full range of qualifications an individual may achieve. Therefore, we have expanded it to separate out individuals with a Master's or PhD degree. This has meant that when the data are grouped by highest qualification, age and sex grouping, an extra qualification has been included within this analysis. Otherwise, the methodology has not changed.

By separating out Master's and PhD degrees from other degrees or equivalent, this causes the UK's human capital overall to be higher. This is because we can distinguish the different earnings people can obtain with higher degrees, such as Master's and PhD degrees, and the probability of everyone obtaining such further qualifications during their working lives. In 2018, this would account for a £380 billion increase in the total UK stock, compared with only accounting for six qualification levels.

Developments of per hour

In a similar way to how a group's human capital is measured, total hours worked is measured by calculating the total amount of hours an individual (by their age, sex and highest qualification grouping) is expected to work while still in the labour market until age 65 years. We then divide this by the amount of lifetime earnings (human capital) they would accumulate over their working life. This provides a number that represents how much human capital an individual has, removing the effect of differing hours and changes in working patterns. From this, we can see when individuals are at their most productive in "earning" human capital, which qualifications are more productive in doing so and when in their life they are most productive.

9 . Why is human capital important?

The concept of human capital allows analysis of the factors influencing economic growth as well as wider sustainability and well-being issues. Human capital is widely recognised to influence future potential output and income, as empirical work on economic growth suggests (for example, The impact of human capital on economic growth: a review). A measure of human capital stock can be a starting point to quantify any potentially reciprocal impact education has on health, crime and citizen engagement outcomes (Health and Human Capital; Education, Work and Crime: A Human Capital Approach; and Does Education Increase Political Participation?). Tracking stock trends also allows analysis of the provision of skills needs for different parts of the economy, whether regional or industry based, which can link education (and other human capital accumulation) provision to business needs.

Our methodology brings together analysis of earnings, labour market demographics and educational outcomes into one framework. This allows us to understand how the evolution of these factors has impacted on the stock estimates, what drives differences in individuals' human capital stock values over time and persistent step differences.

Sustainability is seen as, "what we leave to future generations; whether we leave enough resources, of all kinds, to provide them with the opportunities at least as large as the ones we have had ourselves" (UN, 2012). The capitals approach states that economic, natural, human and social capitals are all resources that matter for the present and future well-being of individuals. This was highlighted in the Report by the Commission on the Measurement of Economic Performance and Social Progress. Our current estimates can give insight into how the UK's skills and knowledge resources are evolving and whether there is a different volume of stock that can productively be used in the economy in the future.

The measures can also be used in the assessment of the impact of an ageing population and changes in retirement ages and in the evaluation of the economic benefits of different levels of education.

10 . Workplan

We recognise there are further ways to measure people's skills, knowledge, competencies and attributes. So in October 2018, we published our workplan of the developments we are aiming to achieve, which have been gathered through user discussions. One of the main developments is our current consultation on measuring human capital through a set of indicators. We would really appreciate your responses, which can be filled in here.

Within the published workplan, we proposed to investigate developing our methodology for measuring stocks through lifetime earnings. Our outlines and work done so far is summarised in Table 1.

Table 1: Planned developments from 2018 published workplan, with work done up to October 2019

Development	What we have done	Further plans
Human capital per productive hour	We derived initial estimates, which are presented within this release.	We can derive further analysis, given user interest. We are interested in user feedback on the methodology applied.
Further qualifications	Within this release, we have derived estimates of Master's and PhD degrees combined. We investigated splitting out Master's and PhD degrees separately , but further work would be needed as the sample sizes are too small to apply the same methodology. We have also investigated the derivation for further breakdown of GCSE or equivalent qualifications as well as of A level or equivalent qualifications, splitting out different types of the equivalent qualifications, such as the subjects taken for GCSEs versus equivalent NVQ-type qualifications. Further work would also be needed here as the sample sizes are too small to apply the same methodology.	Future article focused on deriving further breakdown of GCSE or equivalent qualifications as well as of A level or equivalent qualifications but with more aggregated age groups, similar to the occupation and regional methodology, can be considered, given user interest. The occupation and regional methodology is explained in our previous 2004 to 2017 release and 2015 release.
On-the-job training	Characteristics and benefits of training at work, UK: 2017 showed differences in earnings associated with in-work training depending on occupation, highest qualification and other characteristics. Because we were unable to account for whether training taken on the job results in further formal qualifications or in informal training, more research is required into the optimal way to incorporate training into the current methodology. One way of developing this would be to expand the age coverage of the likelihood of people gaining further formal qualifications during their working lives to encompass people aged over 40 years. Some initial findings on this are presented after this table.	We plan to present a paper on different methods to derive the effect of on-the-job training, with differing impacts from both. One of the two main methods would be to split existing transition probabilities of obtaining further qualifications to also capture the probability of having taken informal on-the-job training, per each qualification level. An alternative way would be to derive a lifetime earnings premium from doing any type of on-the-job training and apportion that out based on whether people did any in the last year. In order to apply these methods, we would need to consider cumulative impacts from several years' worth of training at work. Further, at present, our survey sources capture training at work within the past 4 or 13 weeks but not for the past year as a whole, which would be consistent with the rest of our estimates.

Further earnings differences	Within this development, several elements were considered. In order to fully implement these, we need to make use of not-yet-acquired administrative data, such as the Longitudinal Education Outcomes dataset. However, we have investigated the feasibility of taking account of differential progressions, which is feasible. We will look to derive some experimental estimates of progression using administrative data linked to the 2011 Census, continuing analysis on progressions presented in Inclusive growth: measures and trends and Young people's earnings progression and geographic mobility, England and Wales: tax year ending 2012 to tax year ending 2016. However, there are differences in earnings between administrative sources of earnings and self-reported measures.	Future releases once further data is obtained.
Incorporating human capital into a framework consistent with the national accounts	We presented at the Economic Statistics Centre of Excellence (ESCoE) Conference on Economic Measurement in May 2019 [link to slides] . Our slides are available upon request. We set out our thoughts regarding what needs to be considered in order to assess how human capital and other "missing capitals" can relate to assets and other concepts in the national accounts. We had some useful feedback, and we will continue to develop our thinking as part of the Organisation for Economic Co-operation and Development (OECD) working group on well-being and sustainability and the future of the system of national accounts. We have also commissionsed an ESCoE project to investigate research into this topic, and we are looking to hold workshops around future ESCoE and International Association for Research in Income and Wealth (IARIW) conferences; the ESCoE discussion paper is to be published in the next year, setting out possible options.	Future ESCoE discussion paper to coincide with a wider set of views on what can be done. Also, guidance from the OECD working group should be presented at the IARIW 2020 conference, after which we will consider how to incorporate suggestions and what further research and sources may be needed to fulfil the recommendations.
Other		We have received user requests to analyse human capital by industry and the effects of training at work by industry. We will look to publish this in the future, either as an article or as an ad-hoc release.

Source: Office for National Statistics – Human capital estimates

Notes:

1. <u>Occupation and regional methodology, 2004 to 2017 release</u>

2. <u>Occupation and regional methodology, 2015 release</u>

3. <u>Characteristics and benefits of in-work training</u>

4. <u>Progression in inclusive growth</u>

5. <u>Progression in young people's earnings and geographic mobility</u>

On-the-job training

Individuals earn qualifications later in life, whether resulting in informal or formal certificates. In the current methodology, we assume individuals do not increase their qualifications after the age of 40 years. However, this is increasingly an area of our methodology that does not reflect people's behaviours. Figure 13 presents the initial impact on total human capital stock of capturing people's training for further formal qualifications.

Figure 13: Human capital stock would increase by £1.1 trillion, if taking into account the increased qualifications taken by those aged over 40 years

Human capital stock when taking into account these increased transitions into qualifications and no transitions into qualifications at all, UK, 2018

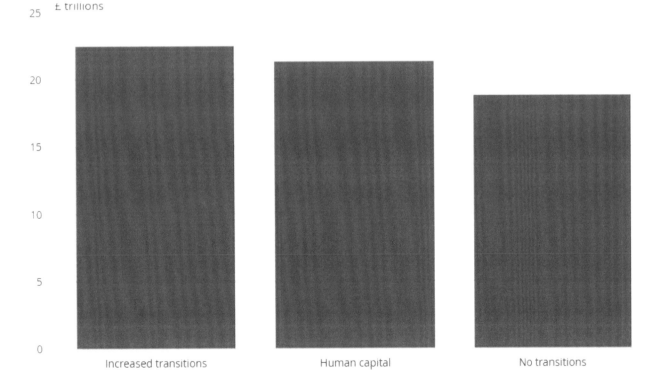

Human capital stock when taking into account these increased transitions into qualifications and no transitions into qualifications at all, UK, 2018

Source: **Office for National Statistics – Human capital estimates**

329

If the further qualifications for people aged over 40 years were taken into account, the UK's human capital stock would increase by £1.1 trillion in 2018, which would be 5% higher. However, if people of all ages did not take any further recognised qualifications after becoming economically active, the UK's human capital stock would have been £2.6 trillion less in 2018, which would be 12% lower.

More information on the likelihood of people obtaining further qualifications can be found in the reference tables.

Statistical bulletin

Disability, well-being and loneliness, UK: 2019

Personal well-being (UK) and loneliness (England) outcomes for disabled adults, with analysis by age, sex, impairment type, impairment severity and country.

Contact:
Joel Jones
life.course@ons.gov.uk
+44 (0)1633456180

Release date:
2 December 2019

Next release:
To be announced

Table of contents

1 . Other pages in this release

The Office for National Statistics (ONS) has explored outcomes for disabled people across a number of areas of life, through a series of bulletins – other pages in this release include:

- Improving disability data in the UK

- Disability and education

- Disability and employment

- Disability and housing

- Disability and crime

- Disability and social participation

Aims of this work

This work aims to present comparable information that uses the Government Statistical Service's (GSS) harmonised definition of "disability", and as far as possible presents UK analysis, alongside intersections with other protected characteristics.

Definition of disability

For the purposes of this analysis, a person is considered to have a disability if they have a self-reported long-standing illness, condition or impairment that causes difficulty with day-to-day activities. This definition is consistent with the Equality Act 2010 and the GSS harmonised definition. For further information on disability and impairment definitions see the Glossary.

Article scope

The Office for National Statistics (ONS) routinely reports on personal well-being but does not routinely disaggregate this information by disability. Related to well-being is loneliness, where disabled people have previously been shown to be at a disadvantage (ONS, 2018).

This bulletin uses the Annual Population Survey (APS) to explore outcomes of personal well-being for disabled adults, aged 16 to 64 years, in the UK, covering the period 2014 to 2019. The Community Life Survey (CLS) is used to explore loneliness for disabled and non-disabled adults, aged 16 to 64 years, in England, covering the period 2014 to 2018.

2 . Main Points

- Disabled people's average ratings are lower than those for non-disabled people for happiness, worthwhile and life satisfaction measures.

- Average anxiety ratings are higher for disabled people at 4.27 out of 10, compared with 2.66 out of 10 for non-disabled people.

- Disabled people with a mental impairment as a main health problem have the poorest well-being ratings.

- Disabled people whose impairments affect them more severely have poorer well-being ratings than disabled people whose impairments affect them less severely.

- The proportion of disabled people (13.3%) who report feeling lonely "often or always" is almost four times that of non-disabled people (3.4%), with the greatest disparity for young adults, aged 16 to 24 years old.

3 . Well-being by disability (UK)

Well-being measures are taken from the Annual Population Survey (APS), using UK data from the year ending June 2019. For time series analysis, the data go back to the year ending June 2014, as this is the earliest period available for disability data using the harmonised definition (see the glossary).

Figure 1: Disabled people report lower well-being levels than non-disabled people

Average well-being ratings for disabled and non-disabled people, UK, 2018 to 2019

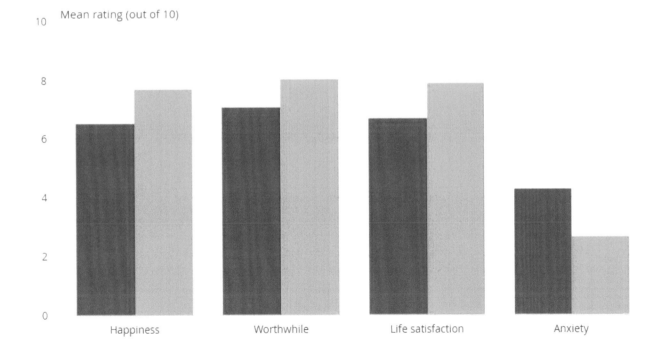

Average well-being ratings for disabled and non-disabled people, UK, 2018 to 2019

Source: Office for National Statistics – Annual Population Survey

Disabled people report lower well-being levels than non-disabled people

On average, disabled adults have poorer ratings than non-disabled adults on all four personal well-being measures. In the year ending June 2019, the mean scores on these measures were:

- for happiness yesterday, 6.54 out of 10 for disabled people, compared with 7.71 for non-disabled people

- for feeling that the things done in life are worthwhile, 7.09 out of 10 for disabled people, compared with 8.03 for non-disabled people

- for life satisfaction, 6.68 out of 10 for disabled people, compared with 7.90 for non-disabled people

- for anxiety yesterday, 4.27 out of 10 for disabled people, compared with 2.66 for non-disabled people (higher numbers equate to poorer well-being in this measure)

Between 2014 and 2019, there were small increases in the average ratings for for happiness, worthwhile and life satisfaction for both disabled and non-disabled people. However, over this period the differences between disabled and non-disabled people on these measures remained consistent. See the Disability and well-being dataset Table 1 for further information.

4 . Loneliness by disability (England)

Loneliness data are taken from the Community Life Survey, using England-only data from the year ending March 2018. For time series analysis, the data go back to year ending April 2014, as this is the earliest period available for disability data using the harmonised definition (see the glossary).

A higher percentage of disabled people feel lonely compared with non-disabled people

The proportion of disabled people who reported feeling lonely "often or always" was nearly four times that of non-disabled people. In the year ending March 2018, 13.3% of disabled people reported that they felt lonely "often or always", compared with only 3.4% for non-disabled people.

Between 2014 and 2018, there were no significant changes in the proportions who reported feeling lonely "often or always" for both disabled or non-disabled people. See the Disability and loneliness dataset Table 1 for further information.

5 . Age

Figure 2: Differences between disabled and non-disabled people in average anxiety ratings decrease with age

Average anxiety ratings for disabled and non-disabled people by age group, UK, 2018 to 2019

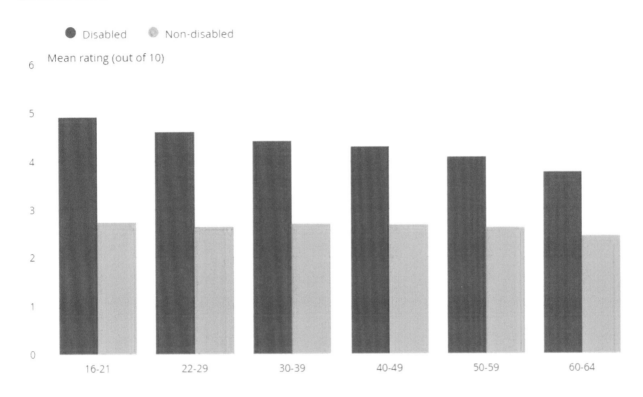

Source: Office for National Statistics - Annual Population Survey

The difference between disabled and non-disabled people in average anxiety ratings becomes smaller in older age groups. In the 16 to 21 years age-group the average rating is 2.19 points higher for disabled people compared with non-disabled people; in the 60 to 64 years age-group the difference is 1.32 points. This effect is also seen with loneliness where disparities between disabled and non-disabled people are smallest in the older age-groups.

However, differences in average happiness, worthwhile and life satisfaction ratings between disabled and non-disabled people have little variation as people get older.

Figure 3: The disparity in the proportion of people who feel lonely is largest in the younger age groups

Proportion of disabled and non-disabled people who feel lonely regularly by age group, England, 2017 to 2018

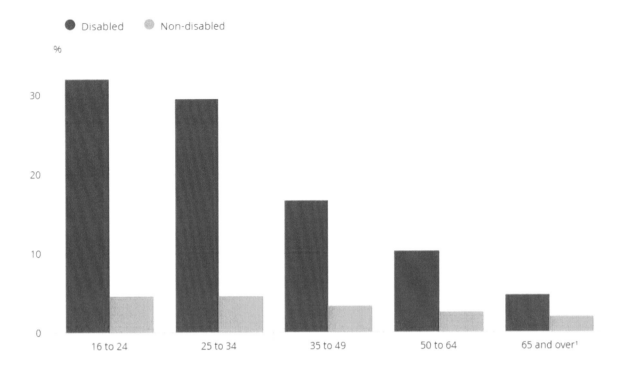

Source: Department for Digital, Culture, Media and Sport – Community Life Survey

Notes:

1. Figures for 65 and over should be treated with caution due to low sample sizes (<31).

In all age groups the proportion of people who felt lonely "often or always" was higher for disabled people than for non-disabled people. The proportion of disabled people who reported feeling lonely "often or always" was largest in the younger age groups and decreased with age.

The disparity between disabled and non-disabled people, in terms of the proportion of people who said that they felt lonely "often or always" decreased with age, from 27.4 percentage points in the 16 to 24 years age group to 2.7 percentage points in the 65 years and over age group.

6 . Sex

Both disabled men and disabled women have poorer well-being than their non-disabled counterparts

The differences between disabled and non-disabled people on all four measures of well-being are similar for both men and women. For disabled men, average happiness, worthwhile and life satisfaction ratings were between 1.03 and 1.32 points lower than for non-disabled men, while anxiety ratings were scored 1.49 higher, at 4.00 out of 10. For disabled women, average well-being ratings were between 0.92 and 1.16 points lower, with anxiety scored 1.65 higher, at 4.46 out of 10.

Average life satisfaction, worthwhile and happiness ratings are higher for women than they are for men and this is true for both disabled and non-disabled people. Conversely, the average rating for anxiety is poorer for women and this is also true for both disabled and non-disabled people.

See the Disability and well-being dataset Table 3 for further information on the analysis of well-being by disability and sex.

Both disabled men and women were more likely to report feeling lonely "often or always", compared with their non-disabled counterparts. When comparing disabled and non-disabled men, there was a difference of 10.5 percentage points. For women, this difference was 9.3 percentage points.

See the Disability and loneliness dataset Table 4 for further information on the analysis of loneliness by disability and sex.

7 . Impairment type

Figure 4: Disabled people with a mental impairment as a main health issue have the poorest well-being ratings

Average well-being ratings of people with different impairment types, UK, 2018 to 2019

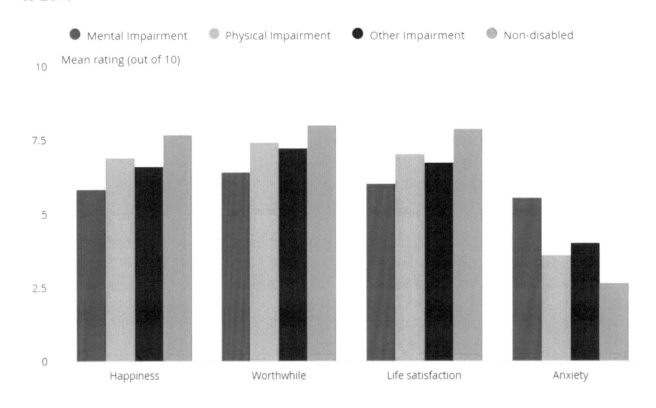

Source: Office for National Statistics – Annual Population Survey

Notes:

1. Main impairment only includes disabled adults aged 16 to 64.

The average well-being ratings of disabled people vary with impairment type. Whilst the average rating for each well-being measure was poorer for disabled people in all impairment types (physical, mental or other), well-being measures were notably poor for those with a mental impairment as their main health problem.

See the Disability and well-being dataset Table 4 for further information on the analysis of well-being by disability and impairment type.

Analysis of loneliness by impairment type has not been included as these data were not collected on the Community Life Survey.

8 . Impairment severity

Figure 5: Disabled people who are "limited a lot" have poorer well-being

Average well-being ratings by impairment severity, UK, 2018 to 2019

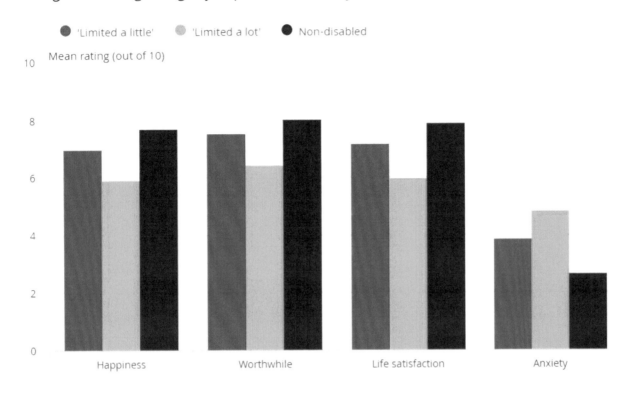

Source: Office for National Statistics – Annual Population Survey

Disabled people who self-report that their ability to carry-out day-to-day activities is "limited a lot" by their impairment have a mean anxiety rating of 4.85 out of 10; this compares with 3.87 out of 10 for disabled people who report their ability is "limited a little" by their impairment and 2.66 out of 10 for non-disabled people. This effect, of poorer outcomes for those "limited a lot" by their impairment, is seen on all four of the well-being measures.

The effect of poorer average well-being ratings in disabled people who are more severely affected by their impairment is present in people of all impairment types: mental, physical and other. The poorest well-being ratings are seen in disabled people who both have a mental impairment as a main health problem and whose ability to carry-out day-to-day activities is "limited a lot".

The greatest disparity is in anxiety ratings where disabled people, whose main health problem is a mental impairment and whose ability to carry-out day-to-day tasks were stated as "limited a lot", have an average rating of 6.13 out of 10, compared with 2.66 out of 10 for non-disabled people.

See the Disability and well-being dataset Table 5 and Table 6 for further information on the analysis of well-being by disability and impairment severity.

Figure 6: The proportion of people who feel lonely is highest in disabled people who are more severely affected by their impairment

Proportion of people who feel lonely "often or always" by impairment severity, England, 2017 to 2018

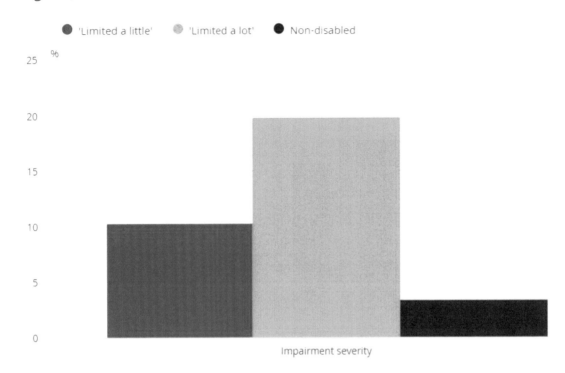

Source: Department for Digital, Culture, Media and Sport – Community Life Survey

Disabled people whose ability to carry-out day-to-day tasks are "limited a lot" (19.8%) are also almost twice as likely to feel lonely "often or always", compared with those who are "limited a little" (10.3%).

9 . Country

Trends vary for each of the well-being measures. The smallest disparities between disabled and non-disabled people were seen in England on all four measures. The differences in average well-being ratings were greater in Wales than in England on worthwhile, life satisfaction and anxiety.

The largest disparities between disabled and non-disabled people were seen in Northern Ireland and Scotland for happiness, life satisfaction and anxiety. Whilst these disparities were not significantly different between these two countries, they were different from the other UK countries.

See the Disability and well-being dataset Table 7 for further information on well-being by disability and country analysis.

10 . Disability, well-being and loneliness data

Well-being data

Disability and well-being dataset
Dataset | Released 2 December 2019

Average well-being ratings of disabled and non-disabled people in the UK, with breakdowns of year, impairment type, impairment severity, age, sex and country.

Loneliness data

Disability and loneliness dataset
Dataset | Released 2 December 2019

The proportion of disabled and non-disabled people in England who feel lonely "often or always", with breakdowns of year, impairment severity, age and sex.

11 . Glossary

Disability

To define disability in this publication we refer to the Government Statistical Service (GSS) harmonised "core" definition: this identifies "disabled" as a person who has a physical or mental health condition or illness that has lasted or is expected to last 12 months or more, that reduces their ability to carry-out day-to-day activities.

The GSS definition is designed to reflect the definitions that appear in legal terms in the Disability Discrimination Act 1995 (DDA) and the subsequent Equality Act 2010.

The GSS harmonised questions are asked of the respondent in the survey, meaning that disability status is self-reported.

Impairment

An impairment is defined as any physical or mental health conditions or illnesses lasting or expected to last 12 months or more. Respondents were presented with a list of impairments and then asked to select all that apply and subsequently their "main health problem". The commentary in this bulletin refers to the main health problem. Analysis is limited to those who are also defined as disabled and does not explore where disabled people experienced more than one impairment. For further details see Volume 3: Detail of Labour Force Survey variables .

Mental impairments

Mental impairments are those with "depression, bad nerves or anxiety", "epilepsy", "learning difficulties" or "mental illness or nervous disorder".

Physical impairments

Physical impairments are those with "problems with arms or hands", "problems with legs or feet", "problems with back or neck", "difficulty in seeing", "difficulty in hearing", "speech impediment", "severe disfigurement, skin conditions or allergies", "chest or breathing problems" "heart, blood pressure, or blood circulation problems", "stomach, liver, kidney or digestion" or "diabetes".

Other impairments

Other impairments are those with "progressive illness not included elsewhere (for example, cancer, symptomatic HIV or multiple sclerosis)" or "other health problems or disabilities".

Severity

Disabled people whose ability to carry-out day-to-day activities is self-reported as "limited a lot" or "limited a little" by their impairment. Respondents were asked: "Does your condition or illness reduce your ability to carry out day-to-day activities?" with the responses, "yes, a lot" and "yes, a little" being taken to indicate severity of disability.

Personal well-being

Personal well-being measures ask people to evaluate, on a scale of 0 to 10, how satisfied they are with their life overall, whether they feel they have meaning and purpose in their life, and about their emotions (happiness and anxiety) during a particular period.

Loneliness

Those who feel lonely "often or always" refers to those who when asked: "How often do you feel lonely?" selected the answer "often or always" from the following list of responses: "often or always", "sometimes", "occasionally", "hardly ever" and "never". These responses have been grouped together into an "other" category. This analysis is available in the datasets.

Statistical significance

Any changes or differences mentioned in this bulletin are "statistically significant". The statistical significance of differences noted within the release are determined based on non-overlapping confidence intervals.

12 . Measuring the data

The Annual Population Survey

Well-being estimates are based on data collected from the Annual Population Survey (APS).

The APS is an annual survey based on data collected in wave 1 and wave 5 on the Labour Force Survey (LFS), combined with an annual local area boost sample run in England, Wales, and Scotland.

The survey does not cover communal establishments, except for NHS staff accommodation. Those living in student halls of residence or boarding school are included as part of their family household. The APS dataset contains approximately 300,000 individuals.

The APS datasets are produced for four different overlapping 12-month periods: January to December, April to March, July to June and October to September. The analysis in this publication was conducted on the July 2018 to June 2019 period as it provides the most up-to-date information.

The Community Life Survey

The Community Life Survey is a household self-completion survey of approximately 10,000 adults aged 16 years and over in England. The survey can be completed either in a paper or online format; the question regarding disability status is asked online only. Data for the 2017 to 2018 year were collected between August 2017 and March 2018.

13 . Strengths and limitations

Causality

The analysis conducted is for the purpose of comparing the outcomes of disabled and non-disabled people. The analysis describes differences in these two populations, but does not explore the cause of this difference. Further analysis, which is outside the scope of this article, is required to make judgements on causality. Please see the "Improving Disability Data in the UK" article for details of our future workplan.

Coverage and population

Analysis using the Annual Population Survey (APS) has been restricted to 16- to 64-year-olds because the survey does not collect data for under 16s and the disability variable is not robust for those aged over 64. Disability status is only collected for people aged 65 years or older at their first contact resulting in less data for this population. The weighting used does not account for the reduced sample size for this age group, making the data not fully representative of the population.

The survey's sampling method excludes communal establishments. Therefore, the findings of this analysis are not representative of disabled people who reside in medical or residential care establishments.

Approximately 100,000 APS respondents are used in the analysis in this bulletin -- this is notably lower than the 300,000 people who are in the survey. This is because of the use of the working age population only and no proxy responses recorded on the well-being modules.

Uncertainty and quality

The results in this bulletin are survey-based estimates, so they are subject to a level of uncertainty as they are based on a sample rather than the whole population. Confidence intervals are provided around every estimate and give an indication of the range in which the true population value is likely to fall. The estimates in this bulletin are supported with confidence intervals at the 95% level. This means that, if we repeated the sample, we would expect the true population value to fall within the lower and upper bounds of the interval 95% of the time (that is, 19 times out of 20).

Impairments

Analysis by impairment is based on the "main impairment" as reported by the respondent. People often experience more than one impairment, but this analysis does not account for co-morbidities or the cumulative impact of living with more than one impairment simultaneously.

Well-being

The Personal well-being in the UK Quality and Methodology Information report contains important information on the strengths and limitations and uses of the data as well as how outputs are created and the quality and accuracy of those outputs. For more information on personal well-being, please see the Personal well-being user guidance and Harmonised principles of personal well-being.

All analysis of well-being measures in this bulletin compares mean scores between groups. Another method of comparing well-being scores between groups is to look at the proportions of people who are within certain thresholds that indicate well-being levels.

Loneliness

Loneliness proportions were calculated using the Community Life Survey, which is used in England only. Links to data for other UK countries are included in the Related links section.

14 . Related links

Personal well-being in the UK: April 2018 to March 2019
Statistical bulletin | Released 23 October 2019
Estimates of life satisfaction, feeling that the things done in life are worthwhile, happiness and anxiety at the UK, country, regional, county and local authority level.

Loneliness -- What characteristics and circumstances are associated with feeling lonely?
Article | Released 10 April 2018
Analysis of characteristics and circumstances associated with loneliness in England using the Community Life Survey, 2016 to 2017.

Community Life Survey: Focus on Loneliness 2017 to 2018 (PDF, 545KB)
Article | Released 17 January 2019
Estimated levels of loneliness in England, using the Community Life Survey, 2017 to 2018.

Scotland's Wellbeing: national outcomes for disabled people
Article | Released 31 July 2019
Analysis of the National Performance Framework (NPF) outcome indicators from the perspective of disability in Scotland.

National Survey for Wales, 2016 to 2017: Mental Wellbeing (PDF, 825KB)
Statistical bulletin | Released 10 October 2017
An overview of mental well-being among adults living in Wales from the National Survey for Wales.

National Survey for Wales, 2016 to 2017: Loneliness (PDF, 1.3MB)
Statistical bulletin | Released 13 February 2018
Detailed analysis of the National Survey for Wales results on loneliness.

Health survey Northern Ireland: first results 2017 to 2018 (PDF, 1.05MB)
Statistical bulletin | Released November 2018
A summary of the main topics included in the 2017 to 2018 Health Survey in Northern Ireland.

Disability pay gaps in the UK: 2018
Article | Released 2 December 2019
Earnings and employment for disabled and non-disabled people in the UK, raw disability pay gaps and factors that affect pay for disabled people.